Interdisciplinary Measures

Literature and the Future of Postcolonial Studies

Graham Huggan

Liverpool University Press

First published 2008 by
Liverpool University Press
4 Cambridge Street
Liverpool L69 7ZU

British Library Cataloguing-in-Publication data
A British Library CIP record is available

ISBN 978-1-84631-109-3 cased
     978-1-84631-110-9 limp

Typeset in Amerigo by Koinonia, Manchester
Printed and bound in the European Union by Biddles Ltd, King's Lynn

Contents

Acknowledgements   vii

Introduction   1

Section I. Literature, Geography, Environment
  1 Decolonizing the Map: Postcolonialism, Poststructuralism
    and the Cartographic Connection   21
  2 Unsettled Settlers: Postcolonialism, Travelling Theory
    and the New Migrant Aesthetics   34
  3 Postcolonial Geography, Travel Writing and the Myth of Wild Africa   49
  4 'Greening' Postcolonialism: Ecocritical Perspectives   64

Section II. Literature, Culture, Anthropology
  5 Anthropologists and Other Frauds   93
  6 African Literature and the Anthropological Exotic   106
  7 (Post)Colonialism, Anthropology and the Magic of Mimesis   130
  8 Maps, Dreams and the Presentation of Ethnographic Narrative   142

Section III. Literature, History, Memory
  9 Philomela's Retold Story: Silence, Music and the Postcolonial Text   155
  10 Ghost Stories, Bone Flutes, Cannibal Counter-memory   166
  11 Cultural Memory in Postcolonial Fiction: The Uses and Abuses
    of Ned Kelly   182
  12 (Not) Reading *Orientalism*   196

Index   210

Acknowledgements

Acknowledgements are due to the following parties for reprinted material: Percy Tresize (photographer) and the Aboriginal custodians of Quinkin Cave (cover image); *Postcolonial Studies* and the Institute of Postcolonial Studies (introduction); *Ariel* and the University of Calgary (chapters 1 and 8); *The Journal of Australian Studies* and University of Queensland Press (chapter 2); *Modern Fiction Studies* and Johns Hopkins University Press (chapter 4); *Comparative Literature* and the University of Oregon (chapter 5); Routledge/Taylor & Francis (chapter 6); *Cultural Critique* and University of Minnesota Press (chapter 7); *Journal of Commonwealth Literature* and Sage Publications (chapter 9); Cambridge University Press (chapter 10); *Australian Literary Studies* and University of Queensland Press (chapter 11); *Research in African Literatures* and University of Indiana Press (chapter 12). Every effort has been made to locate copyright holders in all cases; apologies are given for any oversights here. Most of the work in this book revises or updates previously published work; the original publications are as follows, with thanks to all those involved in giving me permission to reprint material here: 'Postcolonial Studies and the Anxiety of Interdisciplinarity', *Postcolonial Studies* 5.3 (2002): 245–75 (introduction); 'Decolonizing the Map: Post-Colonialism, Post-Structuralism and the Cartographic Connection', *Ariel* 20.4 (1989): 115–31 (chapter 1); 'Unsettled Settlers: Postcolonialism, Travelling Theory and the New Migrant Aesthetics', in *Scatterlings of Empire*. Ed. Wilfred Prest and Graeme Tulloch. St Lucia, QLD: University of Queensland Press, 2001. 117–27 (chapter 2); '"Greening" Postcolonialism: Ecocritical Perspectives', *Modern Fiction Studies* 50.3 (2004): 710–33 (chapter 4); 'Anthropologists and other Frauds', *Comparative Literature* 46.2 (1994): 113–28 (chapter 5); 'African Literature and the Anthropological Exotic', in *The Postcolonial Exotic: Marketing the Margins*. London: Routledge, 2001 (chapter 6); '(Post) colonialism, Anthropology, and the Magic of Mimesis', *Cultural Critique* 38 (1997–8): 91–106 (chapter 7); 'Maps, Dreams, and the Presentation of Ethnographic Narrative', *Ariel* 22.1 (1991): 57–69 (chapter 8); 'Philomela's Retold Story: Silence, Music and the Post-Colonial Text', *Journal of Commonwealth Literature* 25.1 (1990): 12–23 (chapter 9); 'Ghost Stories, Bone Flutes, Cannibal Counter-memory', in *Cannibalism and the Colonial World*. Ed. Francis Barker, Peter Hulme and Margaret Iversen. Cambridge: Cambridge University Press, 1998. 126–41 (chapter 10); 'Cultural Memory in Postcolonial Fiction: The Uses and Abuses of Ned Kelly', *Australian Literary Studies* 20.3 (2002): 142–54 (chapter 11); '(Not) Reading *Orientalism*', *Research in African Literatures* 36.3 (2005): 124–36. Thanks are also due to numerous people for helping and/or encouraging me in this project: these include my colleague Andrew Thompson at the University of Leeds and Anthony Cond, Charles Forsdick and Richard Phillips at Liverpool University Press. A number of mentors have sustained me over the years, including Diana Brydon, Patricia Merivale, Bill New and Craig Tapping at the University of British Columbia; Helen Tiffin and Gillian Whitlock at the University of Queensland; Larry Buell, Jim Engell and Werner Sollors at Harvard University; Chris Balme and Frank Heidemann at the University of Munich; and Ed Larrissy and all my postcolonial colleagues at the University of Leeds. All deserve thanks; and Sabine Schlueter, who knows how difficult I am, deserves the most thanks of all.

Introduction

Postcolonialism as Comparatism

Few research fields can be as contested, not least by their own practitioners, as postcolonial studies, which continues to show every inclination to choose itself as the principal object of its own debates. Perhaps the most obvious thing to be said about postcolonial literary/cultural criticism – and even here there are dissenting voices – is that it is, by definition, a comparative field. That it is insufficiently rigorous in its comparisons is less obvious, though evident enough to have attracted extensive and well-documented critique. John McLeod, for example, in his excellent primer *Beginning Postcolonialism* (2000), runs through a wearily familiar list of comparison-related criticisms. These include (1) that postcolonialism, through its reliance on Western critical-theoretical models, tends to replicate and reinforce the colonialist structures it sets out to dismantle; (2) that it 'creates a ghetto for literature from once-colonised countries within English departments and degree schemes' (McLeod 249); (3) that it is over-dependent on anti-foundationalist theories of knowledge that underestimate or simply overlook the material socio-economic conditions that remain 'the foundation of reality and determine how we live our lives' (McLeod 257); (4) that it represents the premature celebration of an unfinished historical project, collapsing the distinction between 'different countries which have experienced decolonisation at different times and other countries which have not experienced it at all' (McLeod 257); and (5) that it has signally failed to address pressing issues of economic power and class domination, in part because its practitioners are reluctant to concede their own advantaged position within the late-capitalist world system they affect to critique.

This list, McLeod implies, amounts to an attack on an ill-conceived mode of comparative literary/cultural criticism whose practitioners only rarely deliver on the political promises they perhaps never really intended to keep. Now this is to

1

generalize, of course, about postcolonialism's generalizations – an easy rhetorical move that McLeod just as easily counteracts. Postcolonialism, he says, is

> a generalising term, to be sure, but all terms must inevitably generalise [...]
> What word could [postcolonialism's opponents] find to avoid generalisation?
> [...] If postcolonialism is too generalising, perhaps one solution is to use the
> same term in different ways in different contexts. This would reflect contin-
> gent historical, cultural and geographical conditions while offering ways of
> thinking *across* these differences to global, transnational operations such
> as multinational capitalism or US military aggression which inevitably link
> together disparate locations [...] The ability to think *comparatively* and across
> differences can be enabling. (McLeod 254–55; his italics)

The problem remains as to the basis for such broadly thought comparisons, a
problem arguably compounded by postcolonialism's recent forays into such
other, similarly fashionable academic territories as world systems theory,
diaspora discourse and anti-globalization critique. One approach to this
dilemma has been to open up postcolonial studies across the disciplines in
the pursuit of transdisciplinary cultural analysis; another has been to stress the
multilingual dimensions of both postcolonial literatures/cultures and the criticism that is applied to them in the interests of transnational cultural critique.
This 'culturalist' approach to the field has long since become the methodological
dominant, raising the unresolved question of what happens to literature and
literary studies when these are bypassed in the interests of a broader cultural
analysis, or instrumentalized for the purposes of a 'global' cultural-political
critique.

Postcolonialism as Culturalism

The cultural turn in postcolonial criticism has brought it closer to cultural studies
as a perceived challenge to traditional disciplinary configurations and to the
professional specialization implied by 'the conventional separation of auton-
omous and fragmentary knowledges within the human sciences' as a whole
(Easthope 172). While the impact of cultural studies on the Western academy has
perhaps been exaggerated, it is still true to say that its emergence and development have created a series of discernible institutional effects. Among these has
been the reinforcement of a tendency already well established in several fields
of humanities study, namely the focus on *contemporary* social movements and
cultural phenomena. This focus has brought with it a revitalization of interest
in *popular* cultural formations, these latter often being seen somewhat inaccu-
rately as 'the' domain of cultural studies, in keeping with its partial definition
as an oppositional exploration of the multifacetedness of everyday life. While
the oppositionality of cultural studies has sometimes proved misleading, it has
provided a valuable point of contact for postcolonial critics whose work also
appeals to the multiplicities submerged beneath totalizing or exclusivist views

Interdisciplinary Measures

THE UNIVERSITY OF
WINCHESTER

Postcolonialism across the Disciplines

Series Editors
Graham Huggan, University of Leeds
Andrew Thompson, University of Leeds

Postcolonialism across the disciplines showcases alternative directions for postcolonial studies. It is in part an attempt to counteract the dominance in colonial and postcolonial studies of one particular discipline – English literary/cultural studies – and to make the case for a combination of disciplinary knowledges as the basis for contemporary postcolonial critique. Edited by leading scholars, the series aims to be a seminal contribution to the field, spanning the traditional range of disciplines represented in postcolonial studies but also those less acknowledged. It will also embrace new critical paradigms and examine the relationship between the transnational/cultural, the global and the postcolonial.

of national culture. This 'contact zone' (Pratt) has arguably expanded with the more recent shift to *trans*national models of cultural studies, in which the prefix 'trans' is less indicative of a movement *across* pre-constituted national boundaries than of an attempt to conceptualize *beyond* the idea of the nation and the corresponding ideology of the nation-state that it has historically legitimized and maintained.

This move to a transnational, or even 'post-national', understanding of processes of cultural production, mediation and consumption has been registered for some time now in a number of crossover journals, the titles of which already point to the overlap between comparative analyses of cross-culturality, cultural studies approaches to transnational/global mediating processes, and postcolonial political and economic concerns. Probably the best-known of these journals in the postcolonial field is *Interventions*. Founded in the late 1990s by the influential British theorist Robert Young, *Interventions* makes explicit its interdisciplinary and transnational objectives, and its ambition to draw out the connections between colonial and imperial histories and the contemporary politics of multiculturalism and identitary cross-affiliation (represented by such ubiquitous tag-terms as 'hybridity', 'creolization' and 'transculturalism', themselves extracted from a range of disciplinary fields).

Journals such as these operate in the spirit of Homi Bhabha's unashamedly presentist definition of postcolonial criticism as bearing 'witness to the unequal and uneven forces of cultural representation involved in the contest for political and social authority in the modern world order' (Bhabha, 'Postcolonial' 437). Explicit in Bhabha's definition is that postcolonial critical perspectives are designed to 'intervene in those ideological discourses of modernity that attempt to give a hegemonic "normality" to the uneven development and the differential, often disadvantaged, histories of nations, races, communities [and] peoples' (Bhabha, 'Postcolonial' 437). Widely understood as global in both origin and effect, these discourses pave the way for a revised conception of postcolonial studies as at once synchronic survey of the differentiated experiences of global modernity and diachronic index of the changing role of global capital in shaping responses to both the neo-colonial present and the imperial past.

Understandings of postcolonialism such as these appear to have more in common with the conceptually emancipatory, methodologically ethnographic projects of contemporary cultural studies than with earlier, text-centred definitions of postcolonial (literary) studies as a locus of anti-imperial resistance and critique. Reacting to these shifts, some conservatively oriented postcolonial scholars have warned – and not without reason – against new forms of ahistoricism and theoretical self-aggrandisement, or against the implications of a cultural studies 'takeover' in which literary criticism is consigned to secondary, or even explicitly subordinate, status (see, for example, Fraser; Thieme). A further fear is that the expanded disciplinary range of the 'new' postcolonial studies risks exacerbating the methodological confusion that is arguably inherent in the field. Young's list, in his mission statement for the lead issue of *Interventions*, is certainly daunting:

Though produced for the most part from departments of literature and cultural studies, postcolonial academic scholarship has also been significantly dependent on history, anthropology, political science and psychoanalysis, to name only the most prominent of the disciplines in social science and humanities upon which it draws. Essays appearing in *Interventions* will reflect these numerous and varied disciplinary affiliations. At the same time, the journal will direct attention to, draw from, as well as interrogate other fields such as international relations, developmental economics and area studies which, despite their disciplinary proximity, for a variety of reasons have not made 'interventions' in postcolonial studies [to date]. (Young, 'Introducing' 1–2)

Postcolonialism and the Anxiety of Interdisciplinarity

What are we to make of this newfound disciplinary permissiveness, this temperate climate in which postcolonial scholars feel justified in drawing on fields well outside the range of their expertise? To some extent, the opening up of postcolonial studies to multidisciplinary perspectives is merely the practical implementation of a politico-theoretical insight already central to the field. After all, exponents of earlier alternatives to the latest paradigm of choice, postcolonial studies, had already liberally drawn on a number of different disciplines – notably history, geography, sociology and political science – in their efforts to unravel the complex asymmetries, and no less subtle complicities, of imperial rule. What is new is a sense, sharpened no doubt by the institutional successes of cultural studies, that the postcolonial field is rapidly transforming itself into a prime location for the experimental deployment of cutting-edge interdisciplinary methods in the humanities and social sciences as a whole.

Recent postcolonial research has also brought with it the heady perception, also drawn from cultural studies, that self-consciously 'progressive' interdisciplinary work is mounting a challenge to dominant ideologies of disciplinary expertise. This partly self-mythologizing view is well captured in Lawrence Grossberg, Paula Treichler and Cary Nelson's characteristically generous definition of cultural studies as 'an interdisciplinary, transdisciplinary, and sometimes counter-discursive field that operates in the tension between its tendencies to embrace both a broad, anthropological and a more narrowly humanistic conception of culture' (Grossberg *et al.* 4).

This definition begs several questions that seem equally relevant to *postcolonial* cultural studies. What, for example, is the relationship between 'anthropological' and 'humanistic' conceptions of culture, and how do the tensions between these conceptions reflect on methodological choices for analysis (e.g. qualitative versus quantitative research methods, empirical versus textual or discursive concerns)? And what, for that matter, are the connections between 'interdisciplinary', 'transdisciplinary' and 'counter-discursive' research models; does the term 'interdisciplinarity' already imply some at least covert form of resistance to established academic practices and intellectual norms? It is as unwise, I would suggest, to make 'catch-all' claims about the oppositionality of cultural studies as it is to commandeer the entire body of postcolonial research for the radical purpose of anti-authoritarian critique. As Janet Wolff points out in an essay in Grossberg, Treichler and Nelson's collection, cultural studies programmes, however expansively conceived, do not guarantee interdisciplinarity, while the term 'interdisciplinarity' itself is often confused with its non-identical semantic correlates, 'intertextuality' and 'interdiscursivity' (Wolff 713). As Wolff also suggests, interdisciplinarity implies an ideal form of institutionalized cooperation that is belied both by the 'textual excesses' of humanities studies and by the 'continuing inhibitions' of the social sciences towards an analysis of the aesthetics of cultural forms (Wolff 713–14).

Wolff's caveat applies to the field of postcolonial studies in so far as much of the work that goes on within it is inter*discursive* rather than inter*disciplinary* in approach. To make the distinction stick, some initial discussion of terms is necessary. Julie Thompson Klein begins her 1990 study, *Interdisciplinarity: History, Theory, and Practice* by admitting that 'today the interdisciplinary approach is often praised with no clear indication of what it is' (Klein 12). One of the problems, argues Klein, is that the term 'interdisciplinarity' is almost inherently contradictory, at once conveying 'nostalgia for a lost wholeness and a new stage in the evolution of science'; taking in both the historical quest of unified knowledge, stretching back at least as far as ancient Greek philosophy, and the latest developments at knowledge's ever-expanding frontiers (Klein 12). For my purposes here, I will adhere – as does Klein – to the recent, almost impossibly broad definition of interdisciplinarity by the international advisory body, the OECD: 'Interdisciplinarity ranges from the simple communication of ideas to the mutual integration of organizing concepts, methodology, procedures, epistemology, terminology, data, and organization of research and education in a fairly large field' (Berger, qtd in Klein 63).

But even given the breadth of these terms, is postcolonial studies interdisciplinary? Many of its practitioners would like to think so. Most of the state-of-the-art books on postcolonialism to have emerged in the 'boom' period since roughly the mid-1990s seem to take it for granted that postcolonial studies, by definition, is a cross-cultural interdisciplinary practice. 'By definition', perhaps, but definitions themselves have been few and far between. Ato Quayson, one of the few recent postcolonial explicators to have grappled with the concept at all, distinguishes between 'synoptic' (conceptually oriented) and 'instrumental' (pragmatically applied) dimensions of interdisciplinarity in postcolonial studies. According to Quayson, postcolonial studies has been 'highly interdisciplinary in the synoptic sense, borrowing freely from a wide range of fields in a desire both to challenge received assumptions as well as to shed light on the configurations of the present and the future' (Quayson, *Postcolonialism* 25). Although this initial statement isn't especially helpful ('received assumptions' about what? Which particular 'configurations'?), Quayson goes on to provide more specific guidelines. Synoptic interdisciplinarity, it transpires, consists both in the development of 'synthetic theories that operate across [different] disciplines' and in the variegated processes of defamiliarization that force new perceptions of the 'conceptual categories brought to bear on the discussion in the first place' (Quayson, *Postcolonialism* 24, 39). This synoptic view of interdisciplinarity is itself instrumental in so far as it reflects the postcolonial critic's desire to formulate 'open' theoretical models of analysis that are inextricably connected to the need to dismantle systems of domination (notably imperialism) and ossifying habits of thought. Postcolonial interdisciplinarity might therefore be understood as both a descriptive and a problem-solving exercise; as the collaborative, practically oriented attempt, operating across disciplinary boundaries, to come to terms with the historical legacies of imperialism and colonialism, and to 'struggle to transcend the effects [of these legacies] through an engaged and situated [critical and theoretical] practice' (Quayson, *Postcolonialism* 43).

Two observations might be made here. The first is that postcolonial studies, at least to date, has been marked more by the collective desire for cross-disciplinary procedures of analysis than by genuinely collaborative initiatives of the sort pursued by, say, affiliated educational programmes or task-oriented 'think-tanks' and research teams. Interdisciplinarity has been seconded, that is, to a wider reflexive ideology through which postcolonial critics have sought to theorize alternatives to what Edward Said calls the 'paradigmatic fossilization' of traditional disciplinary regimes (Said 131). The second observation, closely related to the first, is that interdisciplinary activity in the field has been restricted, for the most part, to individuals whose ideas and methods, borrowed freely from other disciplines, are retooled to meet the requirements of anti-imperialist critique. This kind of work, while valuable in itself, is interdiscursive rather than interdisciplinary – not a nit-picking semantic distinction but an important indication of the continuing disparity between theoretical ambitions and practical achievements in postcolonial cultural work. (The tendency in the field to use terms such as 'colonialism' and, particularly, 'imperialism' as all-encompassing concept-metaphors illustrates the extent of the problem, compromising the very historical specificity upon which postcolonial critiques of imperial practice are based. The self-consciously utopian theoretical construction of postcolonial studies as a challenge to institutionally maintained 'disciplinary imperialisms', in which the term 'discipline' itself is held to have imperialistic connotations, plays into the hands of those who have accused postcolonial critics of confusing textual and discursive agency with material effect. 'Imperialism', meanwhile, becomes widespread as a term of mutual accusation – a kind of inside trader's insult – for those wishing to expose postcolonialism's inadequacies, with the assertion of personal/ professional credentials assuming more importance than the critical analysis of the material processes and cultural representations of empire itself.)

Postcolonial studies, for these and other reasons, has been subject to the 'anxiety of interdisciplinarity' that is widespread across the humanities, in particular, but also in the university system at large (Coles and Defert). This concern has manifested itself on several different fronts: in the concern that the erosion of traditional disciplinary boundaries might also entail a compromise of hard-won disciplinary knowledge; in the threat posed to institutional identity and the spectre of an irrecoverable loss of intellectual autonomy; in the suspicion that 'the spectacle of intellectual plurality [might] foster a relativist permissiveness that acknowledge[s] the fertility of diverse agendas [but] refuse[s] to discriminate among them' (Thomas 19); in the uncertainty over the effectiveness of interdisciplinary projects ostensibly geared to wider community interests but readily assimilated to narrow academic agendas and self-serving research pursuits; and, not least, in the legitimate fear that increasingly routine calls for interdisciplinarity and cross-departmental affiliation might be the siren-songs that university management uses to lure departments and other larger administrative units into its own Machiavellian cost-cutting schemes. For some, interdisciplinary modes of critical analysis provide the potential to bring different areas of disciplinary knowledge into dialogue and constructive conflict; for others, however, a commitment to interdisciplinarity remains at best a fashionable academic catch-cry, at worst an alibi for dilettantism and a consumerist, 'cafeteria-style' approach to university education as a whole (see, for example, Heckhausen). Thus, while cross-disciplinary research and teaching models are by no means new, the latest interdisciplinary initiatives seem more likely than ever to attract baleful predictions of corner-cutting and an inevitable lowering of academic standards, or to seek worried assurances that interdisciplinarity be founded on the firmest of disciplinary footings: 'to be interdisciplinary you need to be disciplinary first – grounded in one discipline, preferably two' (Foster 162).

It is no surprise that the anxiety of interdisciplinarity looms large in a relatively new field of academic research such as postcolonial studies; all the more so since interdisciplinary measures have so frequently been conscripted to postcolonial studies' collectively anti-imperialist cause. Nor is it surprising that aggressive interdisciplinary, even 'post-disciplinary', claims by a number of contemporary postcolonial practitioners have made them, along with the field they are seen as representing, vulnerable to counterattack. This disciplinary backlash is probably most evident in imperial history and historiography (although, to be fair, history, particularly the popular field of cultural history, has shown plenty evidence of late of adopting postcolonial methods and vocabularies in going through what some of its own practitioners have announced as an 'imperial turn': see, for example, Stoler). Professional historians of empire, by and large, have treated postcolonial forays into their disciplinary territory with suspicion, with some professing dismay or even anger at postcolonial critics and theorists 'claiming squatters' rights over imperial history's unclaimed provinces' (Kennedy 346). Dane Kennedy has summarized some of the most frequent accusations as follows: the stultifying use of indiscriminate jargon used from 'sometimes incompatible sources'; the infuriating recourse to paradoxically dehistoricizing forms of colonial discourse analysis that 'seek to convict historically specific parties of historically specific crimes while exonerating [themselves] of any accountability to historical specificity'; the overwhelming tendency to treat the West as an 'undifferentiated, omnipotent entity, imposing its totalizing designs

7

on the rest of the world without check or interruption'; the stated aim, not just to dismantle 'hegemonic historiography', but to 'break from the premises of historical analysis altogether' (Kennedy 349–53).

'What then', Kennedy concludes, 'does postcolonial theory offer to British imperial history? With its mind-numbing jargon, its often crude essentializations of the West and the Other as binary opposites, and, above all, its deeply ingrained suspicion of historical thinking, one might well wonder if it has anything to offer at all' (Kennedy 353). Surprisingly, given the exhilaration of his own invective, Kennedy believes it does have something to offer. Conceding that the easy metaphor of postcolonial theory as a 'colonizing discipline, subjecting a province of historical studies to its alien rule', is misleading, even destructive, Kennedy points to the valuable contributions it has made to 'recovering the connection between Britain and its imperial dependencies', and to exploring the cultural dimensions of imperialism as a process of mutual interaction 'that inscribed itself on the dominant partner as well as the dominated one' (Kennedy 356). We might be forgiven, though, for seeing this rescue act as a case of too little, too late; for Kennedy's appeal, however heartfelt, for dialogue between postcolonial theory and imperial history/historiography seeks to create an interdisciplinary reciprocity that his admittedly self-distanced recapitulation of the denunciatory language of some of his professional colleagues has already done its best to disallow. At best, it seems, the integrative aims of interdisciplinarity are projected into the future; at worst, its cooperative ideals are grotesquely distorted into caricatured portraits of territorial warfare, while the potential for constructive dialogue across disciplinary boundaries mutates into quotidian exchanges of cross-departmental abuse.

Scarcely less civil has been the exchange between postcolonial criticism/theory and anthropology, with mutual accusations of Eurocentrism, academic careerism and reductive thinking hanging heavy in the air. One of the charges made most often by postcolonial critics is that the disciplinary apparatus of anthropology has effectively rewarded its practitioners for manufacturing imperialist representations of the non-European other (see, particularly in the African context, Miller; Mudimbe). What is remarkable about certain kinds of postcolonial attack on anthropology is that the history of self-criticism that arguably defines the entire discipline has been glossed over or, sometimes, simply ignored (see, for example, Minh-ha; also Torgovnick). Conversely, counterattacks by anthropologists have been apt to oversimplify the major critical debates within postcolonial studies, preferring either to identify a small number of representative scapegoat figures or to conflate the by no means readily compatible views of postcolonial critics and theorists on complex issues of cross-cultural representation and exchange. Surveying the scene, one might well conclude that 'the dialogue between postcolonial criticism and anthropology has descended into a series of sometimes crude myth-making exercises in which each accuses the other of silencing those on whose behalf they wish to speak' (Huggan; see also Ch. 7 of this book). One of the ironies behind this travesty of interdisciplinary communication has been the tendency to adopt an interchangeable discourse on the other; thus, when Trinh T. Minh-ha memorably defines anthropology as a 'conversation of us with us about them' (Minh-ha 65), she appears blissfully unaware that the same phrase might apply to her own (and other postcolonial critics') self-righteous pronouncements on the discipline of anthropology itself. Anthropology, in this sense, is made to act as postcolonialism's silent other, providing on the one hand the hardened disciplinary object against which postcolonial critics and theorists assert their own free-floating authority while preserving, on the other, the cultural capital of 'resistance' through the maintenance of a collectively anti-establishment will.

One of the more notable counterblasts against self-serving postcolonial critiques of anthropology is in Micaela di Leonardo's *Exotics at Home* (1998), her energetically revisionist study of the ethnographic dimensions of modern American life. As di Leonardo argues, 'in the current [US] public sphere … anthropology and its presumed relation to primitives, whether lauded, derided, or neutrally noted, are tools at hand for a wide variety of actors with varying political interests' (di Leonardo 54). Media coverage, for example, of issues of race, ethnicity and the underprivileged social other often borrows 'the appearance, if not the discipline, of anthropological work', donning an 'anthropological costume [which] acts to disguise both its thin knowledge base and its deprecatory intent' (di Leonardo 44). Nor are academics immune from co-opting their own versions of fake ethnography into 'full-dress morality plays' in which the 'evil imperialist anthropologist is brought on stage … to stand in for the bad, white (and often male) West before a usually bellelettristic audience' (di Leonardo 45). Di Leonardo does not shrink from implicating several respected postcolonial scholars. Marianna Torgovnick, for example, sarcastically introduced as a 'self-described progressive critic of anthropology', is found guilty not only of misreading the work of individual anthropologists, but of rushing to negative judgement on the profession as a whole; while Trinh T. Minh-ha, the Vietnamese theorist and filmmaker, is derided for 'substituting complaint for scholarship' and for assuming that 'personal responses to a few carelessly read anthropological texts constitute a critique of an entire discipline' (di Leonardo 41). Even Edward Said, grudgingly admired for the range and quality of his scholarship, is chastised for glossing over a whole history of radical anthropology, as well as for succumbing to the 'synecdochic fallacy' of identifying an entire field with either a handful of 'early colonial collaborators' or an equally small number of more recent '"linguistic turn" practitioners', who confirm the myth of the 'American anthropologist [as] always and forever a postmodernist' (di Leonardo 47).

There is value, no doubt, in di Leonardo's historically contextualized polemic, while in her analysis of the shortcomings of postcolonial critiques of anthropology she undeniably scores a number of palpable hits. There is a level of generalization in Torgovnick's, Said's and Minh-ha's suspiciously self-serving interventions which is likely to strike even the non-specialist reader as, if not unwarranted, then at least unclear. But it seems at the same time as if di Leonardo herself, from a position within her own beleaguered discipline, might have been lured into the synecdochic fallacy, with a few representative cases being deemed sufficient to hold the entire postcolonial field accountable for shoddy scholarship and scattershot critique. Di Leonardo's work, for all its panache, might thus be seen as part of the phenomenon of disciplinary backlash that has impeded postcolonial critics' and theorists' efforts to create the conditions for the type of interdisciplinary practice that might have a lasting impact both on its immediate (academic) environment and on the wider world.

'Second-wave' Postcolonialism

I have dwelt at length on these instances of disciplinary backlash in order to show how difficult it is to overcome the generalized academic territoriality and intellectual one-upmanship that continue to stand in the way of postcolonial studies becoming an accepted form of interdisciplinary analysis and critique. Further problems arise within the field when the question of a disciplinary dominant is considered. In what is sometimes now seen as the 'first wave' of postcolonial criticism (the period between, roughly, the mid-1980s and the mid-1990s), literary modes of analysis were central, and most of the key figures to emerge from this period were trained literary critics, many of them operating in the comparative literature field. This doesn't mean that there was no attempt to work with, or across, other disciplines, but this was generally done with the awareness that the theoretical claim to interdisciplinary analysis often amounted in practice to 'computing with the methodological training of one discipline, however transformed' (Spivak, *Critique* 209). Some well-known critics – Edward Said, for instance – laid claim to what we might call an anti-disciplinary interdiscursivity in which the collocation of disparate sources confirmed both the impulse towards high-cultural intellectual mastery and a paradoxical will to break down the hierarchies that sanction traditional (disciplinary) lineages of Western thought. Others, however – notably Gayatri Spivak – were more suspicious of claims to either inter- or anti-disciplinarity, pointing to the limitations of commodified versions of interdisciplinary practice that did little more than 'neutraliz[e] the vocabulary from another discipline and tak[e] it to describe yet again what happens between reader and text' (Spivak, *Critic* 55).

Spivak and, to a lesser extent, Said made it clear that they were primarily literary critics operating in the border-zones between different disciplines and wary of making over-ambitious claims to multidisciplinary expertise. More recent work, which might do well to heed such advice, is less likely to fret about its own methodological eclecticism, as in the type of 'second-wave', materialist-inspired postcolonial criticism that is more self-consciously interventionist in its approach to current social and political debates. A recent essay by Pablo Mukherjee spells out the distinction between 'first-' and 'second-wave' criticism. '[F]irst-wave postcolonial theorists', claims Mukherjee, 'stressed [...] the importance of the historical specificity of literature and culture. Yet, frequently, their very notion of "history" and "culture" remained textualist/linguistic in conception and their own institutional location [was] undertheorised' as a result (Mukherjee 146). The consequences were (1) that the 'migrant cosmopolitan rather than the migrant refugee was taken to be the paradigmatic figure of contemporary history'; and (2) that texts – usually literary texts – were primarily related to each other, or themselves, even as they were claimed to have worldly value as politicized vehicles of cultural critique (Mukherjee 146). Mukherjee sees 'second-wave' criticism as a corrective to these earlier textualist/culturalist tendencies, not least because the object and impetus of contemporary postcolonial criticism and, with it, the responsibilities of the postcolonial critic have changed. The central issues now, he says, in keeping with his own environmentalist sympathies, are 'how to analyse contemporary postcolonial political crises as being continuous with ecological crises; how to excavate a history of alternative bioregional modernities; [and] how to centre refugee migrants and not "hybrid cosmopolitanism" as the paradigmatic postcolonial framework in the consideration of what kind of silences we appropriate and what kinds of interpretative powers must be devolved in the communication between global elites and subaltern masses' (Mukherjee 149–50).

Mukherjee's analysis, like that of several other self-designated 'second-wave' critics, deliberately misreads the work of 'first-wave' critics, breezily dismissed as ivory-tower scholasticists, in order to clear the space for a more concretely (and, by implication, correctly) 'historico-materialist' treatment of the issues of the day. Behind this move we can see the overdrawn, often tedious debate between (post-)Marxists and poststructuralists that initially arose out of 'first-wave' criticism, and that continues to some extent to split the postcolonial field today (see, for example, Lazarus; Parry). But we can also see the salutary attempt to look towards new models of universalism in postcolonial studies arising out of the tension between shared space and unshared values in the context of globalization, and out of the difficulty of finding an international language of adjudication in the context of continuing struggles over political sovereignty and human/environmental rights.

'Second-wave' criticism, in the end, is not so different from the 'soft' culturalism it denounces, nor is it averse (as Mukherjee's essay, which includes an extended analysis of Amitav Ghosh's novel, *The Hungry Tide*, shows) to using literature as a means of illustrating and reflecting upon contemporary sociocultural debates. What is interesting, in fact, in work like this is the *lack* of anxiety it shows over its own interdisciplinary methods, and the unabashedly symptomatic readings it gives of literary and other cultural texts. The position is summed up by another post-Marxist, Robert Young, who, in staking a claim for postcolonial studies as a form of cultural activism, calls postcolonialism a 'self-conscious political philosophy' aimed at forcing 'its alternative knowledges into the power structures of [both] the west [and] the non-west' (Young, *Postcolonialism* 17, 7). Literature continues to play an important role in these not-so-new forms of postcolonial analysis, both in terms of what Terry Eagleton might call the 'ideology of the aesthetic' (Eagleton) and of the changing relationship between events, both current and recalled, and their representational forms. However, it would probably be true to say that the status of literature and the literary has shifted with the move to a more culturally oriented analysis. What, then, is the value of literature in postcolonial studies today?

Postcolonialism and the Literary

It is ironic that the value of literature is increasingly contested at a time when other disciplines, both within and beyond the humanities, have long since accommodated themselves to their own versions of the literary/linguistic turn. Postcolonial literary studies is a case in point, all too often being condemned as the relic of earlier, now outmoded forms of putatively anti-colonial textual criticism, or damned with faint praise as the enabling forerunner of current, updated models of transnational cultural studies in a global age. As I have suggested above, this common perception flies in the face of what many of postcolonialism's most prominent practitioners have said about the continuing value of literature as a subtle vehicle of anti-imperialist criticism and an equally complex site for the ideological contradictions historically embedded in the imperialist cause. To be sure, literary scholars at large have become the victims of structural changes within the academic profession brought about by recent policies of economic rationalization that are frequently as ill administered as they are ill advised. But by the same token, literary scholars are perhaps too ready to accept the cultural capital that this victim status brings, not ready enough to explain the value of the literary to non-experts both within and beyond the universities where most of them are employed. This situation is arguably exacerbated when the social value of literature is claimed to be self-evident, as is sometimes the case in the type of postcolonial scholarship that relies heavily on a 'culturalist' approach. Two relatively recent interventions, by the literary/cultural critic Ato Quayson and the anthropologist Arjun Appadurai, may be helpful here in showing the linkage between literary and other cultural representations and the constitutive role played by the *imagination* in all aspects of social life.

In a series of books and articles, Arjun Appadurai has emphasized the trans-formative power of the imagination in restructuring the parameters of everyday social life. Even the lives of the poor and disadvantaged, says Appadurai, can be radically re-imagined, since people 'no longer see their lives as mere outcomes of the givenness of things, but [rather] as the ironic compromise between what they [can] imagine and what social life will permit' (Appadurai 54). Appadurai believes, in the context of the contemporary world system, that the imagina-tion has broken free from the 'special expressive space of art, myth, and ritual [to become] part of the quotidian mental work of ordinary people in many societies' (Appadurai 5). Still, he acknowledges the influential role of literature as part of what he calls 'the conceptual repertoire of contemporary societies' in a globalized world (Appadurai 58). 'Readers of novels and poems', after all, 'can be moved to intense action [by their reading], and their authors often contribute to the construction of social and moral maps for their readers' (Appadurai 58).

This view of the social and moral function of literature is supported by Ato Quayson, who, in his eponymous book, uses the term 'calibrations' to denote a method of reading that 'oscillates rapidly' between the literary-aesthetic, social, cultural and political domains (Quayson, *Calibrations* xii). This method allows us to 'wrest something from the aesthetic domain for the analysis and better understanding of the social', which Quayson sees, in contradistinction to 'society', as an 'articulated encapsulation of transformation, processes, and contradictions analogous to what we find in the literary domain' (Quayson, *Calibrations* xv). Like Appadurai, Quayson insists on the transformative power of the imagination – its capacity to envision alternative identities, alternative societies, alternative histories – and on the more specific potential of imaginative literature to produce representations of reality (itself structured by representation) that have a profound effect on our interpretation of social facts. This effect is not merely retrospective; for as Quayson argues, 'the social that is being read for across the literary is [also] part of an anticipatory project [in which] the insights derived from local texts may [...] be translated into different contexts and times' (Quayson, *Calibrations* xxxi).

Appadurai and Quayson both point to the capacity of literature, not only to imagine the ways in which reality has been, or might be, interpreted, but also to affect the ways in which reality is *produced*. This by now fairly conventional view of the literary has been crucially important for postcolonial writers, whose imaginative fashioning of their own, and others', societies and cultures often seeks to break loose from the constrictions of inherited cultural forms. Literature is a vital tool in what the Kenyan writer Ngũgĩ wa Thiong'o calls the 'decolonisation of the mind' (Ngugi); in the continuing struggle to create new possibilities of thinking, as well as living, for previously exploited and dispossessed peoples, literature plays a formative role. However, Appadurai's suggestion that the work of the imagination is by no means restricted to designated spaces of art implies a 'post-disciplinary' view of the relationship between the arts and the (social) sciences – a view, and a relationship, towards which postcolonial studies increasingly aspires. The utopian conception of a post-disciplinary academy – already envisioned some time ago in the work of postcolonial writers such as Wilson Harris – is, like all utopian visions, anticipatory and speculative, but it still gestures towards the social conditions under which the contemporary academy might be imaginatively transformed. This move might be some way off yet, but its future is foreshadowed in synoptic views of interdisciplinarity that work self-consciously towards the decolonization of knowledge and the mutual interaction between nominally separate, but by no means incommensurate, knowledge-forms. Postcolonialism's more immediate future surely lies in a patient, mutually transformative dialogue between the disciplines rather than in triumphalist announcements of the imminent end of disciplinarity *tout court*. Such announcements, like postcolonialism itself, risk being seen as 'prematurely celebratory' (McClintock). Postcolonial interdisciplinarity, like other forms of interdisciplinary practice, still needs to acknowledge the discrepancy between individually generated models of interdisciplinary transgression (often less 'transgressive' than they claim to be, still less 'interdisciplinary' in any rigorous methodological sense) and collaboratively implemented initiatives of the type, more common in the sciences than the humanities, that work towards integrating the different intellectual training and disciplinary perspectives of select groups or teams in pursuit of socially applicable research goals. Maybe, in this context, the final anxiety of interdisciplinarity consists not so much in the threat – ever-present though it is – of institutional territoriality as in the public reluctance to acknowledge academic institutions as privileged forums for productive intellectual exchange. Postcolonial studies is only just beginning to come to terms with its own complex disciplinarity; perhaps, reversing Foster, it can learn to be interdisciplinary first, allowing collective practice to shape and inflect its individually produced theoretical models, and playing its part in the creation of a critically minded, non-hierarchically structured research environment well equipped to address issues of common concern, as well as to pursue a variety of disparate personal goals.

The essays in this book span the best part of two decades: a period that has seen the exponential growth of postcolonial studies as a continually constructive, but persistently contested, research field. Some of the earlier essays reflect my ongoing fascination with the interrelations between literature and geography, while a couple of the later ones show my growing interest in literary history and the connections between (post)colonial and environmental concerns. Most of the essays are literature-led, and are interdiscursive rather than interdisciplinary in the terms described above. Like Gayatri Spivak, I am a contemporary literary critic interested in the broad-based forms of 'transnational literacy' that keep assiduous track, without assuming illusory command, of the changing relationship between global events and local trends in the current world order (Spivak, *Critique*). While transnational literacy is not the same as interdisciplinarity, it still implies a crossing, if hardly an erasure, of traditional disciplinary boundaries. It also requires – although this requirement is not always met at the disciplinary level – a working knowledge of languages other than one's own. I feel strongly that the future of postcolonial studies will be multilingual, as well as interdisciplinary, although my own lack of knowledge of what Spivak calls the 'colonized vernaculars' (Spivak, *Critique*) remains a practical impediment to this personal goal. As for interdisciplinarity, its impact on my work has been in direct proportion to the collaborative projects I have undertaken with colleagues from other disciplines: first at the University of Munich, where I founded an international postgraduate programme in postcolonial studies with colleagues from seven different disciplines; and more recently at the University of Leeds, where I co-direct, along with colleagues from the Schools of History and Modern Languages, the new Institute for Colonial and Postcolonial Studies, which, if not yet interdisciplinary in method, is certainly interdisciplinary in intent. Much of the inspiration for these essays came from colleagues and students participating in these projects and programmes; but the faults are all my own.

The essays in the first section of the book, 'Literature, Geography, Environment', all reflect on what might be loosely called the spatiality of postcolonial analysis: its capacity to undertake a critical exploration of the territorial imperatives of colonialism, and its frequently speculative consideration of alternatives to these imperatives, e.g. in the shape of 'open' and/or 'rhizomatic' cultural cartographies, or more socially and ecologically responsible attitudes towards environment and place. The first essay, 'Decolonizing the Map: Postcolonialism, Poststructuralism and the Cartographic Connection', is also the earliest, having first appeared in 1989: a risky move, perhaps, in a book that claims as much to look to the future of postcolonial studies as to re-assess its past. The essay, however, addresses several concerns that continue to be of central relevance to the field even as its earlier deconstructive vocabulary has shifted: the *conceptual* concern for alternatives to a self-privileging colonial/imperial imaginary, but also the *material* concern for more socially equitable (and, often in the process, locally inflected) attitudes to place. The essay looks forward, in other words, to the recent 'greening' of postcolonial studies – a salutary process that joins the demands of social and environmental justice, and that examines both imaginative and material possibilities for individual and collective transformation in an increasingly globalized world. The final essay in the section, '"Greening" Postcolonialism: Ecocritical Perspectives', is an attempt to think through some of these imaginative/material possibilities, as well as to reflect on specific forms of 'ecological imperialism' (Crosby) that have significant impact on the present, as well as widespread influence on the past. The intervening essays, 'Unsettled Settlers: Postcolonialism, Travelling Theory and the New Migrant Aesthetics' and 'Postcolonial Geography, Travel Writing and the Myth of Wild Africa', are different attempts to work towards a notion of postcolonial geography, a project increasingly engaged by specialist geographers as well as transdisciplinary social and cultural theorists, with both groups arguably sharing a suspicion for excessively metaphorical understandings of social/cultural processes (e.g. colonial settlement) that owe as much to history as to geography, and in which the privileges of the present are co-dependent on the mythologies of the past.

History and geography are brought together, too, in the essays in the second section of the book, 'Literature, Culture, Anthropology'. This section traces the processes by which the self-sustaining cultures of Empire were created and contested, and critically assesses the formative role of anthropology both in supporting and subverting the cultural norms on which colonial/imperial authority rests. Despite its provocative title, 'Anthropologists and Other Frauds', the lead-off essay, is a defence of the critical capacity of anthropology to counteract the self-justificatory myths of imperial power, even as imperialism's obvious abuses were once captured in flagrant ethnographic misrepresentations of supposedly inferior or marginal 'races', classified for the purposes of containment, and subject to the authority of those who sought discursive management of the peoples over whose territories and livelihoods they exerted considerable, if never total, administrative control. The other essays in this section provide variations on these themes, either by showing the implication of *both* anthropology *and* imaginative literature in creating and perpetuating a colonial exotic ('African Literature and the Anthropological Exotic'), or by suggesting the capacity of both to challenge, through unorthodox assemblage ('Maps, Dreams, and the Presentation of Ethnographic Narrative: Hugh Brody's *Maps and Dreams* and Bruce Chatwin's *The Songlines*') or insubordinate agency ('(Post)Colonialism, Anthropology, and the Magic of Mimesis'), the dominating strategies of mimetic representation on which colonial/imperial claims to cultural superiority are consistently based.

The third section of the book, 'Literature, History, Memory', gathers similarly interconnected essays, this time around the themes of history and (cultural) memory in the contexts of widely divergent, sometimes directly competing, ways of representing the colonial/imperial past. Chronologically ordered, the essays in this section to some extent follow the trajectory of postcolonial criticism in the last two decades, from its earlier preoccupation with devising alternative historiographies ('Philomela's Retold Story: Silence, Music and the Postcolonial Text'), to its more recent emphasis on the fraught politics of collective memory ('Ghost Stories, Bone Flutes, Cannibal Counter-memory', 'Cultural Memory in Postcolonial Fiction: The Uses and Abuses of Ned Kelly') and the equally entangled material histories of postcolonial textual practice and cultural critique ('[Not] Reading *Orientalism*'). Such a trajectory might falsely imply a progressivist view of postcolonial literary/cultural criticism, a view explicitly contradicted by postcolonialism's predominantly non-linear, temporally disjunctive approach. Direct opposition to Eurocentric notions of progress, after all, is one of postcolonialism's most readily identifiable features, as for that matter are its critique of reductionist forms of European historicism and its counterassertion of multiple, discontinuous modernities, which challenge those easy temporal categorizations that might divide the world into postcolonial and (pre)colonial, the future and the past. Another word, then, on the subtitle of this book, which might appear to be misleading. 'The future of postcolonial studies' remains one of the field's most reliably contentious topics, sparking any number of debates that, while certainly not lacking in intensity, have probably managed so far to generate more heat than they have light. That caveat aside, three versions of the debate may be briefly presented here. In the first and probably most common of these versions, the future of postcolonial studies is foreclosed, as in the familiar argument that the work of postcolonial criticism, while historically necessary, is now over, with the term 'postcolonial' having been replaced by any one of a number of more conjuncturally appropriate terms ('transnational', 'transcultural', 'global', etc.). Despite the relative merits of all of these terms, the argument strikes me as being as tenuous as it is tendentious, smacking of the very intellectual modishness of which postcolonialism itself stands routinely accused. The ephemerality of postcolonial criticism is largely an effect of the intellectual impatience of those who make the charge, and a sign of the hypercommodified state of (Western) academic life in general. I would have thought, on the contrary, that postcolonial criticism will be with us as long as the global struggle against colonialism continues; and few would deny the impact of colonialisms both past and present on the modern globalized world.

Another, equally blunt way of saying this is that the proper subject of postcolonialism is colonialism, which might well be taken as presenting a second version of the argument: that the future of postcolonialism is the past. This version has the distinct merit of anchoring postcolonial criticism to a particular set of historically verifiable conditions. However, it remains fair to say (even if it is said too often) that the field's broad comparative sweep can work against subtle historical distinctions, and that its theoretical reach has not always been matched by its historical grasp. History, in other words, is invoked in postcolonial criticism – and this book is probably no exception – more than it is actually studied; and Benita Parry, among others, is surely right to emphasize the pressing need across the entire field for more empirical work (Parry). Notwithstanding, postcolonial studies will always have what Homi Bhabha might call an 'aspirational' feature; and if the future of the field *is* the future, then that future will eventually succeed in consigning it to the past. To put this less cryptically: if one of the abiding tasks of postcolonial criticism is to negate its own prefix (for it clearly confronts the *continuity* of colonialism), another of its primary objectives is to work towards a day when its critical interventions will no longer be necessary. Postcolonial criticism, in moving with the times, is irresistibly plural: multi-sited, multilingual, cross-disciplinary. Stubbornly utopian, too, in so far as postcolonialism, that most academic and yet *least* academic of intellectual exercises, commits its seemingly impractical practitioners to the highly tangible pursuits of making colonialism visible in the world, and of helping to make it obsolete.

Works Cited

Appadurai, Arjun. *Modernity at Large: The Cultural Dimensions of Globalization*. Minneapolis: University of Minnesota Press, 1996.

Bhabha, Homi, ed. *Nation and Narration*. London: Routledge, 1990.

——. 'Postcolonial Criticism'. In *Redrawing the Boundaries: The Transformation of English and American Studies*. Ed. S. Greenblatt and G. Gunn. New York: Modern Language Association, 1992. 437–65.

Coles, Alexia and A. Defert, eds. *The Anxiety of Interdisciplinarity*. London: Blackdog Publishing, 1998.

Di Leonardo, Micaela. *Exotics at Home: Anthropologists, Others, and American Modernity*. Chicago: University of Chicago Press, 1998.

Eagleton, Terry. *The Ideology of the Aesthetic*. Cambridge: Blackwell, 1990.

Easthope, Anthony. *Literary into Cultural Studies*. London: Routledge, 1991.

Foster, Hal. 'Trauma Studies and the Interdisciplinary: An Interview'. In Coles and Defert, eds. 157–68.

Fraser, Robert. *Lifting the Sentence: A Poetics of Postcolonial Fiction*. Manchester: Manchester University Press, 2000.

Grossberg, Larry, Paula Treichler and Cary Nelson, eds. *Cultural Studies*. New York: Routledge.

Heckhausen, H. 'Discipline and Interdisciplinarity'. In *Interdisciplinarity: Problems of Teaching and Research in Universities*. Ed. L. Apostel. Paris: OECD, 1973. 83–89.

Huggan, Graham. *Peter Carey*. Melbourne: Oxford University Press, 1996.

Kennedy, Dane. 'Imperial History and Post-Colonial Theory'. *Journal of Imperial and Commonwealth History* 24.3 (1996): 345–63.

Klein, Julie Thompson. *Interdisciplinarity: History, Theory, and Practice*. Detroit: Wayne State University Press, 1990.

Lazarus, Neil. *Nationalism and Cultural Practice in the Postcolonial World*. Cambridge: Cambridge University Press, 1999.

McClintock, Anne. 'The Angel of Progress: Pitfalls of the Term "Post-Colonialism"'. *Social Text* 31.2 (1992): 84–98.

McLeod, John. *Beginning Postcolonialism*. Manchester: Manchester University Press, 2000.

Miller, Christopher. *Theories of Africans: Francophone Literature and Anthropology in Africa*. Chicago: University of Chicago Press, 1990.

Minh-ha, Trinh T. *Woman, Native, Other: Writing Postcoloniality and Feminism*. Bloomington, IN: Indiana University Press, 1989.

Mudimbe, V. Y. *The Invention of Africa: Gnosis, Philosophy, and the Order of Knowledge*. Bloomington, IN: Indiana University Press, 1988.

Mukherjee, Pablo. 'Surfing the Second Wave: Amitav Ghosh's Tide Country'. *New Formations* 59 (2006): 144–57.

Nǧuǧi wa Thiong'o. *Decolonising the Mind: The Politics of Language in African Literature*. London: James Currey, 1986.

Parry, Benita. *Postcolonial Studies: A Materialist Critique*. London: Routledge, 2004.

Pratt, Mary Louise. *Imperial Eyes: Travel Writing and Transculturation*. New York: Routledge, 1992.

Quayson, Ato. *Calibrations: Reading for the Social*. Minneapolis: University of Minnesota Press, 2003.

——. *Postcolonialism: Theory, Practice of Process?* Cambridge: Polity Press, 2000.

Said, Edward. 'Orientalism Reconsidered'. In *Postcolonial Criticism*. Ed. B. Moore-Gilbert, G. Stanton and W. Maley. London: Longman, 1997. 131–42.

Spivak, Gayatri Chakravorty. *A Critique of Postcolonial Reason: Toward a History of the Vanishing Present*. Cambridge, MA: Harvard University Press, 1999.

——. *The Post-Colonial Critic*. London: Routledge, 1990.

Stoler, Laura Ann. *Haunted by Empire: Geographies of Empire in North American History*. Durham, NC: Duke University Press, 2006.

Thieme, John, ed. *The Arnold Anthology of Post-Colonial Literatures*. London: Arnold, 1996.

Thomas, Nicholas. *Colonialism's Culture: Anthropology, Travel and Government*. Princeton, NJ: Princeton University Press, 1994.

Torgovnick, Marianna. *Gone Primitive: Savage Intellects, Modern Lives*. Chicago: University of Chicago Press, 1990.

Wolff, Janet. 'Excess and Inhibition: Interdisciplinarity in the Study of Art'. In Grossberg, Treichler and Nelson, eds. 706–18.

Young, Robert. 'Introducing *Interventions*'. *Interventions* 1.1 (1999): 1–3.

——. *Postcolonialism: A Very Short Introduction*. Oxford: Oxford University Press, 2003.

SECTION I

Literature, Geography, Environment

Decolonizing the Map: Postcolonialism, Poststructuralism and the Cartographic Connection

We're not going to get away from structures. But we could do with some lithe, open, agile, portable structures, some articulating structures [...] We can't all go to the same place [...] we have to go together in different directions.

Robert Bringhurst, *Pieces of Map, Pieces of Music*

The problem with maps is they take imagination. Our need for contour invents the curve, our demand for straight lines will have measurement laid out in bones. Direction rips the creel out of our hand. To let go now is to become air-borne, a kite, map, journey [...]

Thomas Shapcott, 'Maps'

The fascination of Canadian, Australian and other postcolonial writers with the figure of the map has resulted in a wide range of literary responses both to physical (geographical) maps, which are shown to have operated effectively, but often restrictively or coercively, in the implementation of colonial policy, and to conceptual (metaphorical) maps, which are perceived to operate as exemplars of, and therefore to provide a framework for the critique of, colonial discourse.[1] The exemplary role of cartography in the demonstration of colonial discursive practices can be identified in a series of key rhetorical strategies implemented in the production of the map, such as the reinscription, enclosure and hierarchization of space, which provide an analogue for the acquisition, management and reinforcement of colonial power.[2] My initial focus in this chapter, however, will be on a further point of contact between cartography and colonialism, namely the procedures and implications of mimetic representation.

Mimesis, besides providing a theoretical basis for cartographic practice, based now as throughout much of the history of cartography on the possibility of producing a plausible reconstruction of a specific geographical environment, has proved through the ages to be a cornerstone of Western culture. Although the viability of mimetic representation has been repeatedly contested at least

21

since the time of Plato, mimesis has consistently provided a means of promoting and reinforcing the stability of Western culture.[3] Yet, as theorists of colonialism such as Homi Bhabha and Edward Said (among others) have shown, mimesis has also historically served the colonial discourse which justifies the dispossession and subjugation of so-called 'non-Western' peoples; for the representation of reality endorsed by mimesis is, after all, the representation of a particular kind or view of reality: that of the West. In this context, the imitative operations of mimesis can be seen to have stabilized (or to have attempted to stabilize) a falsely essentialist view of the world which negates or suppresses alternative views that might endanger the privileged position of the Western perceiver. Edward Said has related this view to the 'synchronic essentialism' that he envisages as characteristic of Orientalist and other forms of colonial discourse. Said emphasizes, however, that the apparent stability of colonial discursive formations has been placed under continual threat both by historical forces that disrupt or at least challenge the discursive system adopted and applied by the dominant culture (or cultural group), and by internal inconsistencies within the system itself. These inconsistencies, claims Said, are brought to light when the system is imposed on cultures perceptibly different from that of the dominant.

Supporting Said's claim, Homi Bhabha identifies colonial discourse as an agonistic rather than an antagonistic mode whose primary effect is not to reinforce colonial authority, but rather to produce a form of hybridization which mimics that authority. Bhabha correspondingly distinguishes between *mimesis*, an apparently homogeneous system of representation, and *mimicry*, the articulation of a desire for a 'reformed, recognized other [...] as the subject of a difference that is almost the same, but not quite' ('Mimicry' 126). Colonial discourse, Bhabha goes on to suggest, is the site of a clash between the Western desire for a uniform self and the need to define that self against reformed 'others' which, although produced in the self's likeness, are never quite the same; the result is a double articulation in which 'the representation of a difference [...] is itself a process of disavowal' ('Mimicry' 126). The destabilizing process set in motion by colonial mimicry produces a set of deceptive, even derisive, 'resemblances' that implicitly question the homogenizing practices of colonial discourse. Mimicry also invokes a wider challenge to the authority of colonial representation by redefining the desire of the colonial powers to 'fix' its own position as a form of 'fixation,' an obsession which, manifested in the fetishization of the other (through the workings of stereotype, discriminatory classification, etc.), confirms the fear that the supposedly normative values of the colonizer will come to be challenged, and eventually displaced, by the colonized. Thus, argues Bhabha, there is an ambivalence written into colonial discourse through which the informing colonial presence is 'split between its appearance as original and authoritative and its articulation as repetition and difference' ('Signs' 93).

I have dwelt on this inevitably oversimplified paraphrase of Bhabha's theory because it seems to me that the shortcomings of the discursive system he describes are strikingly similar to those of the map, itself split between its appearance as a 'coherent', controlling structure and its articulation as a series of differential analogies. In this context, cartographic discourse can be considered to resemble colonial discourse as a 'narrative in which the productivity and circulation of subjects and signs are bound in a reformed and recognized totality' (Terdiman 156). Yet cartographic discourse, I would argue, is also characterized by the discrepancy between its authoritative status and its approximative function, a discrepancy which marks out the 'recognizable totality' of the map as a manifestation of the desire for control rather than as an authenticating seal of coherence. The 'uniformity' of the map therefore becomes the subject of a proposition rather than a statement of fact; moreover, this proposition comes to be identified with the 'mimetic fallacy' through which an approximate, subjectively reconstituted and historically contingent model of the 'real' world is passed off as an accurate, objectively presented and universally applicable copy.[4]

I stated before that the 'reality' represented mimetically by the map not only conforms to a particular version of the world but to a version that is specifically designed to empower its makers. José Rabasa's critical reading of Mercator's seventeenth-century Atlas, for example, reveals historical links between the 'reality' represented by Western world-maps and a privileged Eurocentric organization of geographic space which 'institute[s] a systematic forgetfulness of antecedent spatial configurations' (6). Corroborating Rabasa's thesis, Gayatri Spivak uses the more recent example of the cartographic reinscription of India by the British Raj to illustrate the colonizer's 'necessary yet contradictory assumption of an uninscribed earth' (133). This assumption, claims Spivak, 'generates the force to make the [colonized] native see himself as other' (133); but as she implies in her use of the word 'contradictory', the desire to appropriate, secure and perpetuate the position of an other or others manifested in the regulatory operations of cartographic discourse and, by analogy, in the stabilizing rhetoric of colonial discourse neither guarantees the effectiveness of colonial rule nor ensures the coherence of the discursive system that underwrites it. To return to Rabasa's reading of Mercator, the apparent coherence of cartographic discourse is historically associated with the desire to stabilize the foundations of a self-privileging Western culture. But this coherence is then contradicted by what Rabasa calls 'blind spots' in the map which, brought to light in a rigorous deconstructive reading, identify the map's supposedly 'universal' mode of representation as a set of rhetorical strategies that reinforces the pre-located authority of its European makers. Furthermore, these blind spots reveal flaws in the overall presentation of the map which allow it to be read in alternative, 'non-European' modes; what passes for 'universal' history therefore remains undecidable 'not on account of a theoretical deconstruction of teleology and eschatology, but due to an everpresent deconstruction of Eurocentric world views by the rest of the world' (12).

Rabasa's application of a deconstructive methodology to the critique of European colonialism suggests that a working alliance may be formed between deconstruction as a process of displacement which registers an attempted dissociation from a dominant discursive system and decolonization as a process of cultural transformation which involves the ongoing critique of colonial discourse. To explore more fully the implications of this alliance, I shall devote the next section of the chapter to a brief commentary on three concepts which suggest the applicability of post-structuralist 'positions' (Jacques Derrida's term) to the critique of colonial discourse. These terms are, respectively, *structure*, *simulacrum*, and *displacement*.

The most succinct discussion of the first of these concepts is in Derrida's seminal essay 'Structure, Sign and Play in the Discourse of the Human Sciences.' His claim is as follows:

> Structure, or rather the structurality of structure [...] has always been neutralized or reduced [in Western science and philosophy] by a process of giving it a centre or referring to a point of presence, a fixed origin. The function of this centre was not only to orient, balance and organize the structure, but above all to make sure that the organizing principle of the structure would limit what we might call the play of the structure. By orienting and organizing the coherence of the system, the centre of a structure permits the play of its elements within the total form [...] [but] the concept of a centred structure, although it represents coherence itself, the condition of the episteme as philosophy or science, is contradictorily coherent. ('Structure' 279)

Derrida's postulation of the 'contradictory coherence' of a discursive system reliant on the concept of a 'centred structure' recalls Bhabha's reading of the ambivalence of colonial discourse; it also undermines the claim to coherence of cartographic discourse by revealing that the exemplary structuralist activity involved in the production of the map (the demarcation of boundaries, allocation of points and connection of lines within an enclosed, self-sufficient unit) traces back to a point of presence whose stability cannot be guaranteed. The 'rules' of cartography, both those which function overtly in the systematic organization of the map and those which are implied in the empowering methods of its production, are duly discovered to pertain to a desire for control expressed by the power-group or groups responsible for the articulation of the map. This desire, however, is controverted by insufficiencies both within the assembled structure and, by implication, within its controlling agency, which is discovered to have laid false claim to the fixity of its own origins and to the coherence of the system it orients and organizes. In this way, cartographic discourse can be seen to play an exemplary role not only in the demonstration of the empowering strategies of colonialist rhetoric, but also in the unwitting exposure of the deficiencies of those strategies.

The 'contradictory coherence' implied by the map's systematic inscription on a supposedly 'uninscribed' earth reveals it, moreover, to be a palimpsest covering over alternative spatial configurations which, once brought to light, indicate both the plurality of possible perspectives on, and the inadequacy of any single model of, the world. Thus, Swift's famous derision of those seventeenth-century European cartographers who 'in their Afric-maps with savage-pictures fill[ed] their gaps' neatly complements Rabasa's deconstructive analysis of Mercator's (contemporaneous) Atlas, which highlights conspicuous gaps, absences and inconsistencies in the presented text as a means of exposing flaws in the wider discursive system it exemplifies. A similar argument can be brought to bear on conceptual maps; as Kevin Hart observes in his gloss on Derrida,

> all maps seek to be both complete and consistent but [...] in each case there are hidden gaps of one kind or another [...] [which] occur because each thinker takes either the material world or the conceptual world to be an instance of full presence; and, as Derrida argues, there can be no such thing: what seems to be a plenitude of presence is always already divided against itself. (110)

The issue is thus not whether deconstruction can somehow provide a 'better' map but the eventual problematization of 'any discourse which proposes itself as an exact map of reality' (113).

Derrida's implied critique of cartographic exactitude involves a reassessment of the relation between structure and simulacrum. The goal of structuralist activity, explains Roland Barthes, is to

> reconstruct an object in such a way as to manifest the rules of its functioning [...] structure is therefore a simulacrum of the object, but a direct interested simulacrum, since the imitated object makes something appear which remained invisible or [...] unintelligible in the natural object [...] The simulacrum is intellect added to object, and this addition has an anthropological value, in that it is man himself, his history, his situation, his freedom, and the very resistance which nature offers to his mind. (Barthes 214–15)

Here again, cartography can be seen to exemplify structuralist procedure. A simulacrum of the world (or part of it) is produced through the participation of the intellect in the abstract reorganization of its 'natural object': the external environment. But this participation is never neutral; thus, turning Barthes's terms against himself in a characteristically deconstructive ploy, we can identify the 'anthropological content' of the map not just in the history, but in the *interested* history of mankind. In Eurocentric maps such as Mercator's, to retain the working example, what the 'imitated object' (the map) 'makes appear' in the 'natural object' it reconstructs (the world) is the anterior presence of the West, which is consequently revealed as the common denominator for the exemplary structuralist activity involved in the production of, and vouchsafing the 'coherence' of, the map.

A deconstructive reading of the Western map, on the other hand, is one which, focusing on the inevitable discrepancy between the 'natural' and the 'imitated' object, displaces the 'original' presence of the West in such a way as to undermine the ideology which justifies its relations of power. This operation of displacement is tantamount to a 'decolonization' of the map, where decolonization entails an identification of and perceived dissociation from the empowering strategies of colonial discourse (including, for example, a rejection of its false claim to a 'universal' history). The result is a dismantling of the self-privileging authority of the West which also suggests that the relations between the 'natural' and the 'imitated' object that inform the procedures of cartographic representation are motivated by the will to power; and, further, that these relations ultimately pertain neither to an 'objective' representation nor even to a 'subjective' reconstruction of the 'real' world but rather to a play between alternative simulacra that problematizes the easy distinction between object and subject. In this sense, Barthes's distinction between the 'natural' and the 'imitated' object is jeopardized from the outset because the metaphorical activity involved in the imitation of an object presupposes a stability and, to use Derrida's term, a 'fullness of presence', which that 'original' object does not possess. Thus, the process of displacement engendered by deconstruction can be seen as one which disrupts the neat distinction between oppositional terms by emphasizing the instability of both the terms themselves and the structural relation between them.[5] The relevance of this disruptive process to the practice of cartography is considerable; for not only is the metaphorical resemblance between the map and the reality it purports to represent invalidated, or at least called into question, by the displacement of the ontologically stable relation between the 'original' and its 'copy', but this proposed resemblance is discovered to be the product of an ideological imposition which traces back to an identifiable rhetorical bias. This bias is related by Derrida to the metaphysics of presence that he associates with Western logocentrism; but as Bhabha, Said and Spivak, among others, have illustrated in their analysis of the figures of colonial discourse, it must always be situated within its specific cultural and historical context.

As Jonathan Culler has observed, the disruptive manoeuvres involved in deconstructionist activity shift emphasis from a conceptual *opposition* based on binary logic to an ideological *imposition* where that logic is used to justify, maintain and reinforce a specific socio-political system based on rigidly defined relations of power (150). The usefulness of deconstruction in exposing and undermining systems of this kind suggests that, rather than being perceived as a decontextualized theory which leads to a form of political quietism through its deferral of the decisions that might engender social change, a form of philosophical anarchism through its insistent refutation of 'standard' wisdoms (Hulme; Felperin), or a paradoxical reinforcement of Western authoritarianism through its disguised relocation of, rather than its alleged dislocation of, Western ontological and epistemological biases, deconstruction can by contrast be considered as a contextualized praxis which enables the exercise of cultural critique and, in particular, the exposure of and resistance to forms of cultural domination.[6] The rest of this chapter concerns itself with a particular aspect of this praxis, namely the ironic and/or parodic treatment of maps as metaphors in postcolonial literary texts, the role played by these maps in the geographical and conceptual de/reterritorialization of postcolonial cultures, and the relevance of this process to the wider issue of cultural decolonization.

The prevalence of the map topos in contemporary postcolonial literary texts, and the frequency of its ironic and/or parodic usage in these texts, suggests a link between a de/reconstructive reading of maps and a revisioning of the history of European colonialism. This revisionary process is most obvious, perhaps, in the fiction of the Caribbean writer Wilson Harris, where the map features as a metaphor of perceptual transformation that allows for the revisioning of Caribbean cultural history in terms other than those of catastrophe or complex. Throughout his work, Harris stresses the relativity of modes of cultural perception; thus, although he recognizes that a deconstruction of the social text of European colonialism is the prerequisite for a reconstruction of postcolonial Caribbean culture, he emphasizes that this and other postcolonial cultures should neither be perceived in essentialist terms, nor divested of its/their implication in the European colonial enterprise. The hybrid forms of Caribbean and other postcolonial cultures merely accentuate the transitional status of all cultures; so while the map is ironized on the one hand in Harris's work as a visual analogue for the inflexibility of colonial attitudes and for the 'synchronic essentialism' of colonial discourse, it is celebrated on the other as an agent of cultural transformation and as a medium for the imaginative revisioning of cultural history.[7]

More recent developments in postcolonial writing and, more particularly, in Canadian and Australian literatures, suggest a shift of emphasis from the interrogation of European colonial history to the overt or implied critique of unquestioned nationalist attitudes which are viewed as 'synchronic' formations particular not to postcolonial but, ironically, to colonial discourse. A characteristic of contemporary Canadian and Australian writing is a multiplication of spatial references which has resulted not only in an increased range of national and international locations, but also in a series of 'territorial disputes' that pose a challenge to the self-acknowledging 'mainstreams' of metropolitan culture, to the hegemonic tendencies of patriarchal and ethnocentric discourses, and implicitly, I would argue, to the homogeneity assumed and/or imposed by colonialist rhetoric. These revised forms of cultural decolonization have brought with them a paradoxical alliance between internationalist and regionalist camps where the spaces occupied by the 'international', like those by the 'regional', do not so much forge new definitions as denote the semantic slippage between prescribed definitions of place.[8] The attempt by writers such as Hodgins and Malouf to project spaces other than, or by writers such as Van Herk and Atwood to articulate the spaces between,[9] those prescribed by dominant cultures or cultural groups indicates a resistance to the notion of cartographic enclosure and to the imposed cultural limits that notion implies.

Yet the range of geographical locations and diversity of functions served by the map metaphor in contemporary Canadian and Australian literatures suggests a desire on the part of their respective writers not merely to *deterritorialize*, but also to *reterritorialize*, their increasingly multiform cultures. The dual tendencies towards geographical dispersal (as, for example, in the 'Asian' fictions of Koch and Rivard) and cultural decentralization (as, for example, in the hyperbolically fragmented texts of Bail and Kroetsch) can therefore be seen within the context of a resiting of the traditional 'mimetic fallacy' of cartographic representation. The map no longer features as a visual paradigm for the ontological anxiety arising from frustrated attempts to define a national culture, but rather as a locus of productive dissimilarity where the provisional connections of cartography suggest an ongoing perceptual transformation which, in turn, stresses the transitional nature of postcolonial discourse. This transformation has been placed within the context of a shift from an earlier 'colonial' fiction obsessed with the problems of writing in a 'colonial space' to a later, 'postcolonial' fiction which emphasizes the provisionality of all cultures and which celebrates the particular diversity of formerly colonized cultures whose ethnic mix can no longer be considered in terms of the colonial stigmas associated with mixed blood or cultural schizophrenia.[10] Thus, while it would be unwise to suggest that the traditional Canadian and Australian concerns with cultural identity have become outmoded, the reassessment of cartography in many of their more recent literary texts indicates a shift of emphasis away from the desire for homogeneity towards an acceptance of diversity reflected in the interpretation of the map, not as a means of spatial containment or systematic organization, but as a medium of spatial perception which allows for the reformulation of links both within and between cultures.

In this context, the 'new spaces' of postcolonial writing in Canada and Australia can be considered to resist one form of cartographic discourse, whose patterns of coercion and containment are historically implicated in the colonial enterprise, but to advocate another, whose flexible cross-cultural patterns not only counteract the monolithic conventions of the West but revision the map itself as the expression of a shifting ground between alternative metaphors rather than as the approximate representation of a 'literal truth'. This paradoxical notion of the map as a 'shifting ground' is discussed at length by the French post-structuralists Gilles Deleuze and Félix Guattari. For Deleuze and Guattari, maps are experimental in orientation:

> The map is open and connectable in all its dimensions; it is detachable, reversible, susceptible to constant modification. It can be torn, reversed, adapted to any kind of mounting, re-worked by an individual, group, or social formation. It can be drawn on the wall, conceived of as a work of art, constructed as a political action or as a meditation. (12)

The flexible design of the map is likened by Deleuze and Guattari to that of the rhizome, whose 'deterritorializing lines of flight' (222) effect 'an asignifying rupture against the oversignifying breaks separating structures or cutting across a single structure' (7–9).

As Diana Brydon has illustrated, Deleuze and Guattari's association of the multiple connections/disconnections of the rhizome with the transformative patterns of the map provides a useful, if by its very nature problematic, working model for the description of postcolonial cultures and for a closer investigation of the kaleidoscopic variations of postcolonial discourse (Brydon 1988). Moreover, a number of contemporary women writers in Canada and Australia, notably Nicole Brossard and Marion Campbell, have adapted Deleuze and Guattari's model to the articulation of a feminist cartography which dissociates itself from the 'oversignifying' spaces of patriarchal representation but which, through its 'deterritorializing lines of flight', produces an alternative kind of map characterized not by the containment or regimentation of space but by a series of centrifugal displacements.[11] Other implicitly 'rhizomatic' maps are sketched out in experimental fictions such as those of Kroetsch and Baillie (in Canada), and Bail and Murnane (in Australia) where space, as in Deleuze and Guattari's model, is constituted in terms of a series of intermingled lines of connection that shape shifting patterns of de- and reterritorialization. In the work of these and other 'new novelists', the map is often identified, then parodied and/or ironized, as a spurious definitional construct, thereby permitting the writer to engage in a more wide-ranging deconstruction of Western signifying systems (one thinks, for example, of Nicholas Hasluck's sly negotiation of the labyrinths of the legal system in *The Bellarmine Jug* or of Yolande Villemaire's playful critique of the semiotics of Western culture in *La Vie en prose*).

If the map is conceived of in Deleuze and Guattari's terms as a rhizomatic ('open') rather than as a falsely homogeneous ('closed') construct, the emphasis then shifts from de- to reconstruction, from map*breaking* to map*making*. The benefit of Deleuze and Guattari's model is that it provides a viable alternative to those implicitly hegemonic (and historically colonialist) forms of cartographic discourse which use the duplicating procedures of mimetic representation and structuralist reconstitution as a strategic means of stabilizing the foundations of Western culture and of 'fixing' the position (thereby maintaining the power) of the West in relation to cultures other than its own. Thus, whereas Derrida's deconstructive analysis of the concepts of 'centred' structure and 'interested' simulacrum engenders a process of displacement which undoes the supposed homogeneity of colonial discourse, Deleuze and Guattari's rhizomatic map views this process in terms of a processual transformation more pertinent to the operations of postcolonial discourse and to the complex patterns of de- and reterritorialization working within and between the multicultural societies of the postcolonial world.

As Stephen Slemon has demonstrated, one of the characteristic ploys of postcolonial discourse is its adoption of a creative revisionism which involves the subversion or displacement of dominant discourses (Slemon, 'Monuments', 'Postcolonial'). But included within this revisionary process is the internal critique of the postcolonial culture (or cultures), a critique which takes into account the transitional nature of postcolonial societies and which challenges the tenets both of an essentialist nationalism that sublimates or overlooks regional differences and of an unconsidered multiculturalism (mis)appropriated for the purposes of enforced assimilation rather than for the promulgation of cultural diversity. The fascination of postcolonial writers, and of Canadian and Australian writers in particular, with the map topos can be seen in this context as a specific instance of creative revisionism in which the desystematization of a narrowly defined and demarcated 'cartographic' space allows for a culturally and historically located critique of colonial discourse while, at the same time, producing the momentum for a projection and exploration of 'new territories' outlawed or neglected by dominant discourses that previously operated in the colonial, but now continue to operate in modified or transposed forms in the postcolonial, culture. I would suggest further that, in the cases of contemporary Canadian and Australian literatures, these territories correspond to a series of new or revised rhetorical spaces occupied by *feminism*, *regionalism* and *ethnicity*, where each of these items is understood primarily as a set of counter-discursive strategies which challenge the claims of, or avoid circumscription within, one or other form of cultural centrism.[12] These territories/spaces can also be considered, however, as shifting grounds which are themselves subject to transformational patterns of de- and reterritorialization. The proliferation of spatial references, crossing of physical and/or conceptual boundaries and redisposition of geographical coordinates in much contemporary Canadian and Australian writing stresses the provisionality of cartographic connection and places the increasing diversity of their respective literatures in the context of a postcolonial response to and/or reaction against the ontology and epistemology of 'stability' promoted and safeguarded by colonial discourse.

I would conclude from this that the role of cartography in contemporary Canadian and Australian writing, specifically, and in postcolonial writing in general, cannot be solely envisaged as the reworking of a particular spatial paradigm, but consists rather in the implementation of a series of creative revisions which register the transition from a colonial framework within which the writer is compelled to recreate and reflect upon the restrictions of colonial space to a postcolonial one within which he or she acquires the freedom to engage in a series of 'territorial disputes' that implicitly or explicitly acknowledge the relativity of modes of spatial (and, by extension, cultural) perception. So while the map continues to feature in one sense as a paradigm of colonial discourse, its deconstruction and/or revisualization permits a 'disidentification'[13] from the procedures of colonialism and other hegemonic discourses and a (re-)engagement in the ongoing process of cultural decolonization. The 'cartographic connection' can therefore be considered to provide that provisional link which joins the contestatory theories of poststructuralism and postcolonialism in the pursuit of social and cultural change.

Works Cited

Atwood, Margaret. *The Handmaid's Tale*. Toronto: McClelland and Stewart, 1985.

Bail, Murray. *Homesickness*. Melbourne: Macmillan, 1980.

Baillie, Robert. *Les Voyants*. Montreal: Hexagone, 1986.

Barker, Francis *et al.*, eds. *Europe and its Others*. 2 vols. Colchester: University of Essex Press, 1985.

Barthes, Roland. 'The Structuralist Activity'. In *Critical Essays*. Evanston, IL: Northwestern University Press, 1972. 213–20.

Benterrak, Krim, Stephen Muecke and Paddy Roe. *Reading the Country: An Introduction to Nomadology*. Fremantle: Fremantle Arts Centre Press, 1984.

Bhabha, Homi. 'Signs Taken for Wonders: Questions of Ambivalence and Authority Under a Tree Outside Delhi; May 1817'. In Barker *et al.*, eds. Vol. 1, 89–106.

——. 'The Other Question: Difference, Discrimination and the Discourse of Colonialism'. In *Literature, Politics and Theory*. Ed. Francis Barker *et al.* London: Methuen, 1986. 148–72.

——. 'Of Mimicry and Man: The Ambivalence of Colonial Discourse'. *October* 28 (1984): 125–33.

Board, Christopher. 'Maps as Models'. In *Models in Geography*. Ed. Richard Chorley and Peter Haggett. London: Meuthen, 1967. 671–725.

Bringhurst, Robert. *Pieces of Map; Pieces of Music*. Toronto: McClelland and Stewart, 1986.

Brossard, Nicole. *Picture Theory*. Montreal: Nouvelle Optique, 1982.

Brydon, Diana. 'Troppo Agitato: Reading and Writing Cultures in Randolph Stow's *Visitants* and Rudy Wiebe's *The Temptations of Big Bear*'. *Ariel* 19.1 (1988): 13–32.

Campbell, Marion. *Lines of Flight*. Fremantle: Fremantle Arts Centre Press, 1985.

Chorley, Richard J. and Peter Haggett, eds. *Models in Geography*. London: Methuen, 1967.

Culler, Jonathan. *On Deconstruction: Theory and Criticism after Structuralism*. London: Routledge, 1983.

Deleuze, Gilles and Félix Guattari. *A Thousand Plateaus: Capitalism and Schizophrenia*. Trans. B. Massumi. Minneapolis: University of Minnesota Press, 1987.

Derrida, Jacques. *Of Grammatology*. Trans. Gayatri Spivak. Baltimore: Johns Hopkins University Press, 1976.

——. 'Structure, Sign and Play in the Discourse of the Human Sciences'. In *Writing and Difference*. Trans. Alan Bass. Chicago: University of Chicago Press, 1978. 279–93.

Felperin, Howard. *Beyond Deconstruction: The Uses and Abuses of Literary Theory*. Oxford: Clarendon Press, 1985.

Godard, Barbara. 'Mapmaking'. In *Gynocritics: Feminist Approaches to Canadian and Quebecois Women's Writing*. Ed. B. Godard. Toronto: ECW Press, 1987. 2–30.

Grace, Sherrill. 'Articulating the Space Between: Atwood's Untold Stories and Fresh Beginnings'. In *Margaret Atwood: Language, Text, and System*. Ed. S. Grace and L. Weir. Vancouver: University of British Columbia Press, 1983. 1–16.

Harley, J. B. 'Maps, Knowledge and Power'. In *The Iconography of Landscape*. Ed. D. Cosgrove and S. Daniels. Cambridge: Cambridge University Press, 1988. 277–312.

Harris, Wilson. *Explorations: A Selection of Talks and Articles 1966–81*. Mundelstrup: Dangaroo Press, 1981.

—— *Palace of the Peacock*. London: Faber & Faber, 1968.

Hart, Kevin. 'Maps of Deconstruction'. *Meanjin* 45.1 (1986): 107–17.

Hasluck, Nicholas. *The Bellarmine Jug*. Ringwood, Victoria: Penguin, 1984.

Hodgins, Jack. *The Invention of the World*. Toronto: Macmillan, 1977.

Hulme, Peter. *Colonial Encounters: Europe and the Native Caribbean: 1492–1797*. London: Methuen, 1986.

Kroetsch, Robert. *Badlands*. Toronto: New Press, 1975.

Krupnick, Mark. 'Introduction'. In *Displacement: Derrida and After*. Ed. M. Krupnick. Bloomington, IN: Indiana University Press, 1983. 1–17.

Lee, Dennis. 'Cadence, Country, Silence: Writing in Colonial Space'. *Boundary 2* 3 (1976): 151–68.

Malouf, David. *12 Edmondstone Street*. London: Chatto and Windus, 1985.

McDougall, Russell. 'On Location:. Australian and Canadian Literature'. *True North/Down Under* (1985): 12–42.

Muehrcke, Philip and Juliana Muehrcke. *Map Use: Reading, Analysis and Interpretation*. Madison, WI: JP Publications, 1978.

Murnane, Gerald. *The Plains*. Ringwood, Victoria: Penguin, 1984.

Pêcheux, Michel. *Language, Semantics and Ideology*. London: Macmillan, 1982.

Rabasa, José. 'Allegories of the Atlas'. In Barker *et al.*, eds. Vol. II, 1–16.

Said, Edward. *Orientalism*. Harmondsworth: Penguin, 1985.

Shapcott, Thomas. *Travel Dice*. St Lucia: University of Queensland Press, 1987.

Slemon, Stephen. 'Postcolonial Allegory and the Transformation of History'. *The Journal of Commonwealth Literature* 23.1 (1988): 157–68.

——. 'Monuments of Empire: Allegory/Counter-Discourse/Postcolonial Writing'. *Kunapipi* 9.3 (1987): 1–16.

Spariosu, Mihai. 'Editor's Introduction'. In *Mimesis in Contemporary Theory: An Interdisciplinary Approach*. Ed. M. Spariosu. Philadelphia: John Benjamins, 1984. I–xxix.

Spivak, Gayatri. 'The Rani of Sirmur'. In Barker *et al.*, eds. Vol. I, 128–51.

Terdiman, Richard. *Discourse/Counter-Discourse: The Theory and Practice of Symbolic Resistance in Nineteenth Century France*. Ithaca, NY: Cornell University Press, 1985.

Tiffin, Helen. 'Postcolonialism, Post-Modernism and the Rehabilitation of Postcolonial History'. *The Journal of Commonwealth Literature* 23.1 (1988): 169–81.

——. 'Post-Colonial Literatures and Counter-Discourse'. *Kunapipi* 9.3 (1987): 17–38.

Van Herk, Aritha. *No Fixed Address*. Toronto: McClelland and Stewart, 1986.

Villemaire, Yolande. *La Vie en prose*. Montreal: Les Herbes Rouges, 1980.

Wright, John. 'Map Makers are Human: Comments on the Subjective in Maps'. *Cartographica* 19 (1977): 8–25.

Notes

1 I shall adopt here Peter Hulme's definition of colonial discourse as 'an ensemble of linguistically based practices unified by their common deployment in the management of colonial relationships' (Hulme 2). For a more detailed account, see the opening chapter of Hulme's *Colonial Encounters*.

2 For an excellent summary of these strategies, and of the relations between cartographic and colonial practices, see J.B. Harley's essay in Cosgrove and Daniels, eds.

3 For a development of this argument, see Mihai Spariosu's introduction to *Mimesis in Contemporary Theory*.

4 The argument is taken up and expanded in Christopher Board's essay in Chorley and Haggett. See also Philip and Juliana Muehrcke's discussion of the limitations of and distortions within cartographic representation, and Wright's early, but still relevant, essay.

5 For an investigation of the multiple implications of the term 'displacement', see the essays in, and particularly Mark Krupnick's introduction to, the collection *Displacement: Derrida and After*.

6 Although I am taking issue here with the excessively negative tenor of Hulme's, Felperin's and Tiffin's critiques of the neo-hegemonic assumptions behind Franco-American deconstruction, I would support their general thesis that applications of deconstructionist and other poststructuralist methodologies should take account of the ambivalent position of poststructuralist theory within self-privileging Western cultural institutions, and, in particular, of its apparent elevation to the status of a new orthodoxy.

7 For a fictional rendition of this argument see Harris's novella *Palace of the Peacock*. Many of the essays in his collection *Explorations* deal indirectly with maps as metaphors within the wide framework of a 'revisioning' of Caribbean (and other

postcolonial) cultural history. For essays which explore the implications of Harris's theories for postcolonial writing, see Slemon and Tiffin.

8 Cf. McDougall's comments on Hodgins in 'On Location: Australian and Canadian Literature'.

9 Cf. Grace's essay on Atwood in Grace and Weir.

10 See Brydon's critique of colonial ethnocentrism in 'Troppo Agitato'; see also Dennis Lee's 'Cadence, Country, Silence' for a discussion of the problems involved in writing 'in colonial space'.

11 See also Barbara Godard's introductory essay 'Mapmaking' in the collection *Gynocritics*; and Benterrak, Muecke and Roe's reading of Deleuze and Guattari within the context of a postcolonial (more specifically, Aboriginal) critique of Western territorial imperatives.

12 The relevance of counter-discursive formations to postcolonial writing is discussed at length in the essays by Slemon and Tiffin. For a definition of counter-discourse (adapted by Slemon and Tiffin), see Terdiman.

13 The term is Michel Pêcheux's; for a discussion of its implications for postcolonial writing, see Slemon and Tiffin.

CHAPTER 2

Unsettled Settlers: Postcolonialism, Travelling Theory and the New Migrant Aesthetics

In this chapter, I want to explore the apparent discrepancy between historical experiences of migration and aestheticized theories of 'migrancy' that have emerged from contemporary cultural studies. I will posit a link between the metaphorization of migration and the often utopian spatial poetics/politics of postcolonial theory. I will then examine this link by looking at two recent works by cultural theorists that attempt, in different ways, to bridge the gap between postmodern 'travelling theory' and postcolonial cultural politics. These works – Paul Carter's *Living in a New Country* (1992) and Iain Chambers' *Migrancy, Culture, Identity* (1994) – can be seen as examples of a new 'migrant aesthetic' which uses poststructuralist theories of displacement to account conceptually for migrating people, goods and ideas within the so-called New World Order. I will assess both the benefits and the limitations of such an approach; finally, I will consider the extent to which the current cultural studies debates surrounding migration shed light on Australia's contested status as a postcolonial settler society.

I want to begin, though, with four no doubt unfairly decontextualized quotations on the subject of migration, the first from a political scientist (Aristide R. Zolberg), the second from a sociologist (Hans-Joachim Hoffmann-Nowotny), the third from an economist (Robert E. B. Lucas), and the fourth from a cultural theorist (Iain Chambers). Here are the quotations, which I will juxtapose without further comment:

> If we conceive of a world which consists, on the one hand, of individuals seeking to maximise their welfare by exercising a variety of choices [...] and, on the other, of mutually exclusive societies, acting as organized states to maximise collective goals by controlling the exit or entry of individuals [...] the deviant character of individual migration is thus seen to be related to a fundamental tension between the interests of individuals and the interests of societies. (Zolberg 7)

* * *

Migration results from structural and anomic tensions [...] and is a process by which such tensions are transformed and transferred [...] [Two cases may be cited. In the first, an] individual may have a more or less balanced status configuration within a societal system, but may experience anomic tension because he or she is a member of a power deficient system [...] In such a case, the member may give up system membership status and migrate to another system with a lower power deficit or a power surplus [...] [In the second, an] individual experiences an anomic tension which can be traced back not to the external position of the system but to the internal status quo. If the individual unit perceives the chance of achieving a reduction of the anomic tension internally as low, the individual can try to achieve an improvement of status configuration by emigrating. (Hoffmann-Nowotny 70)

* * *

It is [...] perhaps natural to consider weighing the pros and cons [of migration] within a cost-benefit framework [...] [T]his type of study would divide the population into various categories: children, semi-skilled men, professional women, and so on. The emigration or immigration of each is then viewed as a project to be subjected to cost-benefit criteria [...] I shall assume the objective is one of efficiency, though in principle it is quite possible to introduce distributional weights recognising perhaps a greater concern for the incidence of costs and benefits on lower income groups. (Lucas 104)

* * *

In the oblique gaze of the migrant that cuts across the territory of the Western metropolis there exists the hint of a metaphor. In the extensive and multiple worlds of the modern city we, too, become nomads, migrating across a system that is too vast to be our own, but in which we are fully involved – translating and transforming what we find and absorb into local instances of sense [...] It is, above all, here, that we are inducted into a hybrid state and composite culture in which the simple dualism of First and Third Worlds collapses and there emerges what Homi Bhabha calls a 'differential communality', and what Félix Guattari refers to as the 'process of *heterogenesis*'. The boundaries of the liberal consensus and its centred sense of language, being, position and politics, are breached and scattered as all our histories come to be rewritten in the contentious languages of what has tended to become the privileged *topos* of the modern world: the contemporary metropolis. (Chambers 14)

The day-to-day struggles of many contemporary migrants within today's so-called new world order encounter a further level of conflict here in the competing jargons of academic prose. This chapter is in part about the difficulty of reconciling the often convoluted language of academic abstraction with the equally complex lived experience, in both past and present, of individual migrants and migrant groups. I will argue (as many academics do) for a dialectical understanding of migration as both adaptable conceptual tool and ongoing socio-historical process; I will also argue – with some reservations – for an inter- and/or multidisciplinary methodology with which to analyse migration as an intricate nexus of social, political, economic and historical forces. This line of thinking tallies with several studies on migration, from the literary/ geographical collaboration *Writing across Worlds: Literature and Migration* (1995) to the multidisciplinary Swedish-based project *International Migration, Immobility and Development* (1997), to Robin Cohen's magisterial multi-authored *Cambridge Survey of World Migration* (1995). What is common to these projects, and several others like them, is the recognition that migration cannot just be seen in terms of the 'transference of human capital', but must also be gauged in terms of cultural impact and the shifting winds of global change (Sowell 391).[1] As Stephen Castles and Mark J. Miller suggest in their somewhat misleadingly titled study *The Age of Migration: International Population Movements in the Modern World* (1993), 'immigration changes demographic and social structures, affects political institutions and helps to reshape cultures' (96). Never more so than today; for while international migration is hardly 'an invention of the late twentieth century [...] [i]t has grown in volume and significance since 1945 and most particularly since the mid-1980s' (Castles and Miller 3), with every chance of further, possibly spectacular, growth in what is now the new millennium. This growth is not merely demographic, but indicates a mounting realization that migration is 'one of the most important factors in [effecting and analysing] global change' (Castles and Miller 4). 'The hallmark of the age of migration', for Castles and Miller, 'is the *global* character of its migration: the way it affects more and more countries, and its linkages with complex processes affecting the entire world' (260, emphasis added).

It is not the place of this chapter to examine these complex global processes, but rather to reflect on the various *discourses* through which ideas about migration are produced, disseminated and consumed. One such discourse pertains to contemporary critical/cultural theory, which, particularly since the work of Edward Said and James Clifford in the 1980s and early 1990s, has had a great deal to say about migrants and migration.[2] What is noticeable in much of this work, which might be loosely bracketed under the fashionable heading of 'travelling theory', is the *metaphorization* of migration as a composite figure for a series of metaphysical, as well as physical, displacements. The metaphor of migration serves a variety of different purposes: to illustrate the increasing fragmentation of subjecthood and subjectivity under (post)modernity; to reflect on the semantic instability underlying all constructions of (personal/cultural/ national) identity; and to insist on the homology between experiences of dislocation and the destabilization of essentialist ideologies and 'fixed' paradigms and patterns of thought. Migration has become a useful code-word for the different kinds of conceptual slippage that are characteristic of postmodern/ poststructuralist approaches towards linguistic and cultural systems; in addition, migration functions as a catalysing metaphor for the exploration of cultural change and the apprehension of new, mobile cultural subjects in the nominally post-national era.[3]

The dangers attendant on the metaphorization of migrant experience are not lost on many of these theorists: the cultural theorist James Clifford, for example, in *Routes: Translation and Travel in the Late Twentieth Century* (1997), warns against 'talk[ing] of travel and displacement in unmarked ways, thus normalising male experience' (258);[4] while the literary/cultural critic Caren Kaplan in her book *Questions of Travel: Postmodern Discourses of Displacement* (1996), makes the valid if obvious point that travel metaphors, including those of migration, risk levelling out discrepant historical experiences, blurring the boundaries between voluntary and involuntary forms of movement, and at worst acting as an alibi for the privileges of a worldly cosmopolitan elite.

As Kaplan suggests, migration and other patterns of human movement in the modern era tend to carry an imperial legacy that is often mystified in the voguish academic categories of nomadism, migrancy and displacement. One might expect these mystifications to be of interest to *postcolonial* critics, who have arguably made it their business to bring imperialism back to the centre of self-involved postmodern debates surrounding language, identity and representation in the present late-capitalist conjuncture. Yet even a cursory glance at some of the latest postcolonial theory reveals a similar propensity to use spatial metaphors loosely, even in some cases interchangeably. A particular culprit here is Homi Bhabha, whose celebrated notion of a 'third space of enunciation' – a space he sees as being occupied by, among others, migrants in the Western metropoles – involves a vertiginous conflation of different metaphors of displacement.[5] Revealingly, in an interview with Paul Thompson for the collection of essays *Migration and Identity* (1994), Bhabha speaks of the emergence of a 'new complex, culturally problematic kind of *cosmopolitanism* [...] of migration, which has a very specific postcolonial and Third World history' (196, emphasis added). Yet it is precisely the *elision* of a certain kind of cosmopolitan privilege that arguably limits – and also locates – Bhabha's project.[6] Postcolonial theorists such as Bhabha have justifiably been criticized for their tendency to mystify the same – uneven – relations of power their work claims to uncover. The same might also be said of some of the writers whose works they discuss; as Elleke Boehmer argues in her introductory study *Colonial & Postcolonial Literature* (1995) (the subtitle of which, appropriately enough, is *Migrant Metaphors*), postcoloniality refers to the emergence of a set of conditions for the globalization of 'migrant writing', which she defines somewhat ungenerously as 'a literature written by elites, and defined and canonised by elites' (239–40). This type of literature, for Boehmer, runs the risk of 'evacuating commitment' in the pursuit of celebrating rootlessness and cosmopolitan *joie-de-vivre* (240). 'To define a literature of migrant floating as the culmination of the postcolonial', Boehmer concludes sardonically, 'does represent something of a diminution in a long tradition of self-consciously political writing' (240).

Boehmer's comments are self-confessedly generalized; but they indicate the anxiety hovering around the edges of postcolonial discourse that 'the postcolonial' may be less a marker, as is usually claimed, of opposition than a kind of brand-name for the palatable 'otherness' purveyed and consumed by metropolitan elites.[7] 'In the 1990s', according to Boehmer, 'the generic postcolonial writer is more likely to be a cultural traveller, or an "extra-territorial", than a national' (233). To trade in migrant metaphors can thus become a profitable business, with rewards handed out to writers who, self-conscious border-crossers, know how to manipulate the transcultural codes of a postcolonial 'migrant aesthetic'. (The best example here is, unsurprisingly, Salman Rushdie, who has always taken care to position himself, both pre- and post-*fatwa*, as a cosmopolitan 'migrant writer' belonging to what he calls 'a world community of displaced writers' (15) that includes such figures as Milan Kundera, Maxine Hong Kingston and Günter Grass.)[8] And yet, I want to suggest, it is not just creative writers who have subscribed, consciously or not, to the pre-set 'geopolitical aesthetic' rules of literary cosmopolitanism (Brennan). A variety of literary critics and cultural theorists have also jumped on the bandwagon, fostering a fraught alliance between the allegedly transgressive manoeuvres of postmodern travelling theory and the putatively oppositional politics of postcolonial cultural practice. The figure – the *rhetorical* figure – of the migrant plays a key role here, allowing both for claims of resistance to dominant (state) formations and for self-liberating linguistic play in the 'borderline engagement of cultural differ-ence' (Bhabha 2; also qtd in Kunow 92).

A good example of this alliance is in Iain Chambers' acclaimed study – part travelogue, part cultural commentary, part philosophical meditation – of the impact of cultural diversity on today's increasingly transnational world. *Migrancy, Culture, Identity* (1994), says Meaghan Morris in a dutifully admiring blurb on the back cover, has enhanced Chambers' reputation as 'the dreamer of contempo-rary cultural studies'. The book's interconnected essays 'tell stories of different worlds that already define our own; moving lightly through border-zones of culture dense with new ideas, they stop to chat with strangers on the way; and they share with us the wise joy in dialogue as a way of working towards a common horizon'. This generous tribute, as blurbs often do, tells us more about Morris's engaging brand of breezy populism than it does about Chambers' project, in which the lyrical ambitions of the author are frequently stymied by turgid prose. (I should probably confess to a certain irritation at the relentless *modishness* of Chambers' writing, its aura of street-smart intellectualism and sophisticated worldly *savoir-faire*. Possibly this signals my no doubt snobbish dis-ease with hypertheorized approaches to popular culture, which risk fetishizing the cultural phenomena they claim to be explaining, and which arguably supplant one form of elitism – the Arnoldian connoisseurship of 'high' culture – with another, the postmodernist unravelling of the complexities of everyday life.)

That said, what exactly is the nature of Chambers' project? Ostensibly, it is an analysis of forms of global movement under modernity – mass migration, the worldwide transportation of consumer goods, the transnational circuitries of capital, and so on – which create a volatile mix that belies (white) European pretensions to cultural superiority and stability. As Chambers puts it:

> When the 'Third World' is no longer maintained at a distance 'out there' but begins to appear 'in here', when the encounter between diverse cultures, histories, religions and languages no longer occurs along the peripheries [...] but emerges at the centre of our daily lives, in the cities of the so-called

'advanced', or 'First', world, then we can perhaps begin to talk of a significant interruption in the preceding sense of our own lives, cultures, languages and futures. (2)

'Migrancy' – a cultural studies neologism I have been unable to trace in any dictionary – describes this condition of 'interruption' and historical disturbance; involving a psychic, as well as physical, shift in which 'neither the points of departure nor those of arrival are immutable or certain, [it] calls for a dwelling in language, in histories, in identities, that are constantly subject to mutation' (Chambers 5). 'Migrancy' registers as much a semantic as a historical disruption, one in which

> the nomadic experience of language [...] is no longer the expression of a unique tradition or history; [in which] thought [itself] wanders [...] migrates, requires translation; [and in which] reason runs the risk of opening out on to the world, of finding itself in a passage without a reassuring foundation or finality. (Chambers 4)

'Migrancy', finally, describes a project of *conversion* through which diverse histories of displacement – often highly painful to those affected – are to be assimilated to an aesthetic of pleasurable intercultural contact.

There are several obvious problems associated with this utopian venture. For one, as Chambers himself recognizes, there is the danger of blurring boundaries between, on the one hand, those coercive forms of dislocation that are

> induced by war, economic deprivation, political repression, poverty [and] racist slavery [...] and [, on the other hand,] that diffuse sense of mobility that characterises metropolitan life, [and that is] charted in the privileged channels of movement represented by the media, information technology, advertising, tourism and a generalised consumerism. (Chambers 28)

For another, there is the risk of overemphasizing the city as the *locus classicus* of migration, the place where different and often contradictory realities mix and mingle. 'Migrancy', as Chambers admits, is very much a *metropolitan* aesthetic, based on the mutability and restless creativity of urban praxis, but also on the potential exclusivism of a view in which 'the model of the city becomes [...] the model of the contemporary world' (Chambers 27).[9] And for a third, there is the tendency to collapse the understanding of cultural difference into the consumption of (multi-)ethnic products whose 'otherness' is easily assumed. Consider the transition in the following passage between political intent and personal pleasure:

> In the migrant landscapes of contemporary metropolitan cultures, de-terri-torialised and de-colonised, re-situating, re-citing and re-presenting common signs in the circuits between speech, image and oblivion, a constant strug-gling into sense and history is pieced together. It is a history that is continu-ally being decomposed and recomposed in the interlacing between what we have inherited and where we are.

In the shifting interstices of this world, whether moving to the acoustic patterns of our bodily beat or the techno-surrealist design of computerised simulations, there exists the opening that redeems and reconstitutes our being [...] It is perhaps something that we can hear when Youssou N'Dour, from Dakar, sings in Wolof, a Senegalese dialect, in a tent pitched in the suburbs of Naples. [Chambers currently lives in Naples, where he teaches at the Istituto Universitario Orientale.] Only six months earlier I had heard his haunting voice in a New York club, this time in the context of the Japanese techno-pop/New Age sound of Ryuichi Sakamoto and No Wave New York guitarist Arto Lindsay. It is surely in these terms, well before intellectual and institutional acknowledgement, that we come most immediately and effectively to recognise the differentiated territories in which the imaginary is being disseminated and the eurocentric voice simultaneously dispersed. (Chambers 14–15)

Chambers is unembarrassed by this transparent assertion of 'conspicuous cosmopolitanism',[10] through which the 'de-colonised landscapes of contemporary metropolitan cultures' provide a stage for the straining affect of a would-be postcolonial sensibility. My diction is no doubt too harsh here, but suffice to say I am unconvinced by Chambers' attempt to wed a putatively radical postcolonial cultural politics to an ambivalently indexed postmodern response to cultural consumerism on a global scale. As I have already suggested, the tensions contained within Chambers' version of a migrant aesthetic are already present within postcolonialism as a contemporary currency of intellectual exchange. (Elsewhere, I have analysed these tensions in terms of the competing 'regimes of value' [Appadurai, *Social Life*] that surround the global production and consumption of culturally 'othered' artifacts and ideas [Huggan, *Postcolonial*]). Theories of 'migrancy' might similarly be seen in terms of the apparent contradiction between explicitly *anti*-colonial imperatives to open up new cultural horizons and implicitly *neo*-colonial designs to keep cultural difference in its place.

I want to turn at this stage to another recent attempt to bridge the differences between migration as historical process and 'migrancy' as aesthetic creed. This is the work of the Australian cultural critic and theorist Paul Carter, best known for his excursions into the field of 'spatial history' (*The Road to Botany Bay*, 1987; *The Lie of the Land*, 1996), but also – as I shall demonstrate – an accomplished, if maverick, aesthetician and philosopher of language. I shall concentrate here on Carter's second book, *Living in a New Country: History, Travelling and Language* (1992), partly because it serves as a useful counterpoint to Chambers' study, and partly because it provides me with a segue into the last part of the chapter, an assessment of Australia's current status as a mixed migrant society and, more controversially perhaps, as a rapidly changing postcolonial settler culture.

Carter's book, as its title announces, is about living in a new country, one which is marked by a certain fluidity – a *provisionality* – of interpersonal exchange (*Living* 5–6). Whereas Chambers, based in Europe, must make the case for rejuvenation, Carter in Australia already assumes it, not so much in the country as it is, but in the ways in which it is seen (*Living* 5). This perception of novelty is implicitly associated with a migrant society in which 'language has [...] yet to detach itself from the contingencies of speaking and hearing'; in which communication involves the continual renegotiation of 'dialogical contracts'; and in which a 'migrant psychology', recognizing the arbitrariness of social/linguistic conventions, both registers and inhabits the gap that inevitably separates names and things (Carter, *Living* 6–7). This migrant sensibility, as Carter notes, has not prevented the vilification of 'foreign elements' in Australia as elsewhere, in the so-called Old World as well as the New. In a global climate in which mass migration co-exists with, and sometimes fuels, recrudescent nationalism,

> it becomes more than ever urgent to develop a framework of thinking that makes the migrant central, not ancillary, to historical processes. We need to disarm the genealogical rhetoric of blood, property and frontiers and to substitute for it a lateral account of social relations, one that stresses the contingency of all definitions of self and other, and the necessity always to tread lightly, [...] to make migratory haphazardness the material out of which [our social fabric] weaves its identity. (Carter, *Living* 7–8)

One recognizes here, if in a more lucid form, the emphasis on intercultural dialogue and the celebratory insistence on the performative basis of identity formation that are characteristic of Chambers' work. One recognizes also the common desire to aestheticize 'migrancy', to posit it as an alternative to the poetics of settled spaces and as a rejoinder to the linear discourses associated, somewhat loosely, with Enlightenment thought.

In Carter's last, astonishing chapter this migrant aesthetic is explored further through a reformulation of the modernist techniques of free association and arbitrary juxtaposition. These techniques are brought together in the rhetorical device of collage. For the modernists, Carter explains, 'collage was a disruptive device, a mechanism for undermining bourgeois notions of representation and tradition'; but in a postcolonial society, which Carter equates in Australia with a migrant society, collage is not anomalous but

> the normal mode of constructing meaning. Everyday speech does not flower out of any deeply held and mutually shared unconscious grammar but is patched together from heterogeneous lexical, syntactic and grammatical sources that are generally produced imitatively, without any sense of context. (*Living* 186–87)

Carter cites the example of Australia's 'major suburban streets, with their eclectic mix of commercial signs, advertising hoardings and historically parodic architectural styles' (*Living* 187). Most of his other examples, though, are less visual than auditory or *phonic*; for the primary effect of what Carter calls 'postcolonial collage' is to 'relocate and sound the spaces in between' different utterances, and to reveal '[w]ithin the ritualised performances of language [...] a deeper poetics, a suppressed association mediated through sound, cadence, rhythm, pitch and stress' (Carter, *Living* 187, 198).

It is in the spaces opened up by migrant (mis)communication that Carter locates a poetics of movement, of productively interrupted speech. Like Chambers, Carter views migration as metaphysical as well as physical itinerary:

> An authentically migrant perspective would, perhaps, be based on an intuition that the opposition between here and there is itself a cultural construction, a consequence of thinking in terms of fixed entities and defining them oppositionally. It might begin by regarding movement, not as an awkward interval between fixed points of departure, but as a mode of being in the world. The question would be, then, not how to arrive, but how to move, how to identify convergent and divergent movements; and the challenge would be how to notate such events, how to give them a historical and social value. (*Living* 101)

This challenge might come as welcome news to historians of migration; but like Chambers, Carter makes little effort to distinguish between different migrant experiences, preferring instead to assimilate these to an overarching migrant aesthetic or, in his ambitious claim, to 'a migrant theory of meaning'. Empirical evidence is abandoned in favour of metaphysical speculation; the ingenuity of Carter's theories (which are, of course, in part a celebration of *migrant* ingenuity) is arguably diminished by his idealist reliance on a generic 'migrant situation'. 'Migrancy', or Carter's version of it, thus risks becoming a totalizing theory even as it accentuates improvisation and the gaps in established systems of meaning and thought.

To be fair to Carter, his is not only a brilliantly *poetical* defence of 'the migrant condition', but also a thoughtful alternative to what he calls the 'prosaic' type of narrative history in which 'the master historian, carefully contextualising, ingeniously iron[s] out differences in the interests of his grand narrative' (Carter, *Living* 191). 'Migrancy' emerges in this latter context less as a theorization of migrant histories than as an attempt to understand the grounds of historical thinking in figurative – that is to say, aesthetic – terms. These terms are closely allied to the principles of travelling theory: the need to understand culture, not as a stable entity but as an intersection of different trajectories (Clifford, 'Traveling Cultures'); the need to understand identity as being formed and reformed on the move; and, not least, the need to understand theory as a horizon of figuration, as a shifting composite of metaphors that travel, as ideas themselves travel, in time and space (Said, 'Traveling'). Travelling theory, in cultural terms, allows for perspectives on global movement that stress the provisionality of all forms of intercultural connection. This raises the complex question of how to fashion group solidarities, and of how to locate agency, in a global cultural economy punctuated by incommensurable 'differences' and 'disjunctures' (Appadurai, 'Disjuncture'). It could be argued against Carter that his aestheticized theory of migrant meaning traps migrants themselves in a semantic loop, propelling them into situations where their adaptive genius, their capacity to improvise and create new meanings, merely reconfirms their disempowerment at the hands of the cultural orthodoxy – and of state authority. If 'migrancy' registers the speculative attempt to apprehend movement 'as a mode of being in the world', it is surely not an answer to those who seek to control (meaning mostly to restrict) migrants' actual movements. The suspicion emerges that 'migrancy' might be a form of anti-essentialist essentialism which disguises the uneven relations of power between different migrant groups – including the power of course to decide who is or is not a migrant. This begs the question of the particular 'migrant situation' in Australia, and of changing definitions and perceptions of migration and of the mixed migrant society.

'We are mostly all migrants', says Carter in his introduction to *Living in a New Country*, 'and even if we have tried to stay at home, the conditions of life have changed so utterly in this century that we find ourselves strangers in our own houses' (7). Yet as I have suggested, this universalization of 'the migrant experience' in travelling theory overlooks often conspicuously hierarchical attitudes towards different migrant groups. In Australia, these attitudes not only indicate a history of selective immigration policy, but also the continuing inequalities of access – to education, economic opportunity, political power and so on – for different migrant communities within a supposedly multicultural society.[11] The two pieces on twentieth-century Australia in Robin Cohen's *Cambridge Survey on World Migration* restrict themselves to immigration patterns for southern Europeans and Asians.[12] This picture is potentially misleading; for while immigration to Australia in the last few decades has certainly derived from southern Europe and, increasingly, Asia, with Asians accounting for some 40 per cent of intakes in the early 1990s, post-Second World War efforts to bring in migrants to Australia focused on *Britain*, operating on a ratio of roughly ten British migrants for every 'foreigner' accepted (Castles and Miller). The tendency to overlook migrants of British (or, more problematically, 'Anglo-Celtic') origin replicates the common view that, while technically the vast majority of Australians are migrants, some – to adapt Lolo Houbein via George Orwell – are more 'migrant' than others.[13] A similar forgetfulness has affected some studies of so-called 'migrant writing' in Australia, in which it is assumed that migrant writers are, by definition, 'non-Anglo-Celtic' (Gunew and Longley). The view of migrant writing as predominantly transgressive or counter-hegemonic merely reinforces ethnic compartmentalization, both by manufacturing a series of 'representative' migrant voices and by homogenizing the target group – 'Anglo-Celtic' Australians – against which they are presumed to speak. Thus, one of the ironies in the otherwise valuable work of anthologizer-critics like Sneja Gunew is that, while they rightly dismiss the view of migrant writing as sociological evidence, sociology itself might provide rather different, possibly corrective, views of their working categories. Certainly, the view of migrant writing as operating against normative 'Anglo-Celtic' practices tends to be founded on a largely essentialized – perhaps even jaundiced – view of 'Anglo-Celtic' culture.[14]

A similar argument might be brought to bear against the view of Australian literature/culture as postcolonial. As Bob Hodge and Vijay Mishra, among others, have suggested, the term 'postcolonial' has been applied in a variety of tenuously comparable contexts, tending paradoxically to obscure the very asymmetries of power its proponents wish to examine. In Australia, these relations of power pertain to a history of internal colonialism, of continuing white discrimination against, especially, Aboriginal people that makes a mockery of the claim that Australia, and its literature, have emerged in opposition to European cultural norms. While the 'postcoloniality' of Australian literature and culture can certainly be contested, Hodge and Mishra's argument – like Gunew's – risks merely substituting one set of essentialisms for another. Thus, Aborigines are to be celebrated, as Gunew endorses 'non-Anglo-Celtic' migrants, as Australia's authentically colonized subjects or as their 'true' dissenting voice.[15] In fact, postcolonial critics and theorists, including many of those whom Hodge and Mishra finger, are only too well aware of the contradictions embedded in Australia's relationship to its colonial past – and its neo-colonial present. Alan Lawson, for instance, in an essay on postcolonial theory and 'the settler subject', points to the ambivalence already inscribed within the terms 'settler' and 'settler culture'. The term 'settler', says Lawson, is a 'tendentious discursive phenomenon [which] foregrounds the slippage from invader to peaceful settler as a strategy within the project of imperialism' (28–29). 'Settler cultures', similarly, are internally conflicted, 'liminal sites at the point of negotiation between the contending authorities of Empire and Native' (Lawson 24). The task of postcolonial theory and criticism is to analyse these internal conflicts and contradictions, in such a way as to demonstrate the inadequacy of the binary constructions (Europe and its others, the colonizer and the colonized, the West and the rest, and so on) that dominate a certain, foundationalist type of anti-colonial critique.

These arguments and counter-arguments, by now, probably have a familiar ring to them. I have rehearsed them briefly here to make a general point about the hazards of literary/cultural labelling, and to illustrate that terms like 'migrant', 'settler' and 'postcolonial' are necessarily political in their descriptive and affective force. It is axiomatic that terms like these are anchored to power structures, and that the effectiveness of each to convey a certain, perhaps subliminal, meaning must depend on those who control the channels of communication at any given point. The value of travelling theory is to destabilize these meanings, disrupting, for example, the ideological opposition between the 'temporary' migrant and the 'permanent' settler by showing the semantic slippage that exists *within*, as well as *between*, each of these terms. Another benefit of travelling theory is to suggest that 'migrancy' is a condition of possibility; that it harbours the potential to transform a historical record of exclusion and discrimination into a utopian aesthetic which suggests that 'it is the figurative possibility in language itself that makes the future possible' (Carter, *Living* 114). The danger always exists that this transformative project may be self-serving, and that the multiple histories it seeks to convert may be misrecognized, even overlooked. Travelling theory – cultural theory in general – certainly needs the support of history, less as an empirical check on its idealist excesses than as a guide to accompany it on its divagatory journeys, down its tangled tracks. Theories of migration and 'migrancy' are a test-case for this companionship: a reminder that theories of displacement are always historically inflected; but equally, that the scattered histories of displaced and relocated peoples are also records of the metaphors they have used to justify their movements – and chart their quests.

In this chapter, I have tried to state a case for the usefulness of cultural theory in approaching the historical experiences of migration, to Australia and elsewhere. While cultural theory's prevarications might seem merely irritating to some historians, its value might lie precisely in its capacity to act as a gadfly to received perceptions of the historical record. If, as I have suggested, the metaphorization of migration sometimes helps to obscure the specificities of historical experience, it also draws attention to what we might call the *metaphoricity* of human life itself.[16] Cultural theory, even of the most extreme relativist variety, has nothing to gain from refuting the factual, or from collapsing historically verifiable events into a play of indeterminate fictions. At its worst, of course, it seems to fall afoul of a kind of sophistry, a perverse determination to complicate issues beyond the reach of historical truths. At its best, though, it provides a set of workable, if often complex, methodologies for an interrogation of the unevenness that cuts across all – necessarily metaphor-laden – forms of human representation. It is perhaps utopian, if nonetheless salutary, to think that history can be remade from below, or that the neglected experiences of migrants might rewrite the narrative of the nation. Yet in present-day Australia, these are more than just saving illusions – as migrants themselves often know, and as historians, cultural theorists and scholar-writers of many different stripes will no doubt continue to make it their business to find out.

Works Cited

Ahmad, Aijaz. *In Theory: Classes, Nations, Literatures*. London: Verso, 1992.

Appadurai, Arjun. 'Disjuncture and Difference in the Global Cultural Economy'. In *Colonial Discourse and Postcolonial Theory: A Reader*. Ed. Patrick Williams and Laura Chrisman. New York: Columbia University Press, 1994. 324–39.

——. ed. *The Social Life of Things: Commodities in Perspective*. Cambridge: Cambridge University Press, 1986.

——. *Modernity at Large: Cultural Dimensions of Globalization*. Minneapolis: University of Minnesota Press, 1996.

Bhabha, Homi K. 'Between Identities: Interview with Paul Thompson'. In *Migration and Identity*. Ed. Rina Benmayor and Andor Skotnes. Oxford: Oxford University Press, 1994.

——. *The Location of Culture*. London: Routledge, 1994.

Boehmer, Elleke. *Colonial & Postcolonial Literature*. Oxford: Oxford University Press, 1995.

Bottomley, Gillian. 'Southern European Migration to Australia: Diasporic Networks and Cultural Transformations'. In Cohen, ed. 386–91.

Brennan, Timothy. *At Home in the World: Cosmopolitanism Now*. Cambridge, MA: Harvard University Press, 1997.

Carter, Paul. *Living in a New Country: History, Travelling and Language*. London: Faber & Faber, 1992.

——. *The Lie of the Land*. London: Faber & Faber, 1996.

——. *The Road to Botany Bay: An Essay in Spatial History*. London: Faber & Faber, 1987.

Castles, Stephen, and Mark J. Miller, *The Age of Migration: International Population Movements in the Modern World*. New York: The Guilford Press, 1993.

Chambers, Iain. *Migrancy, Culture, Identity*. London: Routledge, 1994.

Clifford, James. *Routes: Travel and Translation in the Late Twentieth Century*. Cambridge, MA: Harvard University Press, 1997.

——. 'Traveling Cultures'. In *Cultural Studies*. Ed. Lawrence Grossberg, Cary Nelson and Paula Treichler. New York: Routledge, 1992. 96–116.

Cohen, Robin, ed. *The Cambridge Survey of World Migration*. Cambridge: Cambridge University Press, 1995.

Collins, Jock. 'Asian Migration to Australia'. In Cohen, ed. 376–79.

Gunew, Sneja and Kateryna O Longley. *Striking Chords: Multicultural Literary Interpretations*. Sydney: Allen and Unwin, 1992.

Gunew, Sneja. *Framing Marginality: Multicultural Literary Studies*. Melbourne: Melbourne University Press, 1994.

Hammar, Tomas *et al.*, eds. *International Migration, Immobility and Development: Multidisciplinary Perspectives*. Oxford: Berg, 1997.

Hodge, Bob and Vijay Mishra. *The Dark Side of the Dream: Australian Literature and the Postcolonial Mind*. Sydney: Allen and Unwin, 1991.

Hoffmann-Nowotny, Hans-Joachim. 'A Sociological Approach toward a General Theory of Migration'. In *Global Trends in Migration: Theory and Research in International Population Movements*. Ed. Mary M. Kritz, Charles B. Keely and Silvano M. Tomasi. New York: Center for Migration Studies of New York, 1981.

Houbein, Lolo. 'The Role of "Ethnic" Writers in Australian Literature'. In *Aspects of Australian Culture*. Ed. J. Daalder and M. Fryar. Adelaide: Abel Tasman Press, 1982. 98.

Huggan, Graham. *The Postcolonial Exotic: Marketing the Margins*. London: Routledge, 2001.

Hutcheon, Linda. 'Circling the Downspout of Empire'. In *Past the Last Post: Theorizing Post-Colonialism and Post-Modernism*. Ed. Ian Adam and Helen Tiffin. Calgary: University of Calgary Press, 1990.

Kaplan, Caren. *Questions of Travel: Postmodern Discourses of Displacement*. Durham, NC: Duke University Press, 1996.

King, Russell, John Connell and Paul White, eds. *Writing across Worlds: Literature and Migration*. London: Routledge, 1995.

Krishnaswamy, Revathi. 'Mythologies of Migrancy: Postcolonialism, Postmodernism and the Politics of (Dis)location'. *Ariel* 26.1 (1995).

Kunow, Rüdiger. '"Detached ... from both worlds, not one": Salman Rushdie's *Midnight's Children* and the Postcolonial Novel'. In *The Decolonizing Pen: Cultural Diversity and the Transnational Imaginary in Rushdie's Fiction*. Ed. Liselotte Glage and Rüdiger Kunow. Trier: WVT, 2001, 87–103.

Lakoff, George, and Mark Johnson, *Metaphors We Live By*. Chicago: University of Chicago Press, 1980.

Larsen, Neil. 'DetermiNation: Postcolonialism, Poststructuralism, and the Problem of Ideology'. In *The Pre-Occupation of Postcolonial Studies*. Ed. Fawzia Afzal-Khan and Kalpana Seshadri-Crooks. Durham, NC: Duke University Press, 2000. 140–56.

Lawson, Alan. 'Postcolonial Theory and the "Settler" Subject'. *Essays on Canadian Writing* 56 (Fall 1995): 28–29.

Lucas, Robert E. B. 'International Migration: Economic Causes, Consequences and Evaluation'. In *Global Trends in Migration: Theory and Research in International Population Movements*. Ed. Mary M. Kritz, Charles B. Keely and Silvano M. Tomasi. New York: Center for Migration Studies of New York, 1981.

MacCannell, Dean. *Empty Meeting Grounds: The Tourist Papers*. New York: Routledge, 1992.

Rushdie, Salman. *Imaginary Homelands: Essays and Criticism 1981–1991*. London: Granta Books, 1991.

cultural geography where, with one or two notable exceptions, it hasn't been recognized as a legitimate domain of geography at all. Similarly, ecocriticism, the 'study of the relationship between literature and physical environment' (Glotfelty xix), has not generated as much geographical interest as it might have done, tending to house itself within an English- (often American-) based literary criticism that 'has one foot in literature and the other on land' (Glotfelty xix). More recently, ecocriticism has begun to interest postcolonial scholars, who see productive tensions between the two schools' respective ethical concerns and critical methods, and who foresee the possibilities of a postcolonial ecocriticism that combines the anti-authoritarian sympathies of each, 'not just as a collaborative means of addressing the social and environmental problems of the present, but also of imagining alternative futures in which our current ways of looking at ourselves and our relation to the world might be creatively transformed' (Huggan, 'Greening' 721).[6]

Still another object of academic research that combines the fields of (postcolonial) ecocriticism and travel-writing studies is *eco-travel writing*, that Green branch of travel literature which practises environmental advocacy, and in which nature is more than just a convenient setting or playground in which the adventures of restless/reckless human protagonists are acted out (Holland and Huggan Ch. 4).[7] In what follows, I want to look briefly at two contemporary examples of eco-travel writing that lend themselves to a postcolonial reading. In comparing the two examples – Kuki Gallmann's *I Dreamed of Africa* and Rick Ridgeway's *The Shadow of Kilimanjaro* – I will also ask to what extent they can become viable objects of a postcolonial geography, and whether the postcolonial geography they engage with has the potential to become a fruitful (cross-) disciplinary exercise rather than the dreamchild of a handful of spatial theorists who perhaps claim to know more about geography than they actually do.

Gallmann's and Ridgeway's works are both set in Africa, a continent of contradiction for Western traveller-writers who have struggled to reconcile the conspicuous hardships of local people's daily existence with the self-serving European myth of Africa as 'a refuge from the technological age' and 'a glorious Eden for wildlife' (Adams and McShane xii). East Africa, especially Kenya, bears the brunt of this particular colonial legacy, as captured in such familiar tropes as the Great White Hunter – later turned enthusiastic conservationist – and the Janus-faced vision of the African wilderness as both artificial paradise and area beyond human control (Adams and McShane 6). Wilderness narratives of this type frequently engage the contradictions of colonial Africa as a field for the free play of European conquistadorial fantasy (Hammond and Jablow; Mudimbe), and as a site to be reverentially protected, 'held in trust for future generations [...] as a reminder of our savage past' (Adams and McShane 8). Battling with these contradictions, the Italian expatriate Kuki Gallmann's emotion-soaked memoir of her rise to prominence as a Kenyan landowner, *I Dreamed of Africa* (1991), and the American adventure-traveller Rick Ridgeway's account of his risk-filled journey through Tsavo National Park on foot, *The Shadow of Kilimanjaro* (1999), can both be read as postcolonial homages to the Euro-American literary myth of 'Old Africa' (Ridgeway 236). Kenya duly emerges as a stirring place inhabited by a variety of latter-day Ernest Hemingways and Karen Blixens, all apparently intent on impressing their authority on an uncompromising landscape eventually made to submit to the equal ferocity of their own desire for control. But they are also self-consciously environmentalist texts in which the desire to achieve what Ridgeway describes as a 'visceral feel' for the condition of *wildness* is balanced by an awareness of the need to protect it, both for others and themselves (Ridgeway 199).

Protection, however, means very different things for the two writers. In Gallmann's case, the eventual establishment of her own conservationist foundation, centred on the vast freehold ranch she acquired shortly after moving to Kenya, is inextricably connected with an ideology of proprietorship through which she is able to rationalize her own privileged class position as a powerful expatriate landowner, a self-appointed 'guardian' or 'trustee'. The protection of the environment, for Gallmann, entails a 'balance between the wild and the tame', bridging the apparently incompatible principles of non-interference and domestication (Gallmann 189, 252). Such a balance in turn provides the justification – mediated by that quintessentially domestic form, the memoir – for an expatriate community of controlling European families entrusted not only with the responsible day-to-day management of their own commercial properties but also with the quasi-metaphysical stewardship, apparently vouchsafed by their rich colonial forebears, of the land as a whole. This unashamedly self-privileging version of the white (wo)man's burden is very different from Ridgeway's much more modest, if similarly ambivalent, protectionist mission, which consists in offering moral support to the conservationist cause in East Africa while doing his best, within the time-honoured tradition of extreme adventure writing, to remove the protective barriers around himself, thereby placing his own physical safety at maximum risk. The *untamability*, rather than the *taming*, of the wild is Ridgeway's operating principle, and it is backed by a relatively orthodox travel narrative in which the specific encounter with danger, as well as the generalized apprehension of endangerment, reveals varieties of affective response. To some extent, Ridgeway's narrative is an attempt not just to account for but to aspire to the condition of wildness; by mimicking 'the perpetual alertness of [...] wild animals' (Ridgeway 260), he seeks to minimize the distance between himself and the animal other, going beyond mere recognition to risk the absorption of the other into himself. These works of Gallmann and Ridgeway may be described, then, as narratives united in their self-conscious, partly self-ironic exploration of the myth of wild Africa, but divided by their ideological attitude towards it, as well as by the specific rhetorical strategies they adopt. It is time to look more closely now at some of these strategies and their ideological underpinnings, gauging their effectiveness in conveying either the fiction of attachment (Ridgeway) or the fantasy of entitlement (Gallmann) to the natural world.

Of the two books, Gallmann's is the more obvious crowd-pleaser, situating itself squarely in the European romantic-colonial tradition upheld by such writers as Beryl Markham, Elspeth Huxley and Karen Blixen – a tradition tapped more recently by such commercially viable genres as the nostalgic blockbuster (e.g. *Out of Africa*) and the New Age spiritual quest (e.g. the metaphysical travelogues of Laurens van der Post).[8] Ostensibly a family memoir taking in the early years of Gallmann's transplantation from neo-aristocratic northern Italy to postcolonial East Africa, *I Dreamed of Africa* owes both its tone (melodramatically intense) and its structure (cyclically repetitive) to exotic romance. Africa, as the title of the book implies, is the epitome of the exotic, conjuring up the dreamlike backdrop of 'unbounded freedom, [...] wild open horizons and red sunsets, [and] green highlands teeming with wild animals' (Gallmann 17) against which the domestic dramas of expatriate life, itself conceived as an expression of freedom, are played out.

After a succession of disasters, foremost among them the untimely deaths of her husband Paolo and her son Emanuele, we might conclude that Gallmann eventually learns to live in Africa rather than merely to love it. But in keeping with the spirit of exotic romance, Africa never quite sheds its aura of manufactured mystery. Both spatially and temporally other (predictably, Gallmann's nostalgic preference is for Old Africa), the Kenyan plains can be turned into a home precisely in so far as they are displaced. Local knowledge, in a paradigmatic rehearsal of colonial displacement, is held in check by an imported European poetic sensibility, with the Kenyan landscape, in particular, acting as a conduit for European neo-classical and romantic myths. The customary tropes are all present and correct: 'untouched' landscapes are dramatically unfurled before the panoramic gaze of the new settler (57);[9] wild animals abound; while people, their poverty carefully disguised, their fealty uncritically acknowledged, disport themselves in front of the delighted European spectator in a sequence of resplendent *tableaux vivants*:

> [The Pokot] women were dressed in long skirts of soft hide, greased with a mixture of goat fat and red ochre like their faces and hair. They looked like terracotta statues, agile and feminine with their rows of brass bangles clasping thin wrists and ankles, and with brass rings hung from pendulous ears. [...] Their breasts were greased and bare. Their heads were shaven at the sides, but reddish ringlets sprouted on top, like the crests of exotic birds or manes of wild animals, which gave a surprisingly feminine effect. [...] They snaked their way through the garden and sang as they danced. Their beauty and wildness silenced my European guests, and long into the night the guttural cries mixed, without interference, with the whooping cry of the hyena calling to the moon from the hills. (84)

The effortless control implied in staged ethnic spectacles such as this one reconfirms the host's (Gallmann's) naturalized authority, not just over her awestruck guests, but over 'primitive' peoples whom she seems able to summon up, and whose 'wildness' she can domesticate, at will. Similar patterns can be traced in the Gallmann family's encounters with wild animals. Paolo, a latter-day version of the Great White Hunter (56, 93), plays the role of the noble warrior, his worldview apparently encapsulated in the febrile love-letter he sends his wife in which he imagines their unborn child being 'brought to the centre of an horizon from which one can dominate the world' (130). Emanuele, meanwhile, Gallmann's son by her first marriage, is the inveterate collector, catastrophically killed by one of the snakes he mistakenly believes he has it in his power to control. Kuki herself, finally, is – as one might expect within this transparently romantic structure – the survivor: the nurturing maternal figure who translates the tragic losses of her husband and son into a salvationist mission to protect indigenous wildlife; and whose ranch, a beacon of conservationist goodwill in an increasingly resource-depleted country, is ceremonially transformed into a 'living monument to the memory of the men I had loved' (252).

This gesture of creating a 'living monument', however worthy, character-istically assimilates the collective practice of *conservation* to an individual act of *possession*, an act signed and sealed, like the ranch itself, in the Gallmann family name. The link between conservation and proprietorship had already been clinched at an earlier point in the narrative when Gallmann, contemplating whether to return to Europe to have Paolo's baby, decides to stay on at the ranch to fulfil her self-accorded responsibility as an environmental 'trustee':

> More than anything, I wanted to prove that I deserved my guardianship. [...] Sitting on top of the hill at Mugongo ya Ngurue, looking down at Baringo through the intact cliffs of the Mukutan Gorge, I touched the rough trunk of the old twisted acacia growing there at the edge of the world, as a sentinel to the silent, vast, majestic scenario. That landscape had been there long before our advent. It would still be there after I left. Not only had I no right to spoil it, but I had to be actively involved in protecting it. Special privileges come at a price: and this was my inheritance. (147)

Here as elsewhere, the obligation to protect rationalizes Gallmann's sense of her own entitlement, an entitlement she also ascribes to the tight-knit commu-nity of wealthy European expatriates, most of them substantial landowners, whose company she often shares (38). The bonds that form within this commu-nity are used to establish a patrician lineage confirmed in the nobility of Italian bloodlines and played out in nostalgic colonial rituals, for example the quaint anachronisms of the Club (85–86).

Inherited privileges, however, are not enough to sustain Gallmann, who must persuade herself, in an alien land, that she somehow belongs. Hence the impor-tance of 'guardianship' over the land, a motif invoked in sweeping panoramic vistas (57), as well as in linked images such as the totemic acacia – envisioned by Gallmann, in oracular New Age mode, as an atavistic soulmate – with which the memoir begins:

> There, on the extreme edge of the Great Rift Valley, guarding the gorge, grows an acacia tree bent by timeless winds. That tree is my friend, and we are sisters. I rest against its trunk, scaly and grey like a wise old elephant. I look up through the branches, twisted arms spread in a silent dance, to the sky of Africa. (xvii)

Episodes like this set up what Gallmann later describes as a 'wonderful feeling of being part of the landscape' (80, 145), a reassuringly mutual recognition that reconfirms her natural calling as a 'trustee' (149, 183). 'Trusteeship' comes hand in hand with a sense of loss, reinforced by Gallmann's own domestic tragedies; and with the heartening conviction that conservation has emerged as a new burden for the post-Independence period, as registered in the white (wo)man's 'commitment to keeping the balance between the wild and the tame' (189). This modern-day version of the civilizing mission is a similarly educative enterprise, ridden with residual colonial condescension:

> The average urban African has never seen an elephant; how could these people make a policy which would enable them to protect the environment and at the same time ensure their survival? Was all the wilderness destined to disappear through lack of knowledge and planning? I certainly could not change everything, but I could not tolerate the thought of this happening to Ol Ari Nyiro [her own ranch]. (251)

The mission thus revolves around the establishment of a harmonious micro-environment, overseen by the figure of the benevolent white proprietor, and encompassing '[t]he ranch and its animals, wild and domestic, and its plants, cultivated and indigenous, living in a changing Africa but still remembering – just – their traditional skills' (252).

Needless to say, this microcosmic space re-embodies the wisdom of inherited colonial hierarchies. A conservation system of a different kind, it constitutes a mapping of the Old Africa onto the New, represented in the iconic figure of the white hunter turned conservationist (262–63), and ritually accompanied by the destruction of the ivory pyre – centrepiece of the opening ceremony for Narobi National Park that Gallmann and her friends have helped prepare, and to which they have been invited as guests of honour – that symbolically consigns 'man's thoughtless destruction of the environment' to the past (302). For Gallmann, the burning pyre takes up its place within a wider romantic cycle of purification rituals, not just for the Kenyan nation, but for her own immediate family in whom the fate of the nation is symbolically intertwined: 'It was another ending, another beginning, and it summarized, purified and made sense of all that had happened so far in all our combined lives' (303). Yet this latest death/rebirth is significantly followed by a further ceremony in which, returning home to the ranch, Gallmann and her daughter Sveva are greeted by a band of local Pokot warriors, come to pledge allegiance to the Musungu (white European) and her new conservationist cause:

> Before we knew it, the warriors stopped around us in an almost perfect circle. Sveva and I waited in the middle, on the manicured lawn carved out of the wilderness, among the flowers, our large dogs surrounding us. Our fair skin and hair stood out, and I realized that she and I were the only females present at this ceremony. Our European origin, my position as guardian of this land, gave us, I supposed, the status of men. (308)

Through these two parallel ceremonies, Gallmann achieves the audacious (some might say outrageous) step of ushering in a new enlightened era, in which a combination of sound leadership, mutual trust and cooperative effort will be seconded to correct the environmental abuses of the past. The overriding sense of Gallmann's entitlement, once again, is simply staggering, the self-perpetuating structure of romance being used to shore up and reinvigorate white patriarchal authority in a new conservation-minded Kenya that looks suspiciously like the Old Africa conserved.

A rather different kind of elegy to the Old Africa is the Californian adventure-traveller Rick Ridgeway's *The Shadow of Kilimanjaro*. The text, played out against the spectacular backdrop of Tsavo National Park in Kenya, is an unashamedly nostalgic tribute to an earlier (colonial) era of white park wardens and their antagonists, black hunters, these two groups being brought together in 'the warp and weft of predator and prey' that characterizes nature 'in its wildest state' (Ridgeway 247, 194). As Ridgeway suggests, both of these groups were to play their part in maintaining precarious equilibrium in a social/ecological system since irreversibly disrupted by the modem technologies that accompanied the emergence of the postcolonial nation-state (247–48). The apparently contradictory impulses to conserve and to hunt are similarly intertwined throughout the narrative, as in the triumphal invocation of a rogue's gallery of notorious Great White Hunters 'who celebrated Africa's wild game, who argued for its preservation, who mourned its decline, while, at the same time, hunted it and shot it and each in his own way – directly or indirectly – contributed to its unsustainable harvest' (194). Ridgeway recognizes his own belatedness with respect to these originary mythologies. Yet he still chooses to see his guided journey on foot through East Africa – a variant on the modem ecological safari – as an impossible attempt to recapture the 'oneness with the bush' experienced by the earliest hunter-gatherers, as well as by later generations of white settlers whose sympathies were divided, as are his own, between 'the attraction to hunt' and the 'compulsion to conserve' (256, 246).

Unlike Gallmann, Ridgeway – a temporary visitor to Africa, after all, rather than a permanent settler – has no proprietorial claim to make over the territory through which he travels. He does share her fantasy, however, of a visceral connection with the landscape: '"Contact!" That is what I was looking for on this walk. That is what I came to one of the last few remaining sections of wild Africa to experience. To see it, to smell it, to taste it, to feel it. To be part of it, not apart from it' (262). And contact, distilled through a heightening of the senses, is at its purest when involving *danger*. The exposure to danger, in this case, entails a willed encounter with wild animals in which the tourist's camera is imagined as being interchangeable with the hunter's rifle, and the distance between human and animal is minimized in the reciprocal acknowledgement of hunter and hunted, predator and prey. A charging elephant, for instance, produces an onset of adrenalin rush that borders on elation:

This danger, this possibility of approaching death, is a closing of the distance between two animals, one intent on damaging the other, and it has produced in me an exhilaration that contains neither fear nor regret, and as a consequence it is an exhilaration that feels clear and pure. (193)

By projecting himself into the mindset of the big-game hunter, as well as engaging the sympathies of the modern-day conservationist, Ridgeway aims to produce a travel text that moves beyond sentimentalized empathy for African wildlife – a text which, in positing the historical connection between contemporary forms of 'animal-endorsing' ecotourism and earlier versions of 'animal-destructive' safari, simultaneously succeeds in unravelling the puzzle of the 'apparent irreconcilability between [the] veneration and [the] destruction of wild game' (193).[10] In this context, travel takes the form of a series of proximate experiences and movements, registering the vertiginous effects of what the American anthropologist Michael Taussig calls 'mimetic excess'.[11] In an alternating sequence of historical identification fantasies, Ridgeway imagines what it must have been like to be a colonial game warden, a traditional indigenous hunter, a Victorian adventurer-explorer (Ridgeway 104–05, 218–19, 92). More than any of these, though, Ridgeway aspires to the 'timeless' condition of a wild animal. It is not enough, he implies, for the traveller to mimic 'the perpetual alertness of the wild animals' (Ortega y Gasset, qtd. in Ridgeway 260); rather, his goal must be to 'travel light and unfettered to live wild off the land [...] like a wild animal [itself]' (190). In Deleuze and Guattari's hypertheoretical terms, we might liken this goal to the radical project of 'becoming-animal', a movement beyond the representation of animal drives and instincts to challenge the boundaries between human and animal and, in so doing, to question the very nature of identity and representation itself.[12]

Yet it is the emotional experience, rather than the intellectual apprehension, of 'becoming-animal' that most interests Ridgeway. Here is his attempt, one in a number of italicized dream sequences in the text, to close the gap between himself and the animal other by producing a slow-motion replay of events in which ostensibly opposed human and animal consciousnesses converge to the point of being enmeshed:

> *Her legs trot forward massive yet weightless yet setting down with a force that would break the bones and back and ribs of every great animal that walks this wild land and she deserves her name, the matriarch. This monumental weight coming straight at us has slowed time so that each second is a minute and so in one of these long seconds I consider how she is different from the other elephant who have charged us, that she has a different intent. I run backward at an angle so I am behind Danny as he spins and drops and in the same motion raises his rifle toward his shoulder. All with this same slowing of time, all within this one or two seconds that seem to stretch and stretch and stretch [...]* (192, his italics)

The imaginative connection Ridgeway draws between himself and the charging elephant illustrates his self-confessedly anthropomorphic view of the 'personalities of wild animals' (143), while also lending support to his conviction that 'we have as much to learn about animal behavior from approaching them emotion-ally – from relating to them as one animal to another – as we do from quantified scientific observation' (142). Yet, as throughout the narrative, the sympathetic imagination compensates for the fact that the actual point of contact is not reached. Nor can it be, for the physical contact between humans and animals in the text is imagined as being almost invariably *fatal*, the space of encounter between the two being one in which a life abruptly taken acts as the reverse-image of a life arbitrarily preserved. Ridgeway's professional pursuit of extreme adventure, as previously evidenced in such high-risk sporting activities as mountain-climbing (vi-viii), is translated here into the desire for a brush of death with the animal other. Human and animal – in what amounts perhaps to another version of 'becoming-animal' – are willed to come together, with the result that the human subject, converging with and absorbed into its animal counterpart, risks being physically destroyed.

Hence the voyeuristic fascination in the text with images of eating and being eaten, as in the scene when Ridgeway, imagination inflamed by having recently heard the legendary story of the man-eating lions of Tsavo, transfers the image of a dead buffalo found *en route* onto 'the remains of a human, partly devoured' (108). Self-irony, as befits the modern self-conscious travelogue, often accompa-nies these fanciful imaginings. A good example comes in an early scene, when the wildlife photographer Peter Beard is given pride of place at the centre of a family album in which the masculinist heroics of Old Africa have mutated into a parodic exhibition of accumulated battle-scars:

> There was a photo session with Danny after he'd blown his thumb off in a hunting accident, on the veranda, with the head of a dead cobra we'd chopped off: Peter had Danny hold the snake head next to the remains of his thumb. I have this potpourri of images, all mixed together: old Elui, Dad's Wakamba guide with his scars from leopard attacks and rhino gorings, Dad, with his one squint eye, gaunt from his cancer, and Peter, in the middle of it all, pleased by the extremes. (74)

In passages such as this, Ridgeway's mythicized Africa, closer in spirit to Chatwin's than to Hemingway's, presents an imaginary museum dedicated less to the wonders of the wild than to the enduring curiosities of human wildlife (52, 175, 179).[13] Chatwin's trademark combination of crackpot wisdom and tongue-in-cheek aestheticism can be found, in fact, at several junctures in Ridgeway's narrative, as in the mock-epiphanic moment when, as his party slowly tracks across the boundless Kenyan landscape, he suddenly recognizes that his pasto-ralist desire 'to wander in wildness across open spaces is [somehow] connected to some even deeper urge to follow the herds between their seasonal pastures' (83). Moments like these, registered with an almost comical solemnity, appear to indicate that Ridgeway's text is slyly disabused of the tendencies towards romantic nostalgia it apparently works so hard to affect.

The text demonstrates similar ambivalence in its attitude towards sentimental European conceptions of unpopulated wilderness. Its leisurely discussion, for but unmistakably Western-elitist construction of the Third World as a locus of anti-imperialist resistance, the overpowering rhetoric of which risks silencing the very masses on whose behalf it claims to speak (Loomba).[10] Yet Guha's and Shiva's primary concern is less with the West or Western imperialism *per se* than with the neocolonialist imperatives of the post-Independence Indian state. This 'centralized management system', in pursuing 'a policy of planned destruction of diversity in [both] nature and culture' (Shiva 12), has actively sought to impose a homogenizing late-capitalist vision of economic progress most obviously beneficial to the nation's ruling elite (Guha 195–96). The state's coercive allocation and management of natural resources can be seen as a postcolonial version of ecological imperialism in which it becomes clear that 'the forced march to industrialisation' has had disastrous cultural, as well as ecological, effects (Guha 196). For Shiva, there are thus two symbiotically related crises in postcolonial India: an ecological crisis brought about by the use of resource-destructive technological processes and a cultural/ethnic crisis emerging from an erosion of the social structures that make cultural diversity and plurality possible (12, 235).

Guha and, particularly, Shiva stand behind the work of Arundhati Roy, whose fulminating essays 'The Greater Common Good' (1999) and 'The End of the Imagination' (1998), capitalizing on the runaway success of her Booker prize-winning novel *The God of Small Things* (1997), probably represent the most eye-catching ecocritical intervention to date by a recognized postcolonial writer. The essays – first published separately as cover stories for two mainstream English-language Indian magazines, *Outlook* and *Frontline*, and later repackaged for the international mass market as *The Cost of Living* – are clear attempts to reach out both to a local readership familiar with their controversial issues (the Narmada Valley Project in the first essay, India's decision to go nuclear in the second), and to an international audience possibly unaware of, and probably uninformed on, either issue, but sufficiently attuned to Roy's success to grant her work another look.[11] The essays are deliberately designed, that is, as a politically motivated publicity venture that, riding on the back of Roy's recently accorded literary celebrity status, seeks to attract and, ideally, convert large numbers of readers both in her home country and elsewhere. Now, it would be easy here to categorize Roy as another media-hungry Indo-Anglian cosmopolitan celebrity (Brennan; Mongia), or to see her as placing a well-timed stake in the latest popular humanitarian cause. Certainly, in the first essay mentioned above (on which I shall concentrate here), Roy takes rhetorical liberties with her disempowered Adivasi subjects, converting them into mythologized victims in her own highly personal moral crusade against the tyrannies of the modern Indian state. And certainly, she is aware throughout the essay of the constitutive, but also distortive, role of the global media in constructing the latest, highly visible human/ecological catastrophe as a newsworthy 'event' (Roy 47, 50, 63).[12] But Roy, as in her previous work, is not only interested in manipulating publicity for her own, and other people's, interests, but in showing how publicity – or, in this case, the mediated language of the common good, the *national* interest

– achieves its magical effects. Hence the ironic title of her essay, which reflects on the ways in which a centralized state has not only commandeered national assets and resources, but has also sought through media channels to convey the fiction of a carefully monitored 'national progress'. The fiction of 'national progress' demands that government be 'abstracted out of the messy business of politics', thereby releasing it for the utopian task of 'receiving inputs from all parts of society, processing them, and finally allocating the optimal values for the common satisfaction and preservation of society as a whole' (Chatterjee 160). Technological know-how is an essential instrument of the 'magic of the State' (Taussig, *Magic*). And such expertise, in the hands of the few, requires the self-sacrifice of the many:

> Place all your prayers at the feet of the sarkar, the omnipotent and supremely enlightened state, and they will be duly passed on to the body of experts who are planning for the overall progress of the country. If your requests are consistent with the requirements of progress, they will be granted. (Chatterjee 160)

These, in Partha Chatterjee's appropriately sardonic terms, are the grounds for Roy's ecological fable of the Narmada Valley Development Project: the ill-fated post-independence irrigation scheme, affecting hundreds of thousands of lives, that is usually considered to be 'India's Greatest Planned Environmental Disaster' (Roy 44), and that is sometimes seen, in 'the congealed morass of hope, anger, information, disinformation, political artifice, engineering ambition, disingenuous socialism, radical activism, bureaucratic subterfuge, [and] misinformed emotionalism' that surrounds it (9), as a metonymy for the self-consuming narrative of modern India itself (Preface n.p.).

A few facts may be helpful here. India is the third largest dam builder in the world, having built over 3,000 big dams in the fifty-odd years since independence (Roy, Preface n.p.; McCully). Of these dams, several of the largest and best-known belong to the state-administered Narmada Valley Development Project, spanning three states (Gujarat, Maharashtra and Madhya Pradesh) in central India. This hugely ambitious project, first dreamed up more than forty years ago and still – despite massive protests and a legal stay, now lifted, against further construction[13] – considered to be a viable proposition, conceives of building '3,200 dams that will reconstitute the Narmada [river] and her forty-one tributaries into a series of step reservoirs – an immense staircase of amenable water'. Two of these dams, the giant Sardar Sarovar in Gujarat and the Narmada Sagar in Madhya Pradesh, will hold 'more water [between them] than any other reservoir on the Indian subcontinent' (Roy 33). The project aims to provide electricity and safe drinking water for millions, while irrigating millions of hectares of infertile farming land. From its inception, however, the project has been fraught with problems, proving in many people's eyes to have been massively misconceived. Hundreds of thousands of local people, mostly Adivasis, have been ousted from their land, with irreparable damage being done to their daily lives, their economic self-sufficiency and their culture. Evidence suggests

Jews [Coetzee 20–21, 82–83]) arguably betray a startling lack of cultural sensitivity;[28] while even the most convincing of her critiques reveal authoritarian traces of their own. Hence the irony, presented by one of her opponents, the philosophy professor O'Hearne, that the animal-rights movement she so fiercely supports, deriving as it does from other Western philanthropic movements, risks becoming 'yet another Western crusade against the practices of the rest of the world, claiming universality for what are simply its own standards' (Coetzee 103–04). Hence the irony, acknowledged by Elizabeth herself, that '[a]n ecological philosophy that tells us to live side by side with other creatures justifies itself by appealing to an idea, an idea of a higher order than any living creature [… an] idea, finally […] which no creature except Man is capable of comprehending' (Coetzee 91).[29] And hence the irony that her discourse, for all its altruistic sentiment, frequently betrays self-interested motives, not least by offering a confused mixture of liberal do-goodism and Christian eschatology in which the mission to save lives becomes a displaced quest for self-redemption, and the triumph of the spirit is imaged in symbolic hierarchies of self-denial: from vegetarianism to asceticism, from the abjuration of meat to the mortification of the flesh (Coetzee 65, 107, 117–19).

The lectures can be seen, in fact, as another of Coetzee's forays into the guilt-ridden, occasionally death-driven, territory of liberal thought. Like her closest literary descendant, Elizabeth Curren in *Age of Iron* (1990), Elizabeth Costello appears to embrace her own extinction as the member of an endangered species, a self-acknowledged 'dying breed' (Huggan, 'Evolution'). Certainly, her lectures are permeated with the smell of death, most of all her own (Coetzee 43). As O'Hearne surmises, 'there is […] a collapse of the imagination before death [… which provides the] basis of our fear of [it]' (Coetzee 110). This is the condition, he implies, from which the septuagenarian writer is suffering – a suggestion apparently confirmed in the final scene in which her son John, taking his exhausted mother in his arms and attempting to console her, whispers ambiguously in her ear, taking in 'the smell of cold cream, of old flesh. "There, there," he whispers in her ear. "There, there. It [your life?] will soon be over"' (Coetzee 122). Transformed into another of her own long-suffering animals, Elizabeth herself becomes the subject for a fable – the ironic terminus of a locked debate that, begun in the spirit of defiance, ends on a plaintive note of self-defeat.

Yet if the argument for animal rights seems to rest, here as elsewhere, on human insecurity, the sympathy that Elizabeth invokes, and in turn attracts, is not so easily dismissed. She is sentimental to a fault, but her sentimentalism can still engage us, as in her halting attempt to explain the utopian gesture of embodying animals 'by the process called poetic invention that mingles breath and sense in a way that no one has explained and no one ever will' (Coetzee 89). The literary representation of animals, she suggests in her second lecture, has historically been dominated by anthropocentric conventions. One of these is fabular abstraction, 'where the animals stand for human qualities: the lion for courage, the owl for wisdom, and so forth' (Coetzee 83); another, romantic primitivism, disdains abstract thought in the search to represent embodied experience, yet depends upon it nonetheless (see the discussion of Ted Hughes's 'jaguar' poems in Coetzee 89–90). The attempt to represent the 'natural world' is inescapably Platonic; no surprise, then, that Elizabeth's own literary-critical discourse is caught in similar traps. While her work is primarily concerned with the representation of fictional experience (as in her 'pathbreaking' feminist novel on Joyce's literary anti-heroine Marion [Molly] Bloom),[30] she believes that her success in rendering this experience into words provides conclusive evidence that she can 'think her way into the existence' of any living being:

> If I can think my way into the existence of a being who has never existed, then I can think my way into the existence of a bat or a chimpanzee or an oyster, any being with whom I share the substrate of life [...] [T]here is no limit to the extent to which we can think ourselves into the being of another. There are no bounds to the sympathetic imagination. (Coetzee 49)

This optimism, however, proves to be largely unfounded. The Platonic dilemma remains: in her first lecture, for instance, she becomes, not Red Peter himself, but the *idea* of Red Peter – as if to confirm her own suspicion that there is no access to embodied experience other than through the channels of abstract thought. The ironies begin to multiply again: fables, pushed to their interpretive limits, turn into versions of themselves, thus generating other fables; ecologism itself becomes a fable of the impossible attempt to escape anthropocentric thought (Coetzee 91–93, 99).

These conundrums, as so often with Coetzee, have no rational solution; rather, they require, if the fiction of intersubjective experience is to be sustained, a leap of imaginative faith. In this context, Elizabeth, for all the irony at her expense, may yet be validated. In her first lecture, she quotes disapprovingly from an essay by the American philosopher Thomas Nagel, who maintains that the resources of the human mind, powerful though these are, cannot suffice for us to know what it is like to be another, to grasp 'a fundamentally *alien* form of life' (Nagel 168, qtd. in Coetzee 42, Nagel's italics). Nagel is right, up to a point, but are animals (his main example is a bat) necessarily alien to human consciousness? And what is the imaginative faculty if not the attempt, defying the limitations of human consciousness, to enter the experiences – even the *inner* experiences – of lives other than our own? 'The poet and the philosopher': it seems like the setting for another of Coetzee's ironic fables. But as Nagel grudgingly admits, 'It may be easier than I suppose to transcend inter-species barriers with the aid of the imagination' (172, note 8). In this sense, at least, Elizabeth's claims on behalf of the sympathetic imagination are neither as naive nor as eccentric as some of her opponents might like to think.

Turning now to Barbara Gowdy's prodigiously imaginative novel about the lives of African elephants – and taking a leap of faith myself – I shall ask not so much *whether* she can 'think her way into the existence' of other creatures, but *how* she can, and what might be at stake. In Coetzee's text, animals are functionalized in a drama of human mortality and suffering – one in which the attempt to reach out to the animal world, to inhabit the mental and emotional space of animals' lives through a sustained act of sympathetic imagination, is counteracted by the ironic awareness of animals as objects of human desires and needs: objects of exploitation and abuse, objects of charity and affection. This unresolved dilemma points, in turn, to the problematic of animal representation, registering a tension between what the visual theorist Steve Baker calls (after the philosopher Kate Soper) 'animal-endorsing' and 'animal-sceptical' views of art. The former view, says Baker, 'will tend to endorse animal life itself (and may therefore align itself with the work of conservationists or animal advocacy)'; the latter 'is likely to be sceptical not of animals themselves (as if the very existence of nonhuman life was in question), but rather of culture's means of constructing and classifying the animal in order to make it meaningful to the human' (9). This tension, ever-present in Coetzee's text, is also maintained in Gowdy's novel, which confronts the impossible task of making animals speak without humans speaking for them; of rescuing animals from the 'instrumental characterisation' (Baker 175) to which human history – including literary history – has consigned them, converting them from passive objects for human use into self-willed 'ecological subjects' (Dobson 54–55).[31]

Gowdy goes about her aim, in part, by transforming the literary genre of the animal fable, a genre deployed traditionally to support moralistic, often highly conservative views of the human educational process and, more recently, to prop up the social hierarchies and disciplinary regimes that legitimize imperial rule (Fernandes 7–49).[32] More specifically, Gowdy draws on a source in which both of these aspects come together: Kipling's popular miscellanies for children, the *Just So Stories* (1902) and *Jungle Books* (1894–95). Gowdy's elephants have much in common with Kipling's celebrated jungle creatures: they talk, debate and interact with one another within a stratified social structure; they inhabit a quaintly honour-bound, quasi-Biblical realm of religious legend and cosmogenic myth. But there the resemblance ends. For one thing, Gowdy's elephants, unlike Kipling's beasts, are endowed with a painful consciousness of their condition – a consciousness largely shaped by the memory of who they (individually) are, and what they (collectively) must once have been (Gowdy 83, 148). And for another, unlike Kipling's dutifully rewarded colonial subjects, they are condemned to move through a shiftless post-imperial world defined as much by human as animal savagery – a world in which the fragile network of ecological alliances on which they previously depended for their safety has been thrown violently, perhaps irrecoverably, out of place:

> The emergence of humans did not, as is widely assumed, initiate a time of darkness. On the contrary, in the first generations following the Descent [the advent of human beings, originally descended from elephants], The Domain [Earth] was a glorious place, and this is partly because humans back then were nothing like today's breed. They ate flesh, yes, and they were unrepentant and wrathful, but they killed only to eat [and there] weren't any massacres or mutilations. There was plenitude and ease, and between she-ones [elephants] and other creatures was a rare communion, for [...] all she-ones were mind talkers, and the minds of all creatures were intelligible. (42–43)

Instead, the elephants now inhabit a fallen world in which their collective existence is threatened, and 'a new and stunningly voracious generation of humans', their minds impenetrable, appears intent on their destruction (56, 43). This world, for all its obvious mythic resonances, recalls certain parts of postcolonial East Africa. Here, elephants, while no longer officially endangered, must compete for territory with rapidly increasing human populations, producing a 'conflict of space [that gradually] compresses them into smaller and smaller areas', and threatens to reduce their viable habitat to the relatively protected enclaves of the wildlife parks (Douglas-Hamilton 256). (Ironically, the mythical Safe Place that Gowdy's elephants seek is envisioned at one point in terms of the modern tourist industry, as a wildlife park where peaceful 'hindleggers [humans] [...] [g]ape at she-ones [elephants] [...] [a]ll day long,' as if, by 'star[ing] at us hard enough, they [might] inflate back to what they were. Grow their ears and so on' [74]). Meanwhile, the brutal massacres of the herds – nightmarishly rendered in Gowdy's novel (85–90) – might also be linked to the crisis of the 1970s and 80s, when a sudden rise in ivory prices, allied to the increased availability of guns across the African continent, led to a potentially cataclysmic escalation of the East African ivory trade (Gavron 121).[33]

In the main, however, Gowdy prefers to maintain a guarded, sometimes a deftly ironic distance from both indirect historical analogies and directly cited documentary sources. This is in part because her elephants are mythical as much as world-historical creatures; but it is clear they are also both, and she steers clear, by and large, of the temptation that some of the self-appointed elephant experts on whose work she draws appear unable to resist – the signal urge to co-opt elephants into the type of neoprimitivist morality play in which the elephant becomes a 'noble victim' in a traditional society thrown disastrously off kilter (Baker),[34] and the continuing assault on African wildlife contains within it a history of European imperialist greed. This sentimental view is endorsed by the English journalist Jeremy Gavron, whose travelogue *The Last Elephant* is listed as one of Gowdy's sources (Gowdy 339), and for whom the elephant is nothing less than 'a flesh-and-blood symbol of the most important question of all for Africa: the struggle of ancient traditions and resources to survive and contribute in the modern African world' (Gavron 3). After independence, Gavron claims,

> the first instinct of Africans was to turn around and wipe out their elephant populations: not merely to use the ivory to buy modern material goods, but also, it seems to me, to destroy their world's wildness and danger, to eradicate what many Africans regard as a primitive and shaming past. (xii)

Gavron's view, besides being smugly Eurocentric, risks relegating animals once more either to commodities – the exchangeable trophies of post-imperial conquest – or to the romantic embodiments of an atavistic 'wildness' in which the ambivalent inscriptions of Western modernity on the African continent are strategically erased. While Gowdy's novel is by no means free of the rhetoric of sentimentality – indeed, she makes it clear that she wishes to engage with it

(Gowdy 2) – her aim is neither simply to reproduce the kind of fateful 'declensionist narrative' (Vance 172) in which animals are seen, along with humans, as inhabiting an irreversibly postlapsarian wilderness, nor to revert to the type of mock-historical fable in which animals are enlisted for the nostalgic production of a lost pre-colonial past. Rather, she is concerned to show how both sets of myths may be imaginatively redeployed to articulate a collective non-human consciousness, a unique and by no means wholly unrealistic vision of the world captured from the 'elephant point of view'.

Filtered through the conciousness of several members of the extended herd (including its legendarily gifted 'visionaries, 'link-bulls' and 'mind talkers'),[35] the elephant worldview presented in *The White Bone* balances its faith in a universe saturated with cosmic meaning ('everything exists for the purpose of pointing to something else' [135]) against an ecology of melancholic remembrance in a landscape touched with despair. Precious links to the past have been lost, and different species are now sealed off against one another. The land, previously 'trembling with mystic revelation', has fallen silent; afflicted with the worst drought in living memory, it conjures only visions of 'corpses and dust above which the roar of planes pours down from an illimitable emptiness' (145, 75). Memory, meanwhile, records a litany of losses, while also giving shape to the fleeting visions that link the beleaguered modern herds to a heroic ancestral past:

> 'Every moment is a memory,' [the matriarch, She-Demands, tells two of the young calves in the herd.] [...] 'Everything has been ordained by the She' [the first elephant and mother of all elephants] [...] 'Therefore everything must already have been imagined by the She. We live only because we live in Her imagination. Your life, as you experience it, is the She recollecting what She has already imagined. We are memory. We are living memory.' (83)

Epic memory counteracts the constant fear of annihilation, as the remaining members of the extended herd renew their search for the Safe Place that might guarantee the future of their species. Memories are an elephant's hold on life, the narrator explains, for 'they are doomed without it. When their memories begin to drain, their bodies go into decline, as if from a slow leakage of blood' (1).[36] And yet memories are also reminders of death, reconfirmatory visions of a seemingly preordained destruction, as if each individual elephant were made to carry the burden – were branded with the imprint – of devastating communal loss (148, 270). Memory is mourning, a pathological condition already suggested by the novel's epigraph, taken from Rilke's *Duino Elegies*:

> Yet in the alert, warm animal there lies
> the pain and burden of an enormous sadness.
> for it too feels the presence of what often
> overwhelms us: a memory, as if
> the element we keep pressing toward was once
> more intimate, more true, and our communion
> infinitely tender. (qtd. in Gowdy n.p.)

Rilke's poem, paradigmatically melancholic, uncovers the incurably nostalgic impulses behind the sympathetic imagination. But how is the epigraph to be read in the context of the novel? Is this self-ironic evidence of 'the luxury of pity' that comes from sentimentalizing suffering animals (Scholtmeijer 119), or of the paradoxical detachment that marks attempts to solicit sympathy for animals by making 'them' seem more like 'us', by making their plight our own? Or does it mark the outset of a narrative that attempts to break with anthropocentric/ anthropomorphic conventions by presenting the experience of creatures in a language that can never fully be theirs, nor yet unequivocally our own? As the American ecofeminist critic Linda Vance warns,

> Crafting narratives that will give voice to animals and make humans care about them in appropriate ways is no easy task. We want to avoid anthro- pomorphizing animals even though that has proven itself an effective tactic for mobilizing public sympathy toward them. We need to be faithful to their stories, not our own. The goal is not to make us care more about animals because they are like us, but to care about them because they are themselves. (185)

If this is the task – and I believe it is – that Barbara Gowdy has set herself in writing *The White Bone*, then it is in the very grounds of its impossibility that it contrives to achieve its goal. For *The White Bone* enacts a variation on the utopian narrative in which the 'environmental imagination' (Buell) takes on the force of a performative, conjuring up a semi-mythic, largely non-human world that both presents and transcends ecological catastrophe, and that in so doing gestures towards the conditions under which our own world might be transformed.[37] The nightmare of the present contains within it the dream, now partially occluded, of a possible future (Gowdy 326–27). This dream, already foretold, of a space beyond existing spatio-temporal boundaries requires a new language that reanimates nature in accordance with 'ecotopian' ideals (see Devall and Sessions; also Manes).[38] In *The White Bone*, these ideals appear to correspond to certain strands within Western (Anglo-American) ecofeminism, whose universalist agenda includes the imperative to create greater dialogue between humans and animals by 'translating animal consciousness into a form [that] humans can apprehend' (Vance 183). Certainly, Gowdy's novel has little difficulty matching Vance's requirements for 'ethically appropriate ecofeminist narratives' (182). Narratives about animals, suggests Vance,

> should be informed by both observation and imagination [...]. An animal's life history can be told in factual ways, and it can be told in mythic ways as well. [While] mythologizing has so often been used to objectify animals [...] that objectification [...] is more a function of the world view of the mythmakers than of mythology itself. In dreams, in fantasies, in visions, animals often speak to us – and who is to say that this is not a form of communication? (183)

Similarly, the standard ecofeminist association between the domination of animals and the subjection of women (Warren 4–5) finds echoes in the crude

Pepper, David. *Eco-Socialism: From Deep Ecology to Social Justice*. London: Routledge, 1993.

Platz, Norbert. 'Greening the New Literatures in English: A Plea for Ecocriticism'. In *Anglistentag 1999 Mainz Proceedings*. Ed. Bernhard Reitz and Sigrid Rieuwerts. Trier: Wissenschaftlicher Verlag Trier, 2000. 313–26.

———. 'Literature and Ecology: A Brief Agenda for Exploring the Green Dimension in Canadian Literature'. In *Informal Empire? Cultural Relations between Canada, the United States and Europe*. Ed. Peter Easingwood, Konrad Gross and Hartmut Lutz. Kiel: I & F Verlag, 1998. 229–53.

Pojman, L. P., ed. *Environmental Ethics: Readings in Theory and Application*. Boston: Jones, 1994.

Porritt, Jonathon. *Seeing Green*. Oxford: Blackwell, 1984.

Regan, Tom. *The Case for Animal Rights*. Berkeley: University of California Press, 1983.

Ritvo, Harriet. *The Animal Estate: The English and Other Creatures In the Victorian Age*. Cambridge, MA: Harvard University Press, 1987.

Rosaldo, Renato. *Culture and Truth: The Remaking of Social Analysis* [1989]. Boston: Beacon, 1993.

Rowell, Andrew. *Green Backlash: Global Subversion of the Environment Movement*. London: Routledge, 1996.

Roy, Arundhati. *The Cost of Living*. London: Flamingo, 1999.

Scholtmeijer, Marian. *Animal Victims in Modern Fiction: From Sanctity to Sacrifice*. Toronto: University of Toronto Press, 1993.

Shiva, Vandana. The *Violence of the Green Revolution: Third World Agriculture, Ecology and Politics*. London: Zed, 1991.

Singer, Peter. *Animal Liberation: A New Ethics for our Treatment of Animals* [1975]. London: Jonathan Cape, 1976.

Singh, Satyajit. Introduction. In *The Dam & the Nation: Displacement and Resettlement in the Narmada Valley*. Ed. Jean Drèze, Meera Samson and Satyajit Singh. Delhi: Oxford University Press, 1995. 1–25.

Slaymaker, William. 'Echoing the Other(s): The Call of Global Green and Black African Responses'. *PMLA* 116.1 (2001): 129–44.

Sluyter, Andrew. *Colonialism and Landscape: Postcolonial Theory and Conservation/Development Applications*. Lanham, MD: Rowman, 2002.

Spiegel, Marjorie. *The Dreaded Comparison: Human and Animal Slavery*. New York: Mirror, 1988.

Spivak, Gayatri Chakravorty. *A Critique of Postcolonial Reason: Toward a History of the Vanishing Present*. Cambridge, MA: Harvard University Press, 1999.

———. *In Other Worlds: Essays In Cultural Politics*. London: Methuen, 1987.

Taussig, Michael. *Mimesis and Alterity: A Particular History of the Senses*. New York: Routledge, 1993.

———. *The Magic of the State*. New York: Routledge, 1997.

Vance, Linda. 'Beyond Just-So Stories: Narrative, Animals, and Ethics'. In *Animals and Women: Feminist Theoretical Explorations*. Ed. Carol J. Adams and Josephine Donovan. Durham, NC: Duke University Press, 1995. 163–91.

Warren, Karen J. 'Feminism and Ecology: Making Connections'. *Environmental Ethics* 9.1 (1987): 3–20.

Wise, Steven M. *Rattling the Cage: Towards Legal Rights for Animals*. London: Profile, 2000.

Young, Robert J. C. '"Dangerous and Wrong": Shell, Intervention and the Politics of Transnational Companies'. *Interventions* 1.3 (1999): 439–64.

Notes

1   The anthropocentric versus biocentric dichotomy is central to the different versions of what is generally known as 'deep ecological' thought. One version of the deep ecological view is presented as follows by Jonathon Porritt: 'The belief that we are "apart from" the rest of creation is an intrinsic feature of the dominant world-order, a man-centred or anthropocentric philosophy. Ecologists argue that this ultimately destructive belief must be rooted out and replaced with a life-centred or biocentric philosophy' (206). Deep ecologists, or 'Dark Greens', usually like to distinguish themselves from environmentalists ('Light Greens'), whom they see as being less radical, and as seeking a primarily 'managerial approach to environmental problems' (Dobson 13). (See also Glotfelty, who argues that the prefix 'enviro-' is 'anthropocentric and dualistic, implying that we humans are at the center, surrounded by everything that is not us, the environment' ['Introduction' xxi].) But as Andrew Dobson, among others, has pointed out, there is a tension between the radical aims of deep ecology and 'the reliance on traditional liberal-democratic means of bringing [change] about' (23). See also Pepper for a useful, if overstated, Marxist critique of deep ecology's 'bogus radicalism', and of the misguided – even misanthropic – tendencies of 'one-world' eco- or biocentric philosophies that 'ignore the importance of struggle to change the social order' (141). For a more balanced view of deep ecology, which acknowledges both the diversity within its ranks and its collective commitment to social transformation, see Merchant, as well as note 39 below. See also Curtin, who endorses weak anthropocentrism as a means of combining agendas for ecological freedom and human justice, and who sees the traditional binaries of environmental philosophy (including that between anthropocentrism and biocentrism) as outdated.

2   One of Curtin's examples here is Garrett Hardin's notorious 'ethics of the lifeboat', which elevates First World environmental assets (for example wilderness areas) over and above the value of human life in the Third World, preferring to see the latter as the primary source of the world's potentially cataclysmic 'population crisis' (Curtin 18–20). For a somewhat intemperate attack on the view of overpopulation as a, or even *the*, fundamental threat to 'global ecological balance' – which he considers to be sometimes little more than a euphemism for First World economic/environmental security – see also Pepper.

3   See for example, Gadgil and Guha; Guha; Shiva.

4   See also Curtin 5–7, 18–20.

5   See also Curtin 100.

6   The 'intrinsic' versus 'extrinsic' or, more commonly, the 'intrinsic value' versus 'instrumental value' dichotomies are a staple of environmental philosophy: see, for example, the essays in Callicott, Elliot and Gare, and Pojman. For more relativistic positions, see Curtin and Pepper, the latter of whom attempts, not entirely convincingly, to rescue Marxism from the charge of instrumentalism.

7   The notions of the 'biotic community' and the 'ecosphere' (also called 'biosphere') are associated first and foremost with the work of Arne Naess, the Norwegian founder of deep ecology. The 'biotic community' is a constellation of interconnected human and nonhuman entities; its balance must be preserved, not just for its own sake but to protect the principle of 'biospheric egalitarianism' and to secure the future of the 'ecosphere' as a whole. Naess's nature mysticism goes beyond everyday environmental considerations, registering a Buddhist-inspired commitment to the non-harming of all 'beings', human and nonhuman, sentient and non-sentient alike. Naess's followers, however, are divided on the practical

consequences of his philosophy; critics such as Andrew Dobson have pointed out that Naess's emphasis on ontology rather than ethics suggests the difficulty of bridging the gap between (deep) ecological theory and social practice (54–55).

8 Disagreements between animal-rights and eco/biocentric advocates within environmental ethics and philosophy usually revolve around the latter's view that *all* nature, sentient or not, must be considered as having intrinsic value. Deep ecologists are therefore always likely to be uneasy with an ethical discourse derived, sometimes explicitly, from human duties and rights (see, for example, Regan). For an overview of the issues at stake, see Dobson, especially chapters 1 and 2; see also the later discussion in this chapter of animal-welfare approaches in Coetzee's and Gowdy's work.

9 'Imperialist nostalgia', in the words of the anthropologist Renato Rosaldo, revolves around a paradox: 'A person kills somebody, and then mourns the victim. In more attenuated form, someone deliberately alters a form of life, and then regrets that things have not remained as they were prior to the intervention. At one more remove, people destroy their environment, and then they worship nature. In any of its versions, imperialist nostalgia uses a pose of "innocent yearning" both to capture people's imaginations and to conceal its complicity with often brutal domination' (69–70). Imperialist nostalgia is antithetical, of course, to the contemporary discourses of environmental protest and postcolonial apology; it surfaces from time to time, nonetheless, in functionalized celebrations of 'non-interventionist' precolonial cultures, or in self-serving liberal attitudes towards 'endangered' cultures/ species, intercultural 'reconciliation' and the protection of 'universal' human rights.

10 See also Spivak's *Critique* and *Other Worlds* and O'Hanlon. The debate on how to articulate resistance without either essentializing the dominant society/culture or monumentalizing the oppressed has been integral to the so-called 'Subaltern Studies Project', the collective efforts of a group of mostly Indian and/or Indian-based scholars committed to the task of reversing the traditionally elitist biases of South Asian historiography. For a fairly recent collection of essays in which Subaltern Studies practitioners reflect on the extent to which the project has been complicit in the very 'worlding' of the Third World it originally set out to counteract, see Chaturvedi. See also Guha, who suggests that the Subalternists, in obsessively theorizing their own procedures, have gradually lost touch with the historical experiences of peasants and workers, and that their work has effectively been taken over by *environmental* historians and scholars – like himself (222).

11 It has been suggested, somewhat uncharitably perhaps, that the 'postcoloniality' of Roy's work owes as much to its success on the international market as to its capacity to generate historically situated anti-imperialist critique. However, this is less an accusation of 'selling out' than a recognition of the function of the contending 'regimes of value' that surround postcolonial works and regulate their reception in different parts of the world (Appadurai 4, 14–15). For a more detailed discussion of postcolonial 'regimes of value', see Huggan (*Postcolonial Exotic* 4–8, 28–33); for an incisive analysis of the reception of Roy's work, and the construction of Roy herself as a mythologized literary celebrity, see also Mongia.

12 See also Rowell 282–86. In his study on Chipko, Guha mischievously observes that 'the baton has passed' to Narmada Bachao Andolan (NBA) as India's most globally visible environmental movement (200). Rowell points out, similarly, that Narmada has become a 'national and international hot-spot of controversy' (282), and that the media have played a leading role in conferring glamour on the players of India's own version of the NBA. But as Roy notes, rather more sourly, '[Narmada is] no longer

as fashionable as it used to be. The international camera crews and the radical reporters have moved (like the World Bank) to newer pastures. The documentary films have been screened and appreciated. Everybody's sympathy is all used up. But the dam goes on. It's getting higher and higher' (50).

13 For up-to-date news, as well as useful records, on the conflicted history of the Narmada Valley Project, various websites can be consulted – for example the Narmada Bachao Andolan (NBA) homepage at http://www.narmada.org/html and the site for River Revival (International Campaign for River Restoration and Dam Decommissioning) at http://www.riverrevival.org/html.

14 See Vandana Shiva's similar view of the dam-building industry in general, and the NVP more specifically, as a consortium of 'free trade [...] institutions [...] transnational corporations and [...] development institutions like the World Bank, who are also acting on behalf of corporations, because for every dam they build they are basically generating contacts for the turbine manufacturers and the construction companies' (qtd. in Rowell 286).

15 It is worth noting that while the 90 footnotes to 'The Greater Common Good' are all to non-fictional sources (scientific studies, economic reports, etc.), Roy's essay continually draws attention to itself as a *literary* artifact. Various intertexts come to mind, including Dickens's novels and Swift's satires, but in its combination of righteous indignation and storytelling verve, the essay most recalls the work of Rushdie, particularly the cross-over political allegory/fable/children's-tale-for-adults, itself drawn from multiple sources, that is *Haroun and the Sea of Stories* (1990).

16 See also *God of Small Things*.

17 For an extended documentary version of the heroes-and-villains romance to which radical environmental writers-activists seem particularly susceptible, see Rowell; for a more nuanced, but equally romanticized account of 'TNCs-against-the-people', see also Kane.

18 The self-conferred heroism implicit in media-friendly terms such as the 'eco-warrior' (although generally avoided by environmentalists) has done little to enhance the credibility of the environmental movement as a whole. Roy, although her tongue is clearly in cheek, simply cannot resist: 'All sorts of warriors from all over the world, anyone who wishes to enlist, will be honoured and welcomed. Every kind of warrior will be needed [in the war 'for the rivers and the mountains and the forests of the world']. Doctors, lawyers, teachers, judges, journalists, students, sportsmen, painters, actors, singers, lovers [...] The borders are open, folks! Come on in' (52).

19 See also Fisher and Omvedt, and Gadgil and Guha's (hyper)sociological distinction between 'ecological refugees', who comprise as much as one third of India's total population, 'ecosystem people', perhaps comprising half of the population, who depend on the local natural environment to meet their material needs, and a small minority ('omnivores') who have benefited from processes of national economic development while continuing to 'enjoy and consume the produce of the entire biosphere'. According to Gadgil and Guha's schema, Roy occupies the role of the 'socially-conscious omnivore', a subcategory of mostly urban omnivores who are concerned about the environment, and some of whom have played a valuable role in mobilizing resistance to human rights/environmental abuses (98). For a more critical view of the role of 'urban omnivores' in assuming control of – and representational rights to – rural 'people's' movements, see also Omvedt, for whom the NBA, in particular, is much less democratic than many of its middle-class supporters like to think.

20 Play has of course become a tried-and-tested strategy of radical (especially anarchically inclined) Green movements, which have co-opted the language, and some

of the attributes, of Carnival to their fervent anti-capitalist cause. Play, at least since Bakhtin, has been seen as a powerful force for social disruption; to call Roy's essay 'playful', in this respect, is not to trivialize her arguments, but rather to place them within a wider context where humour and, occasionally, violence meet (see Buettner on Carnival motifs in the contemporary rhetoric of globalization). The self-conscious infantilism that sometimes surfaces in 'The Greater Common Good' arguably belongs to this category of play; even so, it appears at times as if Roy's penchant for aesthetic play might have got the better of her, diverting her text from the material priorities on which it otherwise wishes to insist.

21 Following Michael Taussig, I shall define the sympathetic imagination here as the human capacity –flying in the face of rational limits – to 'yield into and become Other' (*Mimesis* xiii). Speaking *as* and *through* the other raises the irresolvable dilemma of simultaneously speaking *for* the other – a dilemma explored in these 'ventriloquized' lectures and, indeed, throughout the body of Coetzee's work. The sympathetic imagination, as Coetzee makes clear, has profound implications for both the exercise and the dismantling of colonial authority (see also Taussig, *Mimesis* 250–55); it also marks the contradictions of much liberally oriented animal-rights philosophy, where claims made on behalf of animals – particularly *suffering* animals – are contingent on the ability to intuit their experience and, feeling for them without necessarily thinking as them, to somehow make them speak.

22 'Mimetic excess', for Taussig, is 'a form of human capacity potentiated by postco- loniality', which 'provides a welcome opportunity to live subjunctively as neither subject nor object of history but as both, at one and the same time'. Mimetic excess, claims Taussig, 'provides access to understanding the unbearable truths of make- believe as foundations of an all-too-serious serious reality'; it invokes 'the [magical] power to both double yet double endlessly, to become any Other and engage the image with the reality thus imagized' (*Mimesis* 255). While much of Coetzee's work – including these 'made-up' lectures, filtered through another – strikes a chord with Taussig's theories, it bears reminding that the 'magic of mimesis' is not just a resource for postcolonial freedom, but also a source of colonial abuse (see also Huggan, '(Post)colonialism' 8). *The Lives of Animals* thus moves, characteristically for Coetzee, between a celebration of the possibilities of sympathetic magic and an ironical awareness that these possibilities may be more limited, dangerous, and ultimately more irresponsible than Taussig seems to think.

23 See also Singer 231–32 and Wise, especially chapter 1.

24 See the post-lecture discussion of *Guiliver's Travels* in Coetzee (96, 99).

25 See, by way of comparison, Benjamin's poignant essay on Kafka's fables and parables, which he reads, not in terms of metaphysical hope, but a kind of radiant epistemo- logical despair (144–45). Elizabeth Costello's empathy with Red Peter may be seen, in this respect, less as a gesture of defiance than as an admission of failure, still more as a confession of shame at her own atrophied condition: 'Being an animal presum- ably meant to [Kafka] only to have given up human form and human wisdom from a kind of shame – as shame may keep a gentleman who finds himself in a disreputable tavern from wiping his glass clean' (Benjamin 144). For essays that explore the connections between Kafka's and Coetzee's work, see Huggan ('Is There a K?') and Merivale; see also Dovey for perceptive comments on the allegorical dimensions of Coetzee's novels (*The Novels of J.M. Coetzee*; 'Waiting for the Barbarians').

26 Coetzee's work, as several commentators have pointed out, is obviously under- pinned by poststructuralist understandings of the radical instability of language and of the systems of authority – often explicitly or implicitly masculinist – that are made possible by language (Huggan and Watson, Introduction, 5). For examples

of critical work on Coetzee informed by poststructuralist linguistic/philosophical theories, see the essays by Attridge and Parry in Huggan and Watson.

27 As several of Coetzee's critics have pointed out, there is a tension in both his fiction and his critical work between the desire to enter the global mainstream of intellectual debate (as represented, for example, by the various international schools of [post]modernism) and the awareness of being geographically and cultur-ally isolated, of speaking from what Derek Attridge calls 'a marginal location'. Hence the decision, I would argue, to filter his views – with considerable ironic distance – through the figure of an *Australian* writer: a member, like Coetzee, of a Western-oriented 'settler' culture with uncertain links to an exploitative colonial past.

28 The work of some animal-rights activists, notably Peter Singer, is marked by a similarly loose – and potentially dangerous – use of anthropomorphic analogy. In his book *Animal Liberation*, for example, Singer sees vivisection in the same perspec-tive as 'the atrocities of the Roman gladatorial arenas or the eighteenth-century slave trade' (91); even more controversial is the assertion that '[a] chimpanzee, dog, or pig [...] [has] a higher degree of self-awareness and a greater capacity for meaningful relations with others than a severely retarded infant or someone in a state of advanced senility' (22). The implication behind many of Singer's arguments – that we humans should treat animals better because they are like us – ignores considerable social as well as individual differences in animal behaviour; several of his analogies also assume that there are normative standards in *human* physiology and behaviour, thus laying him open to the accusation of a form of 'speciesism' against members of his own kind (7). For a convincing critique of Singer's utilitarian arguments from within liberal animal-rights philosophy, see Regan. For a defence of the right to make analogies between different forms of animal and human mistreat-ment, see Spiegel.

29 Elizabeth attacks ecologism on the grounds that it is implicitly anthropocentric. Animals themselves, she says, 'are not believers in ecology'; it is rather we humans, 'the managers of the ecology', who 'understand the greater dance [and can there-fore] decide how many trout may be shed or how many jaguar may be trapped before the stability of the dance is upset. The only organism over which we do not claim this power of life and death is Man. Why? Because Man is different. Man understands the dance as the other dancers do not. Man is an intellectual being' (Coetzee 92–93). Elizabeth's emotionalism, however, is arguably just as anthro-pocentric, being based on a media-friendly 'empathy' with animals as objects of human pity and affection (Coetzee 93). To conclude, as Elizabeth's son John does, that the animal-rights movement as a whole is prey to woolly-liberal sentimentality is, however, unduly simplistic. For a critical analysis of the reductive binary thinking that so often underlies popular views both *of* and *within* environmental movements ('anthropocentrism' vs. 'ecocentrism', 'intellectualism' vs. 'emotionalism', 'animal-rights liberalism' vs. 'ecological radicalism', etc.), see Dobson, chapters 1 and 2; see also note 1 above.

30 Coetzee is obviously poking fun here at the self-congratulatory aspects of the academic fashion-industry (just as he pokes fun elsewhere at the hypocritical proto-cols of the university lecture and the shallow one-upmanship of academic debate). This playful anti-academicism belongs, however, to a more serious attack on the arrogance of Western rationalism; Coetzee is also making a point here – however tongue-in-cheek – about the writer's capacity to enter and extend the range of other people's creations: a capacity well demonstrated in the prolific intertextuality of his own work. *The Lives of Animals* is no exception, alive with traces from a variety of literary sources, including Coetzee's own novels (notably *Waiting for the Barbarians*

[1980], *Life & Times of Michael K* [1983], and *Age of Iron* [1990]), and engaging several of the themes that traverse his large body of critical work. Special mention should probably be made here of Coetzee's justly acclaimed novel *Disgrace*, published in the same year (1999) as *The Lives of Animals*. With its fictional – frequently ironic – engagement with the consolations of animal welfare and the displaced (Old Testament) symbolism of retribution and sacrifice, *Disgrace* constitutes a useful companion-volume to the more ostensibly 'academic' text.

31 An 'ecological subject', according to Dobson, belongs to a larger biotic community marked by a diversity of life forms and interconnected ecological 'spheres' (54). The postulation of the non-human ecological subject implies that 'the [entire] biosphere [...] has moral standing' (Dobson 55), and that interactions between different species are part of a larger environmental drama in which humans play a contributing, though by no means an inevitably determining, role. Gowdy's elephants are ecological subjects, not just in the sense of being members of an identifiable – and increasingly threatened – biotic community, but also insofar as they are endowed with a finely tuned capacity for moral discrimination that sheds light on codes of environmental practice (and their abuses) as a whole.

32 See also Vance.

33 On the horrors of the ivory trade, see also Ritvo and Eltingham. The trade is now banned in parts of Africa (Kenya, for instance, which lost two thirds of its elephant population in the 1970s alone); poaching, however, remains an ever-present threat, with changing markets, allied to more fully developed military and transportation technologies, ensuring that the demand for ivory and other elephant products can produce sometimes spectacular economic success.

34 See also Scholtmeijer.

35 A 'visionary', according to Gowdy's elephant mythology, is a 'cow or cow calf who is capable of seeing both the future and the distant present'; a 'link-bull' is one who has special insight into 'omens, signs and superstitions'; a 'mind talker' is 'a telepathic cow or cow calf', able to read not just other elephants', but also other animals', if not humans', minds (335–36, 338). Gowdy's elephants, though rendered biologically and culturally plausible, can thus be seen as semi-mythic subjects for a form of zoological primitivism, inhabiting a fully fashioned tribal world of ancient superstitions and ancestral beliefs.

36 Gowdy's use of pronominal shifters, allied to her glossary and battery of 'explanatory' footnotes, suggests her ironic awareness of the impossibility of explaining elephants' lives *either* from the 'outside' (analytical human) or the 'inside' (self-reflexive elephant) point of view. Rather, Gowdy (like Coetzee in *Lives*) uses an array of fictional as well as historically verifiable sources to create the comforting, but by definition self-deceiving, illusion of a non-human world amenable to human understanding.

37 See Buell's *Environmental Imagination* for an in-depth study, mostly devoted to American nature writing, of the capacity of the 'environmental imagination' (Buell's term) to counteract environmental crisis by 'finding better ways of imaging nature and humanity's relation to it' (2). For Buell, as for Gowdy, the environmental imagination requires not only a transformative social/ecological vision but also a rethinking of basic assumptions about the nature or representation itself (2). Gowdy's radical revision of the animal fable is a case in point here (as, for that matter, is Coetzee's use of the fable to reflect on the ethical as well as aesthetic dilemmas posed by 'traditional' ways of representing animals in literature and art).

38 In their book *Deep Ecology*, Bill Devall and George Sessions define ecotopia 'in the broad sense of all visions of a good society placed in the context of deep ecological

norms and principles'. Ecotopian visions, according to Devall and Sessions, are like other utopian visions in that they 'help us see the distance between what ought to be and what now is in our technocratic-industrial society' (162). Gowdy's novel complicates this picture in several ways, not least by filtering such visions through the worldview of non-human species and by stressing the need to account for specific cultural circumstances (for example those in postcolonial Africa) rather than simply asserting global 'technocratic-industrial' norms. Devall and Sessions's book, first published more than twenty years ago, needs to be seen of course in its own historical context, and several of its generalizations would now probably be contested by other deep ecologists: see note 39 below.

39 It would be both inaccurate and unfair, of course, to accuse ecological environmental criticism *in toto* of culture-blindness. Many contemporary ecocritics are conspicuously attentive to social and cultural differences (particularly those associated with social ecology, eco-socialism and the environmental justice movement, but also at least some of those associated with deep and/or spiritual ecology, holistic movements whose practitioners continue, despite their obvious commitment to egalitarianism and social justice, to get a bad press). To some extent, 'Third Worldist' critiques of First World environmental practice suffer from similar tendencies towards overstatement: see, for example, the introduction to Guha and Martinez-Alier's *Varieties of Environmentalism*, which, while rightly questioning the crude opposition between the 'full-stomach' environmentalism of the North and the 'empty-belly' environmentalism of the South, still tends towards an overdrawn distinction between First World conservationist and/or managerial practices and Third World ecological resistance movements, which the authors bracket under the catchy heading of the 'environmentalisms of the poor' (Introduction xxi).

enhancing inter- or transnational medium of communication and exchange; the deployment of Europhone African literatures as ideological weapons in the Independence struggles and in the continuing critical reassessment of African national cultures in the post-Independence era; the emergence of African studies as a viable subject in the Euro-American academy, often presided over by African scholars who have left – in some cases, have been forced to leave – Africa for fairer politico-economic shores; and perhaps most of all, the yawning disparity in material conditions of production and consumption between Africa and the post-industrial First World, especially Europe and America – a situation that has led to metropolitan publishers and other related patrons (commercial sponsors, institutionally based reviewers and accreditation agencies, and so on) being granted a virtual stranglehold, not only over the distribution, but also to some extent the *definition*, of African literature as a cultural field.[1]

All of this suggests that African literature, to some extent a hopeful child of the Independence movements, is also imbricated with larger patterns of structural underdevelopment governing the global knowledge industry (Altbach; Soyinka). It also suggests the unequal state of affairs that arises when

> a hybrid poetics comes into being, combining elements from the historically dominated system (the African one) with elements from the historically dominant one (the English [European] one), and acting as a constraint on the production of literature within the dominated system, while it leaves the dominant system relatively unaffected. (Lefevere 101)

As Andre Lefevere argues in his 1983 essay on the historiography of African literature, African writers are often caught between the desire to achieve recognition, and the financial rewards that come with it, from a wider audience and their awareness of the constraints this might place on their writing and the ways in which it is received. The danger exists, for example, of the edges of a certain, unmistakably politicized kind of writing becoming blunted by a coterie of publishers and other marketing agents anxious to exploit it for its 'exotic' appeal. So much is clear from the three obviously exasperated comments that follow, which indicate the formulaic patterns into which Western publishers have often seemed to want to assimilate African literary works. The first of these is from the Nigerian writer Obi Egbuna, who in a 1974 interview complains:

> What I resent is that once you go to a university and write in English, somebody comes along, like a talent scout from a London publishing house, and asks 'Why don't you just write something for us?' And he expects you to write just like the African author he has published before. So there he is, defining for you what you should do. (Egbuna, in Lindfors, *Dem-Say* 17; also qtd. in Lizarríbar 111)

The second, a year earlier, comes from the then President of the Ghana Association of Writers, Atukwei Okai, who laments the fact that if you [the writer] set out to print anything on your own, the printing costs will stagger you. If you manage to print, the distribution difficulties will blow your mind. If you give your stuff to a local publisher, you will sympathize so much with his problems that you may not write again. [...] So all our best work [...] appears first to an audience which either regards us like some glass-enclosed specimen [...] or like an exotic weed to be sampled and made a conversation piece [...] or else we become some international organization's pet. (Okai 4)

And the third, also in the 1970s, comes from another Nigerian writer, Kole Omotoso, who, bitterly invoking the memory of the Western literary 'discovery' of his countryman Amos Tutuola in the early 1950s, conjures up the Tutuolan image of a 'headless triangle' comprising '[n]ative writer, foreign publisher and foreign audience' (Omotoso 252).

These commentaries, now a good three decades old, are indicative of a mounting resentment among many of the first generation of post-independence African writers that their political views were being consistently diluted, or simply ignored, even as their economic interests were, on the whole, adequately served. This consensus view was to find support in S.I.A. Kotei's ground-breaking study of the parlous state of the African book trade, *The Book Today in Africa* (1981), a work which urgently needs to be brought up to date, and which has certainly not been bettered since.[2] While a systematic study such as Kotei's is unavailable for the 1990s and on into the new millennium, there is little evidence to suggest that the situation for African writers has improved. Many more have found their way into print, to be sure, but most of these with foreign publishers (Heinemann, Longman, etc.), and a workable infrastructure for publishing in Africa – dubbed, in a devastating phrase, a 'bookless society' (Zell) – can still hardly be said to exist.[3] If anything, the patronage systems that underpinned the emergence of African literature in the decades leading up to and immediately following Independence have been consolidated, with the latest 'discoveries' often being skilfully, if not always seamlessly, assimilated to recognizable market trends.

One of the trends through which African literature has been filtered and has acquired a certain market value relates to a phenomenon that might best be described as the anthropological exotic. The anthropological exotic, like other contemporary forms of exoticist discourse, describes a mode of both perception and consumption; it invokes the familiar aura of other, incommensurably 'foreign' cultures while appearing to provide a modicum of information that gives the uninitiated reader access to the text and, by extension, the 'foreign culture' itself. Thus, the perceptual framework of the anthropological exotic allows for a reading of African literature as the more or less transparent window onto a richly detailed and culturally specific, but still somehow homogeneous – and of course readily marketable – African world. Anthropology is the watchword here, not for empirical documentation, but for the elaboration of a world of difference that conforms to often crudely stereotypical Western exoticist paradigms and myths ('primitive culture', 'unbounded nature', 'magical practices', 'noble savagery', and so on). The anthropological exotic might be seen in some sense as exploiting the exotic tendencies already inherent within anthropology, a discipline that even some of its own practitioners have seen as displaying a 'predilection for purveying exotica [...] [and for choosing] the most exotic possible cultural data [...] [and] the most exotic possible readings' for its own research (Keesing 460).[4] Yet anthropology, in the sense I am using it here, is less about the ideological ground rules of disciplinary practice than about the mobilization of a series of metaphors for the reading and writing of 'foreign cultures'. To what extent does African literature deploy, however ironically, these anthropological metaphors? Is it justifiable to read African literature in this (pseudo-)anthropological manner; and what might be some of the implications of such anthropological readings?

It is helpful, before addressing these questions, to turn attention to a longstanding critical debate over the merits and demerits, the viability or otherwise, of anthropological approaches to African literature. The opposing sides of the debate may be represented here by two of the most respected and theoretically informed among contemporary Africanist scholars, Chidi Amuta and Christopher L. Miller. Amuta, in his influential study *The Theory of African Literature* (1989), is dismissive of what he calls Africanist critics' 'unmediated obsession with cultural anthropology' (Amuta 22). For Amuta, this obsession marks the transition from 'outright colonialist criticism to the faintest recognition of the specific socio-cultural character and historical determination of African literature by critics of African literature' (Amuta 22). Not surprisingly, Amuta lists a number of well-known Euro-American critics among the culprits; but equally well-known African scholars, too, are subjected to withering critical scrutiny: Biodun Jeyifo and Wole Soyinka, for instance, peremptorily labelled 'ethno-critics', whose criticism performs the double disservice of 'seeing African literary works [exclusively] in terms of the ethnicity of their authors' and of 'resurrect[ing] decadent ethnic myths and traditionalia, [trying] to project these onto the screen of contemporary literary works' (Amuta 23). Amuta leaves us in little doubt as to his feelings about anthropology, which he, like several of his peers, considers to be irredeemably tainted by its associations with the colonial enterprise in Africa.[5] His anger here, however, is more specifically directed against those literary critics of 'the cultural anthropology school', who tend to see culture in static terms as coherent units or discrete entities, and cultural artifacts as little more than 'museum pieces, chipped porcelain and survivals of animistic social existence to be recovered in long-abandoned caves and the ruins of great walls and moats' (Amuta 22). For Amuta, this type of 'ethnocriticism' subscribes to a hypostatized 'traditionalist aesthetics', usually driven by romantic-idealist notions of 'traditional' African cultures and often allied to an equally spurious 'pan-Africanist universalism' (Amuta 41).

This frontal, at times splenetic, attack is calmly counteracted by Christopher Miller, one of a number of talented American Africanists unfazed by *bolekaja*-style polemics.[6] For Miller, located as he is within the Western institution, 'a fair Western reading of African literatures demands engagement with, and even dependence on anthropology' (Miller, *Theories* 4). The initial rationale for this is disarmingly, even embarrassingly, simple: '[G]ood reading does not result from ignorance and [...] Westerners simply do not know enough about Africa' (Miller, *Theories* 4). But Miller then goes on to provide a sophisticated defence of anthropology, both as a medium of access to 'modes of understanding that emanate from other (non-Western) cultures' (Miller, *Theories* 21) and as a relativizing methodology that allows for the exploration of the link between (local) ethnicity and (global) ethics. Drawing on relatively recent, self-conscious approaches sometimes loosely bracketed under the rubric of the 'new' critical anthropology (including, among others, Geertz's analyses of ethnographic rhetoric, Tyler's postmodern ethnography and Clifford's adaptations of Bakhtinian dialogics), Miller advances the confident argument that '[r]elativism, retooled as contemporary critical anthropology [...] becomes indispensable as a tool of intercultural critique' (Miller, *Theories* 66).[7] This critique, founded on a conversation between the texts of literature and those of ethnography, is tempered by the ironic awareness that 'access to non-Western systems is mediated through a discipline that has been invented and controlled by the West' (Miller, *Theories* 21; see also Mudimbe, ch. 1). Miller still insists, however, that 'without some reliance on anthropological texts, Westerners will not be able to read African literatures in any adequate way' (Miller, *Theories* 21).

Is there any way of reconciling these two seemingly incompatible positions: the hardline anti-idealism of Amuta, which sees anthropological readings of African literature as wedding ethnic particularism to romantic fancy, and the soft-pedal relativism of Miller, which sees anthropology (more specifically, ethnography) as both necessary supplement and potential corrective to textual analysis, and as an instrument with which to understand African literature's important ideological function as intercultural critique? The middle ground is arguably occupied here by critics such as Simon Gikandi, who stop short of rejecting anthropology out of hand as a tool for students of African literature, but who point out the dangers of misunderstanding and/or misapplying anthropological models, which might result in the type of (pseudo-)anthropological reading that assumes literature 'to be a mere reproduction of reality, and language a *tabula rasa* that expresses a one-to-one correspondence between words and things' (Gikandi 149; see also Quayson). It would be easy enough to show that the reception of African literary texts – to give the famous if by now clichéd example of Chinua Achebe's *Things Fall Apart* (1958) – is awash in such anthropological misapprehensions, which have often proved useful in the fuelling and reconfirmation of Western ethnocentric myths (Quayson). The misconceived notion, for instance, that an African text offers unmediated access to an African culture, or even 'African culture', may be reinforced rather than dispelled by inaccurate views of what anthropology is, does, represents. Hence the frequent recourse to exoticizing readings that begin by latching onto the cultural information putatively presented in the text, only to reincorporate that information into an available body of Western cultural myths. These types of readings also tend to succumb to the temptations of naive reflectionism (Gikandi's 'one-to-one correspondence between words and things') and, as

ethnographic authority – outsider expertise and insider experience – while also questioning the boundary between these two apparently divergent interpretive sources. Such a reading, ironically enough, is entirely compatible with current trends in anthropological thinking. In this sense, Head appears less interested than Achebe in exposing the follies of 'cod' anthropology, and in exploring the implications that such aberrant anthropological readings might have for an uninitiated audience eager to translate what they read into more familiar codes; rather, she is concerned to show how anthropology and (oral) literature might enter into productive dialogue – by providing a series of cautionary parables on the illusoriness of absolute cultural understanding, and on the power-politics that underlies contending claims to cultural knowledge.

Things Fall Apart and *The Collector of Treasures* might both be seen as varied examples of a counter-ethnographic impulse within African literature that warns of the dangers of self-privileging anthropological misreadings of literary works. What happens, though, when such anthropological misreadings are reinstated in these works' reception; and when the anthropological exotic forms an integral part of the metropolitan marketing machinery that has helped bring African literature into the limelight, and upon which it still largely depends? It is impossible within the mostly speculative context of this chapter to 'prove' a hypothesis such as this one, which would require considerable (and not always readily available) statistical support. What the remainder of the chapter does, instead, is to trace a set of narrative guidelines that suggests the retention of an 'anthropological fallacy' in African literature at the level of the *institution*. The particular institution I have in mind here is the publishing industry, more specifically the operations of the world's largest publisher and distributor of English-language African literature: the British-based company, Heinemann Books. The Heinemann African Writers Series (AWS) has undoubtedly performed a valuable service, both in fostering the reputations of many gifted African writers and in bringing an increasing number of African literary works – the Series now runs into the hundreds – to the public eye. The emergence of English-language African writing in the 1950s and 1960s, and the wide respect in which it is held today, would be unthinkable without the momentum provided by Heinemann's promotional enterprise, worldwide distributional networks and financial support. But *how*, exactly, has Heinemann chosen to promote African literature? A cursory history of the Series suggests that Heinemann, for all its well-intentioned activities, may have contributed to the continuing exoticization of Africa through misdirected anthropological images; and that the Africa it has promoted by way of its talented literary proteges has been subjected to a self-empowering, implicitly neocolonialist 'anthropological gaze' (Lizarríbar ch. 4).

The development of the Series, established in the early 1960s under the stewardship of its veteran impresario, Alan Hill, must first be understood in the wider context of the African publishing crisis to which I previously alluded. This crisis, as I suggested, might itself be seen as a single component in the vast neocolonial engine that drives relations between Africa and other Third World regions and their First World 'benefactors' today. The publishing industry in Africa, indeed, affords a rueful object lesson in how structural conditions of underdevelopment produce reliance on the very outside sources that reinforce cultural, as well as economic, dependency (Kotei). Low literacy rates; a fragile intellectual infrastructure; the prohibitive costs involved in printing, transporting and purchasing books in such a huge, divided and desperately impoverished continent; the perceived lack of a cultural atmosphere conducive to the development of local production/consumption networks (Irele) – all of these are contributing factors to a history of catastrophically low levels of book production in Africa and to the continuing, largely enforced reliance on importation and outside agencies of support. Yet these are also indicators of a neocolonial knowledge industry: of the educationally reinforced dependency-mechanisms by which many African writers and, by corollary, their local readers are persuaded to believe that cultural value, as well as economic power, is located and arbitrated elsewhere.[17] Camille Lizarríbar, to whose pioneering history of the African Writers Series I am greatly indebted here, sums up the position for many contemporary African writers as follows:

> African authors will often turn to foreign publishers because of a general mistrust in local publishing, and to be assured of a higher quality product. Therefore, both writers and books are geared primarily towards an outside audience. This vicious circle seems to be a well-established mechanism which hinders the growth of an African book industry by continuously directing its resources and products towards an external supplier and consumer. (Lizarríbar 58)

Unquestionably, this state of affairs lies behind the unparalleled success of the Heinemann African Writers Series, and goes some way towards accounting for its (along with other leading Euro-American publishers') virtual monopoly over the distribution of African literature today.

Various myths of origin surround the emergence of the Series. Several of these relate to the formative role played by Chinua Achebe: one of the Series' founding editors; the author of its inaugural and, in several respects, catalytic volume (*Things Fall Apart*); and still far and away its leading generator of revenue (it has been estimated that Achebe's novels alone are responsible for a third of the Series' total sales). Another relates to the landmark decision of Van Milne, an experienced recruit from one of Heinemann's competitors, Nelson, to launch a low-priced trade-paperback series that would effectively piggyback on the existing African educational market. The most important figure, though, and self-designated founder of the Series, was Alan Hill, the then director of Heinemann's lucrative educational branch, Heinemann Educational Books (HEB). As Hill, now retired, relates in his self-congratulatory autobiography, *In Pursuit of Publishing* (1988), the overseas development of HEB was serendipitously connected with the demise of the British Empire. A three-day visit to Bombay in the mid-1950s was enough to persuade Hill that '[t]he India which British soldiers and administrators had lost was being regained by British educators and publishers' (Hill 93), especially Longman and Oxford University Press. Enter HEB and, shortly thereafter, the African Writers Series, which was also to profit from what Hill called 'the winds of [political] change' in Africa (Hill 192).

As Lizarríbar convincingly demonstrates, the self-important, blatantly neo-imperialist rhetoric of Hill's autobiography 'sustains contemporary theories which propose a form of neo-colonialism of Third World countries by the former colonial powers of the West, this time through economic and educational channels' (Lizarríbar 74). *In Pursuit of Publishing* is also remarkable for its redeployment of atavistic 'Dark Continent' imagery in the service of pioneering First World enterprise, as Hill's numerous formulaic allusions to Conrad's *Heart of Darkness* attest. (Here, for example, is our man in Nigeria: 'Periodically we slithered off the wet track into the darkness of the bush; but thankfully we always skidded back on again. Occasionally we would cross a clearing with a circle of primeval mud huts. It seemed like a journey back into a deep past' (Hill 122).) As Lizarríbar concludes of the abundant light-and-dark images that traverse Hill's expeditions of African 'discovery', his vision of the creation of the African Writers Series can be seen as

a mixture of the [...] missionary mentality, which proposed education as the route into the light of Christianity, and [a combination of] western values and his own business savvy, which made him aware of the potential market involved. As a modern missionary, Hill would not merely bring light into the Dark Continent [but] would provide a light that would allow the Dark Continent to reveal its own mysteries through the mediation of literature and good business sense. (Lizarríbar 83–84)

While it would be exaggerating the case to claim that the Series has moulded itself to Hill's self-image, its marketing approach has often shown symptoms of a controlling imperial gaze. This gaze is evident, not just in patterns (especially early patterns) of selection and editorial intervention, but also in the blatantly exoticist packaging of AWS titles, particularly their covers. As emerges from early assessments of titles earmarked for the Series, a certain style and tone were expected, often conforming to Euro-American preconceptions of 'simplicity', 'primitivism' and 'authenticity' (Lizarríbar ch. 4). These preconceptions also hover round the edges of the early titles' covers, several of which feature emblematic images and designs and, in black and white on the back cover, a crudely amateurish photograph of the author for what appears to be ethnic identification purposes. These covers arguably betray a preoccupation with the iconic representation of an 'authentic Africa' for a largely foreign readership, a preoccupation also apparent in appreciative assessments of the works' putatively anthropological content. Hill's triumphal vision of the corrective role to be played by the Series shows this clearly:

In place of the misconceptions of colonialist times, [the African Writers Series] has given us a true picture of African traditional societies as they move into the modern world, depicting their humanity, their artistic achievements, as well as their cruelty and superstition – a mixture very familiar in the history of Western European civilization. (Hill 145)

This pseudo-anthropological view, in which the reconfirmation of exoticist stereotype masquerades as the newly minted expression of a previously misunderstood cultural reality, has been influential in the metropolitan reception of AWS titles – not least because of their insertion into a ready-made educational market. As an offshoot of HEB, the Series was initially intended to function within a residually colonial African educational system modelled on European standards (Lizarríbar 121). As James Currey, in charge of AWS from 1967 until 1984, remarks matter-of-factly: 'This was a series published by an educational publisher and used in Africa for educational purposes, at university as well as at school level' (Unwin and Currey 6). Yet, as soon became clear, the educational function of the Series was by no means restricted to Africa; it could be geared to the education systems of Europe and America as well. And a valuable marketing strategy, particularly though by no means exclusively outside Africa, was to play up the anthropological dimensions of literary texts often touted as virtually unmediated representations of African society, culture and history. Literature emerged as a valuable tool for the student of African customs, a notion reinforced by the provision of glossaries and other paratextual phenomena – introductory essays, photographs and illustrations, the paraphernalia of annotation.[18] Yet this well-intentioned work of sociohistorical explication, still intrinsic to the ethos of the Series, did little to correct stereotypical views of a romantic Africa of 'primitive', even primordial, tribal existence. Hill again on Achebe:

> The great interest of [*Things Fall Apart*] is that it genuinely succeeds in presenting tribal life from the inside. Patterns of feeling and attitudes of mind appear clothed in a distinctive African imagery. [...] Achebe's literary method is apparently simple, but a vivid imagination illuminates every page, and his style is a model of clarity. (Hill 121)

Hill's account of the development of the Series, charted through a series of glibly classified stages or period-movements, oscillates between a diachronic, 'historical' view of African social transformation and a synchronic, 'anthropological' view of a distinctive African culture. Both views, largely essentialized, indicate alternative reflectionist readings of African literature as either a window onto the 'real' Africa or a barometer of its changing culture.

Several caveats, however, should probably be entered here. Hill's philosophy, while influential, can hardly be said to enshrine AWS policy, which, as might be expected, has undergone numerous changes in the five decades of its existence. The Series during that time has expanded far beyond its original educational mandate, and the vision of Africa it presents is far more varied and complex than Hill's suspiciously disingenuous classifications imply.[19] The AWS, while certainly marketed for a foreign and, increasingly, a global audience, has always catered for a sizeable African reading public as well, as is still very much the case today. (This can be seen, for example, in Bernth Lindfors's 1990 statistics on the prevalent use of AWS texts as school/university set texts – Lindfors, 'Teaching', 'Desert Gold') What is more, African writers have chosen by and large to send their works to Heinemann, in the hope not just of financial reward and a large overseas as well as African audience, but also in the legitimate expectation of unbiased treatment and professionally conducted peer review. The view of African literature – to repeat – as an exotically cultivated export product risks falling victim to the same historical inaccuracies and cultural homogenizations of which Hill himself might stand accused. All of these might be considered as extenuating circumstances. For all that, the history of the Series, relaunched in 1987 under Vicky Unwin and still as active as ever, arguably reveals at least some of the characteristic preoccupations of the anthropological exotic: the desire for authenticity, projected onto the screen of a 'real' Africa; the insistence on the documentary value of literary and, especially, fictional sources; the attempt to co-opt African literature into a Euro-American morality play centring on the need to understand 'foreign' cultures; the further co-optation of this educative process for the purpose of lending moral credence to a self-serving romantic quest. Thus, while it remains true that the AWS has done much to provide the working conditions in which African literature continues to flourish, it has done so under circumstances that might be considered, at best, as inconsistent with many of its writers' overtly anti-colonial beliefs. And, at worst, it might even be claimed that the Series has helped, inadvertently no doubt, to project a certain image of an emergent continent, 'expressed' through its literature, that 'reinforces negative stereotypes which have defined the "Dark Continent" and its people to the Western world' (Lizarríbar 140).

As I have suggested, this negative view summons up the image-repertoire of an anthropological exotic which serves to celebrate the notion of cultural difference while at the same time assimilating it to familiar Western interpretive codes. These assimilationist tendencies are also apparent in what Achebe calls 'colonialist criticism': the type of Euro-American response that raids African writing for evidence of 'universal' (read, Western) patterns of human history and behaviour.[20] (Hill's view of the Series as providing a 'mixture [of humanity and cruelty] very familiar in the history of Western European civilization' might be taken here as symptomatic.) But at this point, what should we make of Achebe's own formative role in the development of the Series; or of the respects he pays Hill in his unequivocally appreciative foreword to *In Pursuit of Publishing*? Might there not be a danger here in subscribing to a bifurcated reception model – one in which African writers, through their dealings with Western 'agents of legitimation' (Bourdieu), are inevitably compromised, suckered into successive reinventions of an Africa that the White Man has known all along? While there are several well-documented instances of African writers locking horns with Western publishers, reviewers and critics (within the context of the Series, two names that come immediately to mind are those of Ayi Kwei Armah and Kole Omotoso), it would be unwise to conclude from this that African literature and the Western literary/critical industry are necessarily at logger-heads; that Western publishers and critics inevitably misrepresent Africa, and that Western readers are automatically complicit in such misrepresentations; and that a guaranteed corrective can be provided for these patterns of abuse by the encouragement of homegrown epistemologies, the cultural-nationalist protection of resources, and local ownership of and control over the means of cultural production. Such 'nativist topologies', as Kwame Anthony Appiah calls them, often depend on a binary 'us/them' rhetoric which negates the transculturative potential inherent in a lengthy history of European encounters – however invasive – with Africa, as well as in more recent developments of capitalist globalization – however uneven – that have made an irrevocable impact on the configuration and transformation of African national cultures; which blinds itself to the crucial understanding of modern African literature as a product of the colonial encounter, rather than as 'the simple continuation of an indigenous tradition [or] a mere intrusion from the metropole' (Appiah 69–70); and which risks merely supplanting the Western-academic 'rhetoric of alterity' with a form of 'ersatz exoticism', through which Africans vainly attempt to assert their cultural autonomy by fashioning themselves 'as the image of the Other' (Appiah 72). For Appiah, it is pointless trying to forget Europe by erasing the European traces of Africa's past: 'since it is too late for us to escape each other, we might instead seek to turn to our advantage the mutual interdependencies history has thrust upon us' (Appiah 72).

I would echo Appiah's insistence that Europe is, like it or not, a part of Africa; and that African literature is best regarded as neither celebratory self-expression nor reprehensible Western imposition, but rather as a hybrid amalgam of cross-fertilized aesthetic traditions that are the historical outcome of a series of often violent cultural collisions. The anthropological exotic in which African literature is implicated is, in part, an attempt to convert this violence into palatable aesthetic forms. This attempt perhaps comprises what I would call the 'postcoloniality' of African literature: its global market-value as a reified object of intellectual tourism, or as the reassuringly educative vehicle of a cultural difference seen and appreciated in aesthetic terms (Huggan, *Postcolonial*). But the anthropological exotic is also, like other forms of the exotic, a medium of unsettlement; it contains unwanted traces of the violence it attempts to conceal. As I have suggested in this chapter, the deployment of strategically exoticist modes of representation in African literature, often ironically mediated through an anthropological discourse of 'scientific' observation, has a destabilizing effect on the readers it addresses. Destabilizing in several senses: first, because it reminds these readers of their interpretive limits and of the inevitable biases behind their attempts to construct Africa as an object of cultural knowledge; second, because it redeploys the anthropological technique of participant-observation as the metaphor for a self-empowering, but also potentially self-incriminating, cultural voyeurism; and third, because it illustrates the 'epistemic violence' (Spivak, *Other*) that underwrites the colonial encounter – an encounter of which anthropology, as well as African literature, is the historical product (Asad, *Anthropology*). It has been said, uncharitably no doubt, that the 'literary turn' in anthropology is another variant on the motif of ethnographic salvage: the discipline's attempt, through heightened powers of critical self-reflexivity, to save itself from itself and from its own exoticizing tendencies. I favour the more generous view – also espoused by Miller – that anthropology remains a

the public sphere cannot "read" scholarly commentators' careful historicizations of Others' lives, and so popular representations of Samoa parallel the "timeless" Kalahari and other fictions of "primitive" human lives. [...] What anthropologists have done to the !Kung San and Samoans and so many others has been brought home, deservedly, to anthropology. We are Difference, Otherness, Essence, the Once and Future Anthropologists [...] Anthropology is always the same, and primitives have no history. We are all Stone Age Nisa, all timeless Samoans – exotics at home' (Leonardo 307).

5   For a more detailed discussion of the case against anthropology in colonial Africa, see Adotévi; for a partial rehabilitation, see Falk Moore and, particularly, James. For other useful discussions of the ambivalent role of anthropology in both supporting and critiquing colonial authority in Black Africa, see Mudimbe and the essays in Asad (*Anthropology*); see also the work of Said ('Representing') and Minh-ha – neither of whom has any formal anthropological training – for their influential, if somewhat tendentious, critiques of anthropological 'master narratives'. See also Note 7 below.

6   For an example of *bolekaja* criticism, so named after Nigeria's system of aggressive transport touting, see Chinweizu *et al.*'s memorable tirade in their book *Toward the Decolonization of African Literature* (1983) against interfering Western critics, who are told in no uncertain terms to 'keep [their] hegemonic hands off African literature' (Chinweizu and Madubuike 302).

7   Just how new the New Anthropology is is a matter of some contention within the discipline (see, for example, Marcus and Fischer). The New Anthropology, which is arguably marked by a greater degree of disciplinary self-reflexivity and by an attention to the textuality – the rhetorical constructedness – of ethnography, is no doubt open to misunderstanding partly because it has become the object of attention for literary/cultural studies' scholars from *outside* the field. For a blistering response to ill-conceived, but increasingly fashionable, attacks on anthropology from outside the discipline, see di Leonardo (43–50). See also Note 4 above.

8   On the damaging cumulative effect of several centuries of distorted European representations of Africa, see Hammond and Jablow; see also Mudimbe, who argues convincingly that European discourses of/about Africa, including those derived from anthropology, contributed to nothing less than the *invention* of a 'Dark Continent' that served European psychosexual desires and expansionist needs.

9   The notion that postcolonial literatures involve both deconstructive and recuperative readings is taken from Ashcroft *et al.*, particularly the opening chapter. The tension between deconstructionist theories and the politics of indigenous self-empowerment is central to continuing debates on the political effectiveness of postcolonial criticism.

10   For both the theory and practice of 'contrapuntal' modes of critical reading, see Said (*Culture*). My use of the word 'counter-discourse' here is derived in part from Helen Tiffin, who uses it (via Richard Terdiman) to examine the ways in which postcolonial writers have responded to and creatively transformed the canonized work of their European precursors. For an attempt to apply this term to anthropological, as well as literary, 'classics', see also Huggan ('Anthropologists'). The notion of 'counter-discourse' remains useful in postcolonial studies, even if it has spawned a whole school of 'writing-back' interpretations, including my own, that began some time ago to follow all-too-predictable lines. 'Counter-discursive' approaches to postcolonial literatures have arguably fallen out of fashion; but not so much because they are seen, unfairly I think, as reinstalling the European dominant but rather because literature-based approaches have themselves lost ground during the institutional turn to postcolonial cultural studies.

11   Pratt uses 'autoethnography' in her book *Imperial Eyes* (1992) to refer to 'instances in which colonized subjects undertake to represent themselves in ways that engage with the colonizer's terms' (Pratt 7). Autoethnography thus necessarily implies a dialectical relationship between 'foreign' codes of representation and 'indigenous' experiences – a dialectic maintained, often for ironic purposes, in several contemporary African literary works.

12   For an explanation of Du Bois's term and its applicability to literary works intended for reception by both 'in-group' and 'out-group' audiences, see Sollors.

13   For supplements to Marcus and Cushman's list, see Marcus and Fischer; see also Geertz's considerations of ethnographic rhetoric, particularly in *Works and Lives: The Anthropologist as Author* (1988). For a useful discussion of possible areas of overlap between literature and ethnography, see also Krupat, esp. the first chapter.

14   The classic essay here is 'The Novelist as Teacher' (first published in 1965); see also Achebe's own contribution to *Teaching Things Fall Apart* (Lindfors, *Approaches*).

15   See Clifford's explication of the trope of 'ethnographic salvage' in his essay 'On Ethnographic Allegory' in Clifford and Marcus. As Clifford suggests, the idea of rescuing putatively 'vanishing' cultures is best seen as a romantic popularization of an anthropological paradigm that has itself arguably vanished. But the idea, nonetheless, has retained its ideological force, especially outside the discipline: 'The rationale for focusing one's attention on vanishing lore, for rescuing in writing the knowledge of old people, may be strong […] I do, however, question the assumption that with rapid change something essential ("culture"), a coherent differential identity, vanishes… Such attitudes, though they persist, are diminishing […] [b]ut the allegory of salvage is deeply ingrained' (Clifford 112–13).

16   In other, non-fictional works, Head herself arguably occupies this intermediate position. See, for example, her sociological/anthropological portrait of village life in *Serowe: Village of the Rain Wind* (1981).

17   For different, but equally impassioned, diagnoses of this dilemma, see the essays by Soyinka and Omotoso; in the wider context of literary publishing in the Third World, see also Altbach.

18   A more detailed treatment is urgently needed of the ideological function of 'the paratextual apparatuses' (Genette) surrounding postcolonial literary works. Introductory studies such as Ashcroft *et al.*'s make occasional mention of paratextual devices such as glossaries, arguing that these may serve both to inform the reader and, by drawing attention to what s/he otherwise would not understand, to install cultural difference into the text (Ashcroft *et al.* 56–57, 61–64). Equally, however, glossaries and other translational mechanisms might be seen as ways of *domesticating* the text, making it available for what might be euphemistically called 'general consumption'. To date, the only essay that I have come across that deals in any detail with ideological effects of the paratextual is Wendy Waring's.

19   See, for example, Adewale Maja-Pearce's unabashedly celebratory overview of the first three decades of the AWS: 'In Pursuit of Excellence: Thirty Years of the Heinemann African Writers' Series' (*RAL* 1992), in which he lauds 'the increasing diversity of voices that have emerged from the continent in recent years' (Maja-Pearce 130). As Maja-Pearce – who has himself played an important editorial role within the Series – suggests, 'The genesis of the African Writers' Series has become part of the mythology of modern African literature itself' (125). While this is true, it may also be – as Lizarríbar suggests – part of the problem. The constitutive role played by the AWS in the creation of 'the mythology of modern African literature' is itself in need of critical analysis, precisely the kind of analysis Lizarríbar – however provocatively – presents.

20 See Achebe's eponymous essay in the collection *Hopes and Impediments* (1989). The question of colonialist biases in Western criticism of African literature is far from resolved, even though the angriest exchanges – often *ad hominem* –probably belong to the period from the late 1960s to the early 1980s.

CHAPTER 7

(Post)Colonialism, Anthropology and the Magic of Mimesis

Situating itself at the interface between critical theory and cultural studies, this chapter addresses the theoretical problem of the relationship between *mimicry* and *mimesis*, two terms which are often seen as being virtually interchangeable but which may, as I will argue here, have different cultural functions. Its point of departure, however, is the so-called cultural studies project, whose twin imperatives are, first, to redefine culture not as the privileged domain of an intellectual elite but as an arena for the everyday practices of conflicting social groups; and, second, to turn the exoticist gaze of anthropology back on the viewer, recognizing in the process that the study of culture might best begin at home.

Both of these objectives are, of course, open to question. In the first instance, it might be said that cultural studies' fetishization of 'the popular' is no less elitist than the Arnoldian paradigm of artistic excellence it seeks to replace; in the second, it could be argued in defence of anthropology that the discipline, traditionally concerned with documenting 'other' cultures, has always dialectically performed a self-critique.[1] A test case here is anthropology's alleged complicity with various projects of colonialism, which observers outside the discipline have been more than eager to attack. Anthropology has been accused of conspiring in imperialist representation (Mudimbe), and of silencing those on behalf of whom it claims the right to speak (Said, 'Representing'; Spivak). Most damagingly, perhaps, the discipline has been seen as a tacit form of self-aggrandizement: as the Vietnamese filmmaker Trinh T. Minh-ha has famously pronounced, anthropology is 'a conversation of "us" with "us" about them' (65), a dialogue aimed at settling scores between white men and, less often, white women who bicker about each other's ethnocentrism under the banner of native equality.

Unsurprisingly, professionals within the field have tended to bristle at such polemical judgements. For instance, Talal Asad suggests in his introduction to a collection of essays on anthropology and the colonial encounter that it would be fair to say that anthropologists 'have [...] contributed, sometimes indirectly, towards maintaining the structure[s] of power represented by the colonial system', or that their analyses have at times been affected by the 'readiness to adapt to colonial ideology'. However, he goes on to say that it would be unfair to conclude from this that anthropology was, or is, the 'simple reflection of colonial ideology', or that its primary function in the colonial era was as 'an aid to colonial administration' (17–18). Wendy James, in the same volume, carries Talal Asad's argument further, asserting that anthropologists in the colonies were mostly 'frustrated radicals aware that their work was bound up in, and accountable to, dominant systems, but providing the methodological tools for those systems' self-critique'.[2]

A similar argument might be made for some of their late-twentieth-century counterparts, whose work is carried out in a nominally postcolonial context, but who are often reliant (as were their predecessors) on government or corporate funding and who know (as did their predecessors) that the cultural encounters intrinsic to their research are based on often conspicuously asymmetrical relations of power (Huggan, 'Anthropologists'). This charting of complicities is an integral part of postcolonial criticism, informing the approach of several contemporary anthropologists like Nicholas Thomas, who attempts to use postcolonial theories of the fractured subject to interrogate those falsely homogenizing representations which obscure both 'the multiplicity of colonizing projects and the plurality of potential subversions of them' (195); or like Mary Steedly, who adapts the Marxist feminist strictures of Gayatri Chakravorty Spivak to the examination of gendered relations of power in (post)colonial Indonesia; or, more controversially, like Michael Taussig, who rehabilitates the shamanic powers of indigenous societies that he sees as lurking behind the rationalist technologies of Western imperial science.[3]

Due to its ambitious scope, Taussig's project merits closer critical scrutiny. From his early work on shamanism to his study of spirit possession, Taussig – in his own highly maverick way – has been concerned with *magic*: the magical capacity of technology to reproduce voices and images; and, above all, the magic that comes from a sensuous apperception of the world, from a heightened relationship to and with the life contained in objects. Taussig takes his cue, here as elsewhere, from the work of Walter Benjamin, one of whose tasks had been to show the 'primitive' strain within modernity – the impossible attempt to re-enchant the world through technical reproduction, through the mediated pursuit of a wished-for immediacy of experience. Like Benjamin, Taussig remains critical of Western myths of progress and alert to the susceptibility of modern technologies to ideological manipulation. Likewise, Taussig laments the waning of the sacred: the atrophying of religious experience in late-capitalist Western culture, or, more accurately, the transference of that experience onto the fetishized commodity, which assumes the magical status once accorded to sacred objects.[4]

More particularly, Taussig concerns himself with the magic of *mimesis*: with the capacity of people to see or create resemblances between themselves and others or to identify uncannily with their object of representation. In *Mimesis and Alterity* (1993), he uses ideas drawn in part from Benjamin's essays on the mimetic faculty to illustrate the magical power deriving from the process of *replication*, a process during which the copy 'affect[s] the original to such a degree that the representation [comes to] share in or acquire the properties of the represented' (47–48). Taussig here explores not just the process but the politics of mimesis – the ways in which mimesis operates strategically in colonial contexts, as a means both of relating the self to others and of usurping others' power. For him, then, colonial *mimesis* is indistinguishable from *mimicry*, and he draws his examples accordingly from Darwin's 'first-contact' encounter with the Fuegian Indians, in which mimetic prowess was seen as a property of the so-called 'savage races', and from the wooden Cuna Indian figurines 'mimicking' the whites who have historically exploited them, an instance in which mimicry appears to implement a kind of simulated exorcism: a paradoxical means by which the Cuna deliver themselves from their oppressors by mockingly reproducing them in their own colonial mode.

If Taussig tends to conflate the terms mimicry and mimesis, he also effects a slippage between their respective, interlinked functions. In mimicry, the dominant function is that of mischievous imitation: the kind of *imitation* that pays an ironic homage to its object. However, mimesis (although its function has always been disputed) usually refers to a wider process of *representation* that involves the mediation between different worlds and people – in essence, between different symbolic systems (Gebauer and Wulf). Taussig sees little difference between the Cuna's mimicry of the white man and their mimicry of the white man's mimetic representation of them. In his reading of the Cuna figurines, mimicry serves a dual function, both driving out the collective demons of colonialisms past and present, and appropriating, for curative purposes, the colonizers' representational power. The figurines fascinate Taussig, too, for the light they shed on anthropology. As they cannot be conceived of as conventional 'primitive artifacts', they demand an apprehension that gainsays ethnographic knowledge:

> If I take the figurines seriously, it seems that I am honor bound to respond to the mimicry of my self in ways other than the defensive maneuver of the powerful by subjecting it to scrutiny as yet another primitive artifact, grist to the analytic machinery of Euroamerican anthropology. The very mimicry corrodes the alterity by which my science is nourished. For now I too am part of the object of study. The Indians have made me alter to my self. (8)

And Taussig, apparently dazzled by the brilliance of his own insight, launches into a pseudo-native chant all of his own:

> And here where pirates arm, in arm with Darien
> Indians roamed,
> Of their bones is coral made.
> What Enlightening spirits can I sing into Being

colonial officers. *Hauka*, like *mbari*, had its heyday in the 1920s, a time when European imperial rule in Africa was arguably at its height. During this period, *Hauka* characterized 'embodied resistance' (Stoller, *Embodying*), strategically using mimesis to re-present the cultural 'other' and thereby symbolically taking over the body of the French occupying force. Or such is Stoller's reading; Taussig's interpretation, however, proves somewhat different. As before, Taussig emphasizes the mimicry of mimicry: the means by which the *Hauka* actors not only ape the 'civilized' French but also ape the French aping them in all their pre-European 'savagery.' As Taussig notes,

> It's the ability to become *possessed*, the ability that signifies to Europeans awesome Otherness if not downright savagery, which allows them to assume the identity of the European and, at the same time, stand clearly and irrevocably [...] apart from it. What's being mimicked is mimicry itself – within its colonial shell. (*Mimesis* 24, emphasis in original)

Taussig's point here is most interesting because of the apparent desire for recognition it presupposes – as if mimicry, of whatever order, fixates on its object, enhancing its visibility while draining its force. Taussig views 'possession' as a variation on colonial mimicry: a mimicry that is aimed (as previously) at impersonating him. This mimicry, however, can be reappropriated through the 'magical' technologies of the white man, more specifically, in this case, film: hence Taussig's admiring reading of *Les maîtres fous* (1953), Jean Rouch's landmark ethnographic film about the *Hauka* ceremonies. The film, according to Taussig, who continues to conflate mimicry and mimesis, reappropriates Songhay mimicry, 'borrow[ing] from the magical practice of mimesis in its very filming of it' (242). What is recognized here is not so much the Songhay's mimetic powers as the capacity of the camera, in turn, to 'repossess' them. 'The primitivism within modernism', says Taussig, warming to his topic, 'is allowed to flower. In this colonial world where the camera meets those possessed by gods, we can truly point to the Western rebirth of the mimetic faculty by means of modernity's mimetic machinery' (242). But this machinery arguably also serves to *restore* the Songhay to 'exotic' status; Rouch's film (and Taussig is well aware that the irony also applies to him) effectively reinstates alterity through a secondary mimesis. *Hauka*, in the process, is divested of its anti-colonial impetus through the film's colonialist gesture of recapturing the power of the colonized. The mimetic capacity of *Hauka* to represent an indigenous worldview is assimilated to the European desire to witness images of itself.[9]

Another instance of such a double bind can be found on a different continent, Australia, though in a similar context – the playing out of colonial relations of power. I am referring here to the widely praised compilation *Reading the Country* (1984), a collaborative venture by the Moroccan painter Krim Benterrak, the (white) Australian theorist Stephen Muecke, and the Aboriginal storyteller Paddy Roe. *Reading the Country*, taking its cue from the 'nomadology' of Deleuze and Guattari, registers an attempt, through the dismantling of Western verbal and visual models, to reproduce mimetically an Aboriginal view of Australian landscape. The life of a nomad, says Muecke, is intermezzo: 'The nomad [unlike the settler] does not try to appropriate the territory, there is no sense in enclosing it and measuring it as did the early [white] surveyors. What is important to know are the ways of representing the tracks which cross it' (224). Enlisting the help of Benterrak's irregular landscape paintings, which provide hybrid variations on 'standard' Western topographic maps, and Roe's circuitous stories, which provide ironic counterpoints to the linear flow of Western narrative plots, Muecke sets out to present a 'nomadological' text which aims to 'repeat the experience of the [Western Australian Roebuck] Plains in its own structure' (14).

Like Taussig, Muecke appears to want to perform a kind of sympathetic magic. But his exercise in mimicry, again like Taussig's, might be seen as ironically self-serving. Is Muecke's primary goal to mimic an Aboriginal way of seeing or is it to co-opt Aboriginal codes into Western theoretical discourse? The text that he co-produces is certainly nothing if not derivative; it effectively mimics Aborigines mimicking Deleuze and Guattari mimicking nomads. But as Paul Carter points out in his critique of *Reading the Country*, this infinite regress of mimicry does not succeed in rescuing the text from the obvious charge of ethnocentric bias. In his view, *Reading the Country* is at best 'a valuable record of the dismantling of certain white historical myths: to suppose there is a natural correspondence between this and the "nomadic discourse" of the Aborigine is to be guilty [...] of an imitative fallacy' (348).

The Aboriginal writer Mudrooroo Nyoongah goes still further, taking Muecke to task for staging an Aboriginal side-show for his own benefit and for imprisoning Roe's stories between 'fat slabs of academic prose' (*Writing from a Fringe* 151). This criticism, as often with Mudrooroo, is taking things too far. But as evidenced by the heavily ironic portrait of the Christian missionary Fada in his own Tasmanian-based historical novel, *Master of the Ghost Dreaming* (1991), Mudrooroo clearly has little patience for what he sees as the posturing of trendy Western cultural theorists or for the inscriptions their historical counterparts made on so-called primitive cultures. Dispatched from London to save the souls of his 'sable brethren', Fada has quite explicitly taken it on himself to rescue their putatively 'vanishing' culture:

> The missionary and the anthropologist uneasily shared his soul. The stern Christian knew that [the Aborigines'] pagan ceremonies had to go, whilst the anthropologist (and the romantic) found a natural joy in them. Was there a middle way which accepted both Christian duty and scientific enquiry? (18)

And, while pondering this dilemma, Fada sets his mind to planning his latest paper for the Royal Anthropological Society back home. Throughout Mudrooroo's novel, Fada's amateur anthropology and its evolutionist thinking serve as the subject of unrelenting satire. Mudrooroo also pokes fun at modern forms of cultural relativism, as evidenced in the stunning opening sequence that sets the scene for the rest of the novel. In it, the Aboriginal shaman, Jangamuttuk, orchestrates a corroboree in which his tribespeople paint their bodies in a simulacrum of European style:

[T]he women subjected to the new Christian faith wore a long skirt, but above their waist to perfect the ceremony, they had painted in a lattice work of white lines that signified a bodice lowcut as in formal European wear. There was even the appearance of a necklace dangling above the cleavage of the breasts [...]. To complete their costume, they wore flowers and leafy twigs plaited into their hair and shaped like European women's hats. (2)

The men are no less bizarre, with their hair arranged

into the shape of flat European hats, or piled [...] up around a piece of wood or rolled up cloth so that it might appear in the fire light to be the high helmet of a European soldier. Their body painting had been designed to signify European fashion, both civilian and military. The stripes of military jackets were painted across chests; lapels and buttons, even pockets had been painted with an attention to detail that was quite startling – that is if there were European eyes present to be startled; but for that moment there were none, and even if there had been, it was highly doubtful that the signifiers could have been read. What was the ultimate in a sign system, might still be read as primitive. (3)

The preceding passage reads like a cross between Clifford Geertz and Roland Barthes: the interpretation of culture mediated through the semiosis of fashion systems. However, by assuming the perspective of the canny Aboriginal shaman, the narrator produces not so much a mocking tribute to colonial refinement as a counter-ethnographic reading of the indigenous culture:

He [Jangamuttuk] was not after a realist copy, after all he had no intention of aping the European, but sought for an adaptation of these alien cultural forms appropriate to his own cultural matrix. [...] He, the shaman, and purported Master of the Ghost Dreaming, was about to undertake entry into the realm of the ghosts [the white men]. Not only was he to attempt the act of possession, but he hoped to bring all of his people into contact with the ghost realm so that they could capture the essence of health and well-being, and then break back safely into their own culture and society. This was the purpose of the ceremony. (3–4)[10]

The ceremony provides another example of indigenous mimesis; it does not aim, through mimicry, to subvert someone else's agenda but, through a process of interculturative adaptation, to create its own. European cultural signifiers are assimilated to the indigenous sign system, and the resulting control of semiotic codes becomes the prelude to 'possession': the temporary journey into the spirit-world provides an instance of contact through which the possessed attempt to incorporate the symbolic power of their oppressors and to use it (as the Cuna do with their curative wooden figurines) for the purpose both of healing themselves and of revitalizing their culture. Mimesis here emerges as a self-empowering representation, a stage-managed encounter that mediates between alternative symbolic worlds. It is as if Mudrooroo's text wished to *disabuse* itself of mimicry: of the desire, through simulated service, to resist the dominant culture.[11] The text operates, instead, within its *own* cultural frame of reference, refusing to see itself as a second-order cultural product and rejecting the imagined priority of cultures other than its own. This is not to say that the text subscribes to some version of nativist authenticity; it avoids the move by which it might effect a 'salvage ethnography' of its own (Clifford, 'Ethnographic Allegory'). Instead, it recognizes 'culture' as a site of contestation, as a continual recoding of contingent signifying systems. In this recognition at least, Mudrooroo would surely agree with Michael Taussig and with Walter Benjamin, for whom the mimetic faculty, passing into verbal language, effects a shift based not on 'essential' – recognizable – cultural properties but on the intermittent signals ('flashes', Benjamin calls them) of nonsensuous correspondence ('Mimetic Faculty' 335–36).[12]

In conclusion, I wish to contemplate the puzzle of 'culture' and to show how cultural studies, in moving between connected disciplines, emphasizes both the relational nature of cultural production and the contingencies that affect all forms of cultural exchange. In this chapter, I have attempted to restore the importance of anthropology to cultural studies, not least because anthropology, for all its (not so) hidden biases, remains a valuable agency of cultural critique and also because anthropology, in its more enlightened moments, has the 'worldliness' (Said, *World*) – the understanding of the global effects of cultural practices – that cultural studies, for all its Marxist-inflected politics, often lacks. With certain strands of contemporary anthropology, cultural studies shares the premise that cultural representations are enmeshed in power. Further, it offers a theorized analysis of these relations of power, an analysis that recognizes that theory is itself always political and that, as such, it is best adapted to emancipatory social ends. Theory and politics are not, and cannot be, mutually exclusive. And if cultural studies relies too often on mimetic theories of representation, risking being seen as tendentiously reductionist in its textual analyses, it also provides an antidote to what Stuart Hall calls 'deconstructive ventriloquism' (286): the kind of ingenious mimicry that ossifies into mundane magic and, in repeating its formulas, mantra-like, for a highly select audience, makes the mistake of attempting to substitute intellectual work for politics (286).[13]

Works Cited

Adorno, Theodor. *Aesthetic Theory*. Trans. C. Lenhardt. London: Routledge, 1984.

Asad, Talal, ed. *Anthropology and the Colonial Encounter*. Atlantic Highlands, NJ: Humanities, 1973.

Barthes, Roland. *The Fashion System*. Trans. Matthew Ward and Richard Howard. New York: Hill and Wang, 1983.

Benjamin, Walter. *Illuminations: Essays and Reflections*. Ed. Hannah Arendt. Trans. Harry Zohn. New York: Schocken, 1968.

———. 'On the Mimetic Faculty'. In *Reflections: Essays, Aphorisms, Autobiographical Writings*. Ed. Peter Demetz. Trans. Edmund Jephcott. New York: Schocken, 1978. 333–36.

Benterrak, Krim, Stephen Muecke and Paddy Roe. *Reading the Country: An Introduction to Nomadology*. Fremantle, Australia: Fremantle Arts Centre Press, 1984.

Bhabha, Homi. 'Of Mimicry and Man: The Ambivalence of Colonial Discourse'. *October* 34 (1985): 126–33.

Brunt, Rosalind. 'Engaging with the Popular: Audiences for Mass Culture and What to Say About Them'. In *Cultural Studies*. Ed. Grossberg *et al.* 69–80.

Carter, Paul. *The Road to Botany Bay: An Exploration of Landscape and History*. New York: Knopf, 1988.

Clifford, James. 'On Ethnographic Allegory'. In *Writing Culture: The Poetics and Politics of Ethnography*. Ed. James Clifford and George E. Marcus. Berkeley: University of California Press, 1986. 98–121.

Deleuze, Gilles, and Félix Guattari. *A Thousand Plateaus: Capitalism and Schizophrenia*. Trans. Brian Massumi. Minneapolis: University of Minnesota Press, 1987.

Donaldson, Ian, and Tamsin Donaldson, eds. *Seeing the First Australians*. Sydney: Allen and Unwin, 1985.

Fiske, John. 'Cultural Studies and the Culture of Everyday Life'. In *Cultural Studies*. Ed. Grossberg *et al.* 154–73.

Gebauer, Günter, and Christoph Wulf. *Mimesis: Culture/Art/Society*. Trans. Don Reneau. Berkeley: University of California Press, 1995.

Geertz, Clifford. *The Interpretation of Cultures*. New York: Basic, 1973.

Grossberg, Lawrence, Cary Nelson and Paula Treichler, eds. *Cultural Studies*. New York: Routledge, 1992.

Hall, Stuart. 'Cultural Studies and its Theoretical Legacies'. In *Cultural Studies*. Ed. Grossberg *et al.* 277–94.

Horkheimer, Max, and Theodor Adorno. *Dialectic of Enlightenment*. Trans. John Cumming. New York: Seabury, 1972.

Huggan, Graham. 'Anthropologists and Other Frauds'. *Comparative Literature* 46.2 (1994): 113–28.

——. 'A Tale of Two Parrots: Walcott, Rhys, and the Uses of Colonial Mimicry'. *Contemporary Literature* 35.4 (1994): 643–60.

James, Wendy. 'The Anthropologist as Reluctant Imperialist'. In *Anthropology and the Colonial Encounter*. Ed. Talal Asad. Atlantic Highlands, NJ: Humanities, 1972. 41–70.

Jay, Martin. 'Martin Jay Replies to Michael Taussig and Paul Stoller'. *Visual Anthropology Review* 10.1 (1994): 163.

——. 'Unsympathetic Magic: Review article on *The Nervous System* and *Mimesis and Alterity*'. *Visual Anthropology Review* 9.2 (1993): 79–82.

MacKenzie, Scott. 'Mad Priests and the Mimetic Faculty'. *CineAction* 33 (1994): 12–22.

Marcus, George E., and Michael Fischer. *Anthropology as Cultural Critique*. Chicago: University of Chicago Press, 1986.

Minh-ha, Trinh T. *Woman, Native, Other: Writing Feminism and Postcoloniality*. Bloomington: Indiana University Press, 1989.

Mudimbe, V. Y. *The Invention of Africa: Gnosis, Philosophy, and the Order of Knowledge*. Bloomington: Indiana University Press, 1988.

Mulvaney, D. J. 'The Darwinian Perspective'. In *Seeing the First Australians*. Ed. Ian and Tamsin Donaldson. Sydney: Allen and Unwin, 1985. 68–75.

Nolan, Maggie and Carrie Dawson. 'Who's Who? Hoaxes, Imposture, and Identity Crisis in Australian Literature'. Special issue of *Australian Literary Studies* 21.4 (2004).

Nyoongah, Mudrooroo. *Master of the Ghost Dreaming*. North Ryde, NSW: Angus and Robertson, 1991.

——. *Writing from the Fringe: A Study of Modern Aboriginal Literature*. Melbourne: Hyland, 1990.

Said, Edward. 'Representing the Colonized: Anthropology's Interlocutors'. *Critical Inquiry* 15.2 (1989): 205–25.

———. *The World, the Text, and the Critic*. Cambridge, MA: Harvard University Press, 1983.

Scott, David. 'Criticism and Culture: Theory and Post-Colonial Claims on Anthropological Disciplinarity'. *Critique of Anthropology* 12.4 (1992): 371–94.

Spivak, Gayatri Chakravorty. *In Other Worlds: Essays in Cultural Politics*. New York: Methuen, 1987.

Steedly, Mary. *Hanging without a Rope: Narrative Experience in Colonial and Postcolonial Karoland*. Princeton: Princeton University Press, 1993.

Stoller, Paul. 'Double Takes: Paul Stoller on Jay on Taussig'. *Visual Anthropology Review* 10.1 (1994): 155–62.

———. *Embodying Colonial Memories: Spirit Possession, Power, and the Hauka in West Africa*. New York: Routledge, 1995.

Taussig, Michael. *The Devil and Commodity Fetishism in South America*. Chapel Hill, NC: University of North Carolina Press, 1980.

———. *The Magic of the State*. New York: Routledge, 1997.

———. 'Michael Taussig Replies to Martin Jay'. *Visual Anthropology Review* 10.1 (1994): 154.

———. *Mimesis and Alterity: A Particular History of the Senses*. New York: Routledge, 1993.

———. *Shamanism, Colonialism, and the Wild Man: A Study in Terror and Healing*. Chicago: University of Chicago Press, 1986.

Thomas, Nicholas. *Colonialism's Culture: Anthropology, Travel, and Government*. Princeton: Princeton University Press, 1994.

Young, Robert. *Colonial Desire: Hybridity in Theory, Culture, and Race*. New York: Routledge, 1995.

Notes

1   For useful introductory discussions of the meanings of 'the popular' in cultural studies, see essays by John Fiske and Rosalind Brunt in Grossberg *et al.*; for a defence of the critical faculty of anthropology, see Marcus and Fischer.

2   For an overview of colonialist issues in anthropology, see Thomas; and for a critique from outside the discipline that covers many of these issues, see Said, 'Representing'.

3   For a piece that assesses the relevance of postcolonial theory to anthropology, see Scott.

4   Benjamin's crucial essay on commodity fetishism is 'The Work of Art in the Age of Mechanical Reproduction', in *Illuminations* (217–52). To understand how commodity fetishism is a central topic in much of Taussig's anthropology, see in particular the early study *The Devil and Commodity Fetishism in South America*.

5   For a thoroughgoing, even excessive, critique of Taussig's imitative fallacy, see Martin Jay's review of *Mimesis and Alterity* in *Visual Anthropology Review*. Also in *Visual Anthropology Review*, one finds Taussig's no less caustic reply, Paul Stoller's attempt to make the peace, and Jay's insistence on having the final word.

6   On 'organized mimesis', see Horkheimer and Adorno, especially pages 180–84. Adorno's *Aesthetic Theory* contains most of his ideas on mimesis, which he cryptically defines as 'the non-conceptual affinity of subjective creation with its objective and unposited other' (80). Taussig's fairly sketchy discussions of Adorno and Horkheimer are in *Mimesis and Alterity* (66–69, 86–88); in his review, Jay is particularly hard on Taussig for his 'misreading' of Adorno.

7   See, particularly, Young's discussion of the dynamics of colonial desire (chap. 7), of the mechanism by which 'a culture in its colonial operation becomes hybridized,

alienated and potentially threatening to its European original through the production of polymorphously perverse people who are, in [Homi] Bhabha's phrase, white, but not quite' (175).

8   For a more detailed discussion of this process of simulated subordination, see my own essay on colonial mimicry, 'A Tale of Two Parrots'.

9   Scott MacKenzie, in his interesting essay on Rouch's film in *CineAction*, defends it, as does Taussig, for its demonstration of the counter-hegemonic potential of mimesis. However, as MacKenzie notes in a later commentary on Indigenous 'self-documentary' video, the Western *technological* control of Indigenous (self-)representation is apt to produce a mimetic discourse that is inadvertently patronizing.

10 Note in the above quotation that Mudrooroo (as Taussig does in *Mimesis and Alterity*) plays ironically on the word 'ape'. Mudrooroo is no doubt aware that, later in the (nineteenth) century, the Tasmanian Aborigines would be seen as living proof of Darwin's evolutionary theories. See, for example, the following excerpt from Edward Tylor's preface to H. L. Roth's *The Aborigines of Tasmania* (1890): 'Looking at the vestiges of a people so representative of the rudest type of man, anthropologists must join with philanthropists in regretting their unhappy fate. [...] We are now beginning to see what scientific value there would have been in a minute careful portraiture of their thoughts and customs' (Preface to Roth, vii; qtd. in Donaldson and Donaldson, 73). Tylor here reveals himself as a follower of the 'philanthropic' Fada (although, it must be said, he is a much more learned anthropologist). See Mulvaney's essay 'The Darwinian Perspective' for a useful summary of the influence of Darwinian evolutionary theory in the Aboriginal context.

11 Ironically, after this piece was published it emerged that Mudrooroo himself was something of a mimic, claiming an Aboriginal status that was not necessarily his own. Opinions are divided on the validity of this; for recent views, see Nolan and Dawson, 'Who's Who?'.

12 For Benjamin, language represents the highest level of mimetic behaviour. It is language, with its network of 'nonsensuous similarities', that has replaced the earlier, physical forms of mimetic production. As Mudrooroo suggests in *Master of the Ghost Dreaming*, however, the semiotics of the *body* provides a link between the pre-verbal and verbal modes of mimesis – a link that disrupts the 'evolutionary' chain of 'oral'/'literate' cultures.

13 I would like to thank Charitini Douvaldzi and Martin Roberts for their helpful commentaries on earlier versions of this article.

CHAPTER 8

Maps, Dreams and the Presentation of Ethnographic Narrative

In his 1987 study of the role of the anthropologist as author,[1] Clifford Geertz examines the variety of rhetorical strategies deployed in the presentation of ethnographic material. Geertz's is by no means an isolated project; it reflects, rather, the general shift of emphasis in anthropological studies from an analysis of the documentary product (the ethnography as record) to an exploration of the discursive process (the ethnography as narrative).[2] That boundaries have increasingly become blurred between the discursive practices of anthropology and those of fiction is borne out in the significant similarities between two works from the 1980s: Hugh Brody's *Maps and Dreams* (1981) and Bruce Chatwin's *The Songlines* (1987). Brody provides a good example of the anthropologist as author: a professional ethnographer whose alertness to the rhetorical impact of his work is demonstrated in the unconventional but persuasive presentation of his ethnographic narratives. Chatwin, by contrast, provides an example of the author as anthropologist: a professional raconteur and travel writer whose personal experience is skilfully transcribed into the contours of pseudo-ethnographic fiction. *Maps and Dreams* and *The Songlines* have similar subjects: the critical comparison of Western and Indigenous patterns of territoriality and land use. But Brody and Chatwin have more in common in their respective works than their impassioned defence of Indigenous land rights; for not only do both writers have a strong thesis to present, but also they share a heightened awareness of the narrative means at their disposal.

I shall argue in this chapter that *Maps and Dreams* and *The Songlines* can be seen both as sharply worded condemnations of Western materialism and as finely crafted examples of, and inquiries into, ethnographic discourse. In this context, the apparently straightforward titles of each work are disarming; for what seems initially in *Maps and Dreams* to be a blunt, even naive distinction between a predominantly Western conception of space (the map) and a predominantly non-Western conception of time (the dream) turns out to be a subtle inquiry into the manipulation of time–space metaphors in Western ethnographic discourse. Chatwin's *The Songlines* is similarly surprising; for while the Aboriginal songlines are discovered, like Western maps, to be forms of territorial negotiation, they are also discovered to be metaphors for the nomadic instincts common to (if, in many cases, unacknowledged by) the human species. Both titles have metaphorical as well as literal significance, indicating Brody's and Chatwin's shared concern for the impact of cultural bias on spatial perception and their more immediate interest in the relation that exists in different cultures between graphic (written) and graphemic (non-written) modes of spatial representation.

An example of the former mode of representation is the Western map. 'It is hard to be completely relativistic about maps', claims the art historian E. H. Gombrich, because the mistakes in them can be 'systematically rectified' (188). Nonetheless, it remains clear that the diagrammatic representation of the environment provided by the map owes much both to the disposition of its makers and to the expectations of its readers. The optical data codified in a map constructs a model, not a copy, of the phenomenal world which facilitates our orientation in it. But the model also encompasses, and permits the reconstruction of, an historically specific set of social and cultural attitudes; furthermore, a discrepancy exists between the inevitably approximate function of the map and its frequently absolutist status. As the geographer Philip Muehrcke has noted, 'maps impress people as being authoritative and tend to be accepted without qualification' (333), but while they present themselves as 'truths', the visual 'evidence' they afford is necessarily 'filtered through the perception of the map-makers' (339).[3] In this sense, maps provide good examples of what James Clifford calls 'discursive partiality':[4] they are incomplete but persuasive accounts of the environment they set out to define and delineate. It is worth asking here what kind of discursive partiality maps possess. If we accept the (loose) definition that Western maps are graphic representations of a specified environment, we are in a position to understand the abiding Western preference for graphic over graphemic modes of representation; for the considerable authority invested in the map eventually traces back to the perceived supremacy of the written over the spoken word.[5]

In Aboriginal Australian and North American Native Indian cultures, however, maps tend to be perceived primarily as a means of spoken expression. They support a social system the spatial coordinates of which are graphemically, rather than graphically, represented: the knowledge gained from the map, like the knowledge which informs it, is communicated orally. But this distinction between Western and Indigenous maps is by no means as clear-cut as it seems. Brody and Chatwin both contrast Western patterns of land use, which are based on the principle of material acquisition, with Indigenous patterns, which are based on the principle of collective experience. They take care to point out, however, that the land use of Indigenous (Native Indian/Aboriginal) societies is far more complex than is often supposed.

Brody begins his study by describing the early maps of the European pioneers in British Columbia which, like their treaties and trap-lines, 'encircle[d] the Indians with legal and territorial limits' (115). These maps, suggests Brody, were instrumental in the formulation of a project in which 'potential settlement and resources [became] the subjects of a new Northern mythology' (115). While later European settlers strove to fulfil a dream of progress in which the North was increasingly characterized as a 'place of limitless material possibilities' (115), the Indians adhered with an obstinacy coloured by fatalism to a holistic view of their territory. Their land use, like the maps which conceptualized it, thus expressed the desire for coherence and co-operation, rather than the hope for (or confirmation of) personal gain. A distinction duly emerged between an allegedly 'objective' representation of space in Western (European) maps which supported the notion of territory as a capital good,[6] and a more obviously 'subjective' representation of space in Native Indian maps which reflected their collective experience of the phenomenal 'life-world'.

This distinction still holds good today, as Brody demonstrates by comparing patterns of land use among the various entrepreneurs and corporate conglomerates of the contemporary industrial Northwest with those of Indigenous hunter-gatherer societies like the Beaver Indians. Ironically, the former group is revealed to be the more 'predatory'. More predatory, but not necessarily more sophisticated, in its interactions with the environment; for as Brody suggests, the superior technologies developed by modern industrial societies have not necessarily helped those societies understand the complexity of their natural surroundings. In this sense, modern topographical maps may be considered symbolic of the essentially limited nature of environmental perception in a commercial ecosystem based on narrow profit motives and on an efficient management of natural resources which leads to the inequitable division of material spoils.

The Indian hunters' maps analysed in Brody's text share neither this conception of 'planning' nor this overriding concern for material acquisition. At first sight, the maps appear imprecise and confused, but, as Brody suggests, such impressions are the value-judgements of Western readers whose discriminating rationalism potentially inhibits their appreciation of the richness of the life-world. In fact, says Brody, the maps of the Beaver Indians chart not so much the vagaries as the complex variables of hunting behaviour: 'to disconnect the variables, to compartmentalize the thinking, is to fail to acknowledge its sophistication and completeness' (37). A Western conception of planning, explains Brody, would merely 'confound the flexibility' of the hunters' view of their environment, for

> [the hunter's] course of action is not, must not be, a matter of predetermination. If a plan constitutes a decision about the right procedure of action, and the decision is congruent with the action, then there is no space left for a 'plan,' only for a bundle of open-ended and non-rational possibilities. (37)

The multiplicity of available options does not preclude the possibility of a coherent pattern, however; for the hunters' maps are both composite and communal,

reflecting a wealth of collective experience of the land. Although Brody acknowledges that composite maps like these may 'obscure changes in the pattern of
land use that have occurred' (153), he emphasizes the continuity and consistency of their underlying territorial imperatives, which arise from the collective
consciousness, but also from the collective unconscious, of the people.

To clinch this last point, Brody draws a comparison between the terrestrial
maps of the hunters and the celestial 'trails to heaven' of the people's designated 'dreamers'. The 'dreamers' are those few truly 'good' men within the
band who, having devoted their lives to the welfare of others, are eventually
rewarded with 'the heaven dream'. Strong dreamers are the spiritual guides of
the band: their dreams are then transformed into maps, so that other members
of the band may recognize and seek out their own trails to heaven. Brody takes
care to point out that the maps of the dreamers and the maps of the hunters
are indissociable, for the location of heaven is 'to one side of, and at the same
level as, the point where the trails to animals all meet' (47). The making and
reading of maps thus depends both on the specific knowledge of individuals
within the society and on a nexus of collective beliefs within the culture. The
hunters' maps complement the dreams of the designated dreamers which, in
turn, revive and embellish the dreams of the Ancestors. In this way, maps play
an active role in the preservation or, more accurately, the successive recreation
of the cultural history of the people: they are valuable artifacts which, passed
down from father to son, symbolize and reinforce the values of a predominantly
oral culture. Brody's distinction between the maps and dreams of the Native
(Beaver) Indians and those of the Western (European) settlers amounts to more,
then, than a perceived conflict between two forms of territorial imperative, the
one atavistic and proprietorial, the other teleological and mercantile; it also
registers the clash between two different cultural systems, the one supported
by oral consent, and the other by written contract.

A similar clash informs *The Songlines*, Bruce Chatwin's fictionalized account of
his travels in Australia in the mid-1980s. *The Songlines* charts a double journey:
Chatwin's thought-filled meandering through the Australian outback and his no
less tortuous progress towards a discovery of the nature and implications of the
Aboriginal 'Dreaming-tracks'. In the process, he encounters several guides, one
of whom, the ironically named Russian Australian Arkady,[7] explains to him

> how each totemic ancestor, while travelling through the country, was thought
> to have scattered a trail of words and musical notes along the line of his
> footprints, and how these Dreaming-tracks lay over the land as 'ways' of
> communication between the most far-flung tribes. A song, he said, was both
> map and direction-finder. Providing you knew the song, you could always find
> your way across the country. (13)

The Aboriginal Walkabout, says Arkady, is a reconstruction of the Aboriginal
Dreamtime: 'The man who went walkabout was making a ritual journey. He
trod in the footprints of his Ancestor. He sang the Ancestor's stanzas without
changing a word or note and so recreated the Creation' (14). The circuitous

nomadic routes of the Aborigines reflect the complexity both of their individual Dreamings and of the collective Dreamtime. Like the Beaver Indians', the Aborigines' negotiation of space is also a reaffirmation of their spiritual beliefs. To map the country is to dream it: the forward journey through space and the backward journey through time converge in the configurations of the Dreaming-tracks.

Chatwin's next mentor, ex-Benedictine priest and Aboriginal rights activist Father Flynn, reminds Chatwin of the distinction between Western and Aboriginal perceptions of the land. White men, claims Flynn, often made the mistake of assuming that

> because the Aboriginals were wanderers, they could have no system of land tenure. This was nonsense. Aboriginals, it was true, could not imagine territory as a block of land hemmed in by frontiers, but rather as an interlocking network of 'lines' or 'ways through'. (56)

The songlines, explains Flynn, constitute trade routes in which songs, not things, 'are the principal medium of exchange. [...] A man's verses were his title deeds to territory. He could lend them to others. He could borrow other verses in return. The one thing he couldn't do was sell or get rid of them' (57). Flynn distinguishes between the prevalent Western view of land as a capital good which can be freely bought or sold at market prices, and an alternative, Aboriginal view of land as a shared resource, the terms of which fluctuate in accordance with a flexible system of verbal exchange rather than in response to the latest market demands. This distinction reflects ironically on the attempt of Kidder, the Australian community leader, to 'deprogramme' the sacred knowledge of the Aborigines by returning artifacts and documents to their rightful owners (43). To Kidder, this sacred knowledge is 'the cultural property of the Aboriginal people' (43): it has considerable commodity value. But as Father Flynn explains,

> Aboriginals, in general, had the idea that all goods were potentially malign and would work against their possessors unless they were forever in motion [...]. 'Goods' were tokens of intent: to trade again, meet again, fix frontiers, intermarry, sing, dance, share resources and share ideas. (57)

The alternative viewpoints of Kidder and Flynn inform much of the rest of *The Songlines*: the first, a well-intentioned but misguided attempt to help the Aborigines based on a Western conception of capital gains and losses, the second an attempt not so much to recover the 'cultural property' as to discover the fundamental philosophical precepts of Aboriginal people.

Let me return here to the notion of the map. In my reading of Brody's *Maps and Dreams*, I suggested that the graphic display provided by the standard (Western) topographical map affords not only a means of orientation in the environment it represents, but also an instrument for the eventual appropriation of that environment or a justification for the terms of its tenure. The map can be said in this sense to symbolize a Western desire for, or to reinforce Western myths of, territorial expansion. In Aboriginal cultures, on the other hand, territory tends to be conceived, perceived and represented in graphemic terms, a generalization which seems to hold true both in hunter-gatherer societies such as the Beaver Indians of British Columbia and in nomadic societies such as the Aboriginal people of Central Australia. In *Maps and Dreams* and *The Songlines*, the graphemic representation of space in predominantly oral cultures is shown to pertain to a system of verbal exchange, whereas the graphic representation of space is shown to amount to a system of capital accumulation prevalent among predominantly literate cultures.

If the distinction were as hard and fast as I have involuntarily implied, Brody and Chatwin would then be faced with a seemingly insurmountable problem: in brief, how can the writer convey an intended critique of Western consumer culture in book form, when the book not only is a primary artifact of that culture but might even be considered to be an epitome of that culture? Brody's and Chatwin's approach to the problem is to interweave 'spoken' and 'written' modes into the narrative presentation of their texts in such a way as to suggest that the schematic division between 'oral' and 'literate' cultures may itself be the product of cultural bias, a strategic means by which literate Western cultures have promulgated their superiority over their non-Western 'others'.[8]

Brody first comments on the structure of his text in the preface to *Maps and Dreams*, where he states that 'the odd-numbered chapters try to follow a route selected by the people' (xvi), whereas the even numbered chapters deal more with his own 'research schemes and agendas' (xvi). This contrapuntal structure is combined with the interpolation into the text of a series of palimpsestic maps in which the Native Indians' hunting routes are superimposed onto the standard Ordnance Survey grid. Brody thus illustrates his attempt to alternate between cultures; by switching between the operations of scientific record and those of personal memoir, he further suggests the intersubjective nature of ethnographic inquiry. In the odd-numbered chapters, he explains,

> I have chosen to use fictitious names and have in other ways sought to conceal the identification of both people and places. I refer to the community as the Reserve, intending thereby to suggest that it has a general as well as a specific significance. (xvii)

Brody comes close here to James Clifford's suggestion that ethnographies be read not as 'objective' scientific documents but as multivalent allegories.[9] Brody's fictionalized field-notes also suggest that his concern as an ethnographer extends beyond the written presentation of audio-visual material to the palpable construction of historical narrative. Within the framework of this narrative, Brody continually shifts modes: the realistic docudrama, the homiletic parable, the ironic confession, and so on. As a result of these shifts, and of the interplay of voices in the narrative, Brody attempts to achieve a polyphonic ethnography in which no single voice, point of view, or cultural stance is privileged over the others. The flexible design of *Maps and Dreams* also indicates Brody's concern to break down the traditional dichotomies of ethnographic discourse by 'laying bare' the artifices of narrative presentation. Conscious of his compromised position as a white ethnographer 'intruding' into a non-white culture, Brody wishes to avoid the condescending gesture of delivering a nostalgic paean to an 'oral' culture which finds itself diminishing in the face of an ever-expanding 'literate' one.[10] Instead, he demonstrates the relativity of modes of cultural production in different societies. The implications are clear: speech and writing are relative concepts; their nature and function needs to be considered in international, multicultural contexts rather than within the necessarily limited framework of a single nation or culture.[11]

Chatwin is no less aware than Brody of the cultural biases and uneven power relations that underlie a supposedly 'neutral' scientific approach to ethnography. Like *Maps and Dreams*, *The Songlines* is a polyphonic narrative. Chatwin's cast is wider and more cosmopolitan than Brody's, but his quirky blend of the popular travelogue and the pseudo-philosophical treatise has a similarly relativizing effect to that of the contrapuntal structure of Brody's text. Chatwin's most striking narrative device is his interpolation into the text of a clutch of travel notes liberally sprinkled with anecdotes, conjectures and epigrammatic shafts of wisdom. The effect is mimetic: Chatwin's thesis that migratory instincts are not particular to nomadic societies, but are common to the human species, gains support from the 'migratory instincts' of his own narrative.[12] Chatwin's notes thus effectively sketch a songline of his own, a concatenation of semi-connected voices charting the uneven territory of the text. Significantly, the majority of these notes are clustered together in the central part of the narrative. Apart from the obvious connection here between his physical and his philosophical quests (a variant of the 'journey-into-the-interior' paradigm), Chatwin also decentres his text: first, by interrupting the flow of the narrative; and second, by dispersing the ethnological, philosophical and sociohistorical content of the dissertation.

In sum, the flexible format of *Maps and Dreams* and *The Songlines* suggests that both writers are aware of the thin dividing-line between the ethnography as document and the ethnography as fiction. Brody and Chatwin choose the map as the principal spatial paradigm informing their respective works, but they simulate alternative spatial patterns which break down the traditional Western conception of the map as a linear graphic representation to assert, instead, an Aboriginal conception of the map as a network of interconnected voices. Neither project is entirely successful. It is difficult at times to tell whether Brody and Chatwin are speaking *with* the 'other' or *for* the 'other': the 'intersubjectivity' of Brody's text and the 'polyphony' of Chatwin's remain rhetorical strategies by Western writers to bridge the gap between themselves and cultures that continue to be interpreted by outsiders rather than being allowed to represent themselves.[13] The self-conscious design of either text indicates, however, that both writers are well aware of the contradictions inherent in ethnographic narrative. As a professional ethnographer, Brody seeks to ally himself with a culture that remains irrevocably 'other'; as a travel writer, Chatwin parodies, but also reinstates, the exoticism of a foreign culture whose social customs and philosophical outlook are very different from his own, but whose differences are ironically reabsorbed within the same master theory (of nomadism) that promotes and celebrates them. For Brody, the ostensibly non-fictional text relinquishes its claims to neutrality without ever really coming to terms with its own biases; for Chatwin, the ostensibly fictional text parades its own biases but ultimately fails to distinguish its writer's desire for self-parody from his impulse towards self-congratulation. The shortcomings of Brody and Chatwin's texts, then, are considerable; but they should not be allowed to override the genuine concern of both writers for cross-cultural ethnographies which, in highlighting the close relation in different cultures between cultural perception and spatial representation, go some way towards accounting for the alternative ways in which cultures dream and map space.

Works Cited

Benterrak, Krim, Stephen Muecke and Paddy Roe. *Reading the Country: An Introduction to Nomadology*. Fremantle: Fremantle Arts Centre Press, 1984.

Brody, Hugh. *Maps and Dreams*. Vancouver: Douglas & McIntyre, 1981.

Bruner, Edward. 'Ethnography as Narrative'. In *The Anthropology of Experience*. Ed. Victor Turner and Edward Bruner. Urbana: University of Illinois Press, 1986. 139–55.

Brydon, Diana. 'Troppo Agitato: Writing and Reading Cultures'. *Ariel* 19.1 (1988): 13–21.

Chatwin, Bruce. *The Songlines*. Harmondsworth: Penguin, 1987.

Clifford, James. 'On Ethnographic Allegory'. In *Writing Culture: The Poetics and Politics of Ethnography*. Ed. James Clifford and George Marcus. Berkeley: University of California Press, 1986. 98–121.

——. *The Predicament of Culture*. Cambridge, MA: Harvard University Press, 1988.

——. and George Marcus, eds. *Writing Culture: The Poetics and Politics of Ethnography*. Berkeley: University of California Press, 1986.

Deleuze, Gilles and Félix Guattari. *A Thousand Plateaus: Capitalism and Schizophrenia*. Trans. B. Massumi. London: Athlone, 1987.

Derrida, Jacques. *Of Grammatology*. Trans. G.C. Spivak. Baltimore: Johns Hopkins University Press, 1976.

——. 'Structure, Sign and Play in the Discourse of the Human Sciences'. In *Writing and Difference*. Trans. A. Bass. Chicago: University of Chicago Press, 1978. 278–93.

Foucault, Michel. 'What is an Author?'. In *Textual Strategies*. Ed. Josué Harari. Ithaca, NY: Cornell University Press, 1979. 141–60.

Geertz, Clifford. '"From the Native's Point of View": On the Nature of Anthropological Understanding'. In *Meaning in Anthropology*. Ed. K. H. Basso and H. A. Selby. Albuquerque: University of Mexico Press, 1976. 221–37.

——. *Works and Lives: The Anthropologist as Author*. Stanford, CA: Stanford University Press, 1987.

Gibson, Ross. *The Diminishing Paradise: Changing Literary Perceptions of Australia*. Sydney: Angus & Robertson, 1984.

Gombrich, E. H. *The Image and the Eye: Further Studies in the Psychology of Fictional Representation*. Ithaca, NY: Cornell University Press, 1952.

Goody, Jack. *The Interface Between the Written and the Oral*. Cambridge: Cambridge University Press, 1987.

Harley, J. B. 'Maps, Knowledge, and Power'. In *The Iconography of Landscape*. Ed. Denis

Cosgrove and Stephen Daniels. Cambridge: Cambridge University Press, 1988. 277–312.

Malinowski, Bronislaw. *A Diary in the Strict Sense of the Term*. Stanford, CA: Stanford University Press, 1989.

Mandel, Eli. 'Imagining Natives: White Perspectives on Native Peoples'. In *The Native in Literature*. Ed. Thomas King, Cheryl Calver and Helen Hoy. Oakville, Ont.: ECW Press, 1987. 34–49.

Muehrcke, Philip. *Map Use: Reading, Analysis, and Interpretation*. Madison: JP Publications, 1978.

Mukerji, Chandra. *Graven Images: Patterns of Modern Materialism*. New York: Columbia University Press, 1983.

Ong, Walter. *Orality and Literacy: The Technologizing of the Word*. New York: Methuen, 1982.

Tuan, Yi-Fu. *Topophilia*. Englewood Cliffs, NJ: Prentice Hall, 1974.

Webster, Steven. 'Ethnography as Storytelling'. *Dialectical Anthropology* 8 (1983): 185–205.

Notes

1 The phrase is Geertz's: like Geertz, Brody and Chatwin are both concerned to undermine the misconceived authority of traditional ethnography. They are influenced in this deconstructive process by Foucault, whose seminal essay 'What is an Author?' calls into question the privileged status of the individual author and draws attention instead to the variety of discursive practices that constitute the 'author-function' of any given text.

2 For essays that chart this shift, see those in Clifford and Marcus. Essays that deal more specifically with ethnography as narrative include those by Bruner and Webster.

3 For an account of cultural biases in the history of cartography, see Tuan (esp. the chapter 'Ethnocentrism, Symmetry, and Space'). On the political ramifications of mapping, see also Harley.

4 See Clifford's introduction to the essays in Clifford and Marcus for a further discussion of 'discursive partiality' in ethnographic texts.

5 My argument here is indirectly related to Derrida's (e.g., in the opening section of *On Grammatology*). The revisionist ethnography of Brody and the pseudo-ethnographic fiction of Chatwin both appear to draw on Derrida's discussion of the relation between ethnology and (Western) logocentrism: see his essay 'Structure, Sign and Play' in *Writing and Difference*.

6 For a discussion of the growing importance of the map as a capital good (from early modern European times onwards), see Mukerji.

7 Arkady with a 'k', not a 'c'. Arkady's celebratory exposition of the ancestral beliefs of the Aborigines is ironic in light of the current, ravaged state of their culture. It is doubly ironic in light of the discrepancy between romantic European images of Australia as a land of Arcadian innocence and the harsh realities of convict and free settler life. Historical encounters between the early European settlers and the Aborigines merely serve to confirm the discrepancy. For a fuller account of the tensions generated by the confrontation between European conceptual vocabulary and a land that persistently challenged or even contradicted that vocabulary, see Gibson.

8   The argument is expanded in Goody, and is discussed in a relevant literary context by Brydon.

9   See Clifford's essay 'On Ethnographic Allegory', in Clifford and Marcus.

10 The problem of legitimacy in the (white) representation of (non-white) Native cultures is discussed at length in the essays in Clifford and Marcus; also in a useful essay by Mandel, which calls into question four foundational myths underlying the representation of Indigenous cultures in Canadian 'ethnographic fiction': namely, the myth of the primitive, the myth of origins or ancestors, the myth of the frontier in which the Native is identified with landscape, and the myth of marginality 'that seeks the identification of writer, Native, and place' (36). Brody and Chatwin are both well aware of the pitfalls involved in representing Indigenous cultures from an outsider's point of view, although it might be argued that the attempt in their respective texts to avoid a dichotomous relation between (observing) 'self' and (observed) 'other' leads them to subscribe to a suspect 'myth of marginality' which ironically reinscribes their own authority. See my discussion of this issue above.

11 See Goody, also Ong. The latter's apparent faith in the superior skills of 'literate cultures' – improved upon rather than compromised by the technological advancements of the Electronic Age – unfortunately hinders his appreciation of the different kinds of skills, and different ways of looking at the world, provided by cultures that retain an oral basis. Despite the perceptiveness of an analysis that stresses the relativity of oral/literate modes in contemporary 'developed' and 'developing' societies, Ong seems to fall victim to his inability, or reluctance, to connect the idealistic rhetoric of the Global Village with the hegemonic practice of the multinationals, for whom the project of 'world literacy' admirably serves their own economic interests.

12 Chatwin's thesis is derived in part from Deleuze and Guattari's treatise on 'nomadology'; it is subsequently channelled through the collaborative work of Benterrak, Muecke and Roe, which uses the theories of Deleuze and Guattari to promote a 'nomadic' perception of the land among Aboriginal societies that militates against set (Western) patterns of territorial enclosure. Following Deleuze and Guattari, Muecke defines nomadology as 'an aesthetic/political stance [which] is constantly in flight from ideas or practices associated with the singular, the original, the uniform, the central authority, the hierarchy, without for all that ascribing to any form of anarchy' (15). The definition serves equally well for Chatwin, whose work continually undermines its own authority, and to a lesser extent for Brody, who shares Chatwin's concern to break the self/other dichotomy of traditional Western ethnography.

13 See Geertz's essay 'From the Native's Point of View', in Basso and Selby, for a characteristically sarcastic account of the difficulties involved in interpreting anthropological information, and in ascertaining whose 'point of view' is being represented in the process. For a critique of Geertz's interpretive anthropology, and for what he sees as a more 'dialogic' approach to the relationship between (White) anthropologist and (Native) informant, see the opening section of Clifford's *The Predicament of Culture*. Brody and Chatwin's questioning of the ethnocentric attitudes underlying white incursions into Native cultures owes much to the debate (re-opened by Geertz and continued by Clifford) in *Malinowski's Diary* which explodes the 'myth of the chameleon field-worker, perfectly self-tuned to his exotic surroundings, a walking miracle of empathy, tact, patience, and cosmopolitanism' (Basso and Selby 222). It is worth noting, however, that Brody and Chatwin's attempts 'to follow a route selected by the people' (Brody xvi) do not dissuade the former from providing his own, dominant exegesis of Native culture, or the latter from relying on white,

rather than Native, 'informants'. (It could be argued in Chatwin's defence that he is a travel writer, not an anthropologist, but as I have tried to suggest in this essay, the crucial issue is not the one of what qualifies as 'correct' anthropological practice but the broader one of what constitutes the legitimate representation of a 'dominated' culture by a 'dominating' one.) The self-critiques incorporated into Brody's and Chatwin's ethnographic narratives are salutary, but the critical self-consciousness of either writer, and the variety of points of view they present in their respective texts, do not alter the fact that the weight of anthropological interpretation is carried in both cases by a representative (or representatives) of Western culture.

Literature, History, Memory

CHAPTER 9

Philomela's Retold Story: Silence, Music and the Postcolonial Text

During the reign of Pandion of Atticus, war broke out with the Atticans' long-standing adversaries, the Boeotians. Pandion eventually managed to secure a vital alliance with the Thracian King, Tereus, by offering his eldest daughter, Procne, in marriage. Lonely in Thrace, Procne pleaded with Tereus for her younger sister, Philomela, to come out and join her. Tereus agreed and went to fetch Philomela. He brought her back to Thrace, but not before he had forced his affections on her, raped her and, to prevent her from complaining, cut out her tongue. Philomela still found a way of making herself understood, however, by embroidering a tapestry which reconstructed the story of her rape. Realizing what had happened, Procne plotted her revenge, treating Tereus to a succulent meal – consisting of his own son. Bursting with rage (and indigestion?), Tereus went after the two sisters with an axe. Sympathizing with their plight, the gods saved Procne and Philomela by turning them into birds: Procne became a swallow, Philomela a nightingale. Tereus, for his sins, became a hoopoe.

The story of Philomela, or rather the story of Philomela's retold story, is one of the best-known of the Attic legends, a source of inspiration for many beleaguered poets who have used the legend to celebrate, or lament, their own insufficiently acknowledged ability. But more recently, the legend has taken on a different, allegorical significance; for in the work of several contemporary postcolonial writers, Philomela's story has become a paradigm for the re-enactment of colonial encounter, for the articulation of a violent history of dispossession and depri-vation which circumstances dictate must be told in another way. By providing these writers with an alternative framework for the expression of an otherwise repressed, or censored, history, the Philomela legend allows them to confront and imaginatively transform the past. The conversion in the legend of silence into song also provides a motivation for postcolonial writers seeking to overcome the imaginative legacy of their colonial past.[1] The affiliation between silence and music in several postcolonial texts can be seen in this context as providing alternative, non-verbal codes that subvert and/or replace those earlier, over-determined narratives of colonial encounter in which the word is recognized to have played a crucial role in the production and maintenance of colonial hierarchies of power.[2] But ironically, silence and music may also function as instruments of colonial domination, as collaborative agents of an imposed regime that seeks to manoeuvre its subjects into positions of passive obedience. Silence and music are thus profoundly ambivalent media in postcolonial writing which may serve either to subvert or to support the dominant discourses of the colonial system. My emphasis in this chapter will be on those postcolonial texts in which silence is converted into music in a regenerative process which, even though it cannot transcend the colonial history in which all postcolonial literatures are grounded,[3] at least transmutes that history into an alternative pattern that allows it to be seen in terms other than those of repeated dispossession or defeat.

To illustrate the operations and counter-operations of silence and music within the postcolonial context, I will briefly discuss three texts: Anita Desai's *Clear Light of Day*, the lyrical account of a Hindu family's struggle to survive in the ravaged aftermath of Indian Partition; Keri Hulme's *the bone people*, the moving and often alarming story of a delinquent child's attempt to overcome a catastrophic past; and J. M. Coetzee's *Foe*, a characteristically enigmatic reworking of *Robinson Crusoe* in circumstances that point to, if they also reach beyond, the politics of censorship in contemporary South Africa. Clearly, the social and cultural contexts for each of these texts are widely divergent; it is possible nonetheless to see all three as extended parables of colonial mastery/enslavement in which the compulsive, even masochistic desire to retell the story of a traumatic past is counterbalanced by the therapeutic effect of its telling. What emerges in each case from the dual action of silence and music in the text is the conversion of a sequential history of personal failures and familial/societal disruptions into an overarching myth that neither absolves those failures nor definitively repairs those disruptions, but rather reincorporates them within a larger pattern that suggests the possibility of a more integrated, or at least a more fully understood, future.

I will begin with Desai's novel which, like its two leading characters, sisters Bim and Tara, literally 'seeth[es] with unspoken speech' (9). Bim's rented, rundown house in Old Delhi becomes the site in the novel for a dramatic re-enactment of the past, a drama impelled forward in spite of the agonized reticence of its players. The plot builds on the entangled relations of a middle-class Hindu family whose personal lives seem inextricably linked with the turbulent events surrounding Indian Partition in 1947. Significantly, the violent forces unleashed during this unruly period of Indian history are downplayed in the novel, repressed like the dark secrets of a family that contains within it the cruel knowledge of division, betrayal and madness. The selective agency of memory is called upon to blur and distort, but it cannot erase, and indeed memory becomes the precarious medium through which personal and political experiences are eventually melded together in a union which, though painful, allows a destructive past to be confronted and creatively transformed.

That this confrontation should find expression through the articulation of silence is one of the many paradoxes of the novel; but as I have suggested, Desai is not interested in presenting silence as an absence of or incapacity for speech but rather as a different kind of speech which, like music, offers a viable alternative to the treacherous medium of verbal language. Desai remains well aware, however, that both silence and music are themselves deceptive, and potentially destructive, media. That the retreat into silence, or the recourse to music, may prove injurious to rather than protective of the self is well illustrated in Desai's portrayal of Bim and Tara's retarded brother, Baba, the ironically named 'black sheep' of the family. Baba's record collection, rescued from the abandoned house of former family neighbour and mentor, Hyder Ali, appears initially to offer him solace by providing an 'elemental, primitive rhythm' (13) to his life that shelters him from the unspoken horrors of the outside world. But it becomes increasingly clear that Baba's reclusive existence, regulated by the alternate 'sounds' of silence and music, amounts to an illusory escape from a society with whose rapid changes and violent conflicts he simply cannot cope. A conspiratorial alliance emerges between Baba and his sister Bim in which both ironically take refuge in a past that entraps them; for far from providing a release from the past, Baba's 'old-time' music merely recycles and reinforces the past. A further irony derives from the fact that the records Baba plays so obsessively are products of the West: his acquiescent silence is thus broken only by the addictive recourse to a music that ensnares him into seeking inspiration in a world controlled and dictated by others.

Is music condemned, then, to repeat the enclosing patterns of the past, and silence to acknowledge those patterns; or can this stifling alliance between silence and music be creatively transformed? Desai suggests that it can, and once again Baba plays a key role in that transformation. This depends to a great extent on the other members of his family altering their earlier views of him as a social misfit, a 'mad relation' or a 'perpetual baby' (130), and accepting him instead as one of their own. Baba's unarticulated silences initially seem to contain the 'illicit' details of a family that knows itself, as it knows the country it inhabits, to be torn apart by personal rivalry and political conflict. Not so torn apart, however, that the divisions produced by these conflicts need only be seen as irremediable losses; on the contrary, Desai suggests that the very divisions that split the country, the family, and the individuals within it may eventually contribute to a greater sense of mutual understanding. Baba's silence need not be perceived, then, as a negative articulation of the desire for escape or as an attempt to hide the fear of failure; instead, it may undergo a transformation in which the self-absorbed silence of personal withdrawal is converted into the exchanged silence(s) of friendship and mutual recognition.

In the final scene of the novel, a new allegiance is thus formed between silence and music in which the 'consenting' silence of Baba and Bim as they sit enraptured by the songs of their neighbour, Mulk, and his venerable guru contributes to the expression of a collective culture framed by the figure of the extended Hindu family:

> They sat in silence [...] for now there seemed no need to say another word.
> Everything had been said at last, cleared out of the way finally. There was
> nothing left in the way of a barrier or a shadow, only the clear light of day
> pouring down from the sun. They found the courage, after all, to float in it
> and bathe in it and allow it to pour onto them, illuminating them wholly,
> without allowing them a single shadow to shelter in. (177)

The flawed but passionate songs of Mulk and his guru operate as a vehicle
for collective memory, so that in the ancient school of music from which they
both emanate, and which contains within it the combined knowledge of the
'immature disciple' Mulk and his 'aged, exhausted guru with all the disillusion-
ments of his long experience', it becomes possible for Bim at last to see

> how her own house and its particular history linked and contained her as well
> as her whole family with all their separate histories and experiences – not
> binding them within some dead and airless cell but giving them the soil in
> which to send down their roots, and food to make them grow and spread,
> reach out to new experiences and new lives, but always drawing from the
> same soil, the same secret darkness. (182)

The same 'secret darkness' that had previously been guarded by silence, or
averted through the cultivated pleasures of (Western) art, is now paradoxically
revealed as the wellspring of a collective culture. The triumphant return to
indigenous (Hindu) traditions does not entail a rejection of Western artforms, for
Baba will no doubt continue to play his European and American records, and Bim
to recite her European and American verse; but it does entail a re-incorporation
of these artforms within a wider, cross-cultural framework. It is within that
wider framework that the alternate rhythms of silence and music can contribute
towards a transformation of the past. Music no longer entails the morbid recollection of, or fruitless escape from, an unwanted history, and silence no longer
seeks to repress what cannot, or should not, be told. Instead, both cooperate,
as Philomela transmutes her silence into song, in the imaginative conversion of
a story of violence and despair into a tentative call for hope.

A similar conversion takes place in Keri Hulme's novel, *the bone people*. As in
Clear Light of Day, the personal and the political interfuse: the story of a young
delinquent boy's struggle to overcome his nightmarish past contains within it the
allegory of New Zealand's often painful attempts to come to terms with a history
of colonial dependence and with continuing tensions between its Indigenous
(Maori) and European (Pakeha) communities. As in Desai's novel, a key role is
played by an emotionally disturbed character whose muteness can be perceived
either as a form of self-protection or as a gesture of resistance to prescribed social
'norms'. Equally ambivalent is the music with which this silence is affiliated. The
connection is clear enough; the novel begins with the coming together of silence
and song in Simon's expression of conciliatory good will:

> He walks down the street. The asphalt
> reels by him

> It is all silence.
> The silence is music.
> He is the singer.
> The people passing smile and shake their
> heads.
> He holds out a hand to them.
> They open their hands like flowers,
> shyly.
> He smiles with them.
> The light is blinding: he loves the
> light.
> They are the light. (3)

The rhapsodic tone of this opening is not always matched by what follows, however, underscoring the consistent tension in Hulme's novel between alternative impulses towards harmony and discord. Music, like silence and its other non-verbal counterpart, gesture, is shown to be an ambivalent medium: like Desai, Hulme is obviously well acquainted with Nietzsche's connection between the divine inspiration provided by music and the Bacchanalian compulsion towards severance and dissolution.[4] It is significant here that the song Kerewin dedicates to Simon is called 'Simon's Mead Reel'; for although the reel is a syncretic musical form well-suited to celebrating the union between Simon, Kerewin and his foster-father, Joe, and the commingling of their already-mixed cultural ancestries, it also warns of the dangers of intoxication and recklessness. The reel thus offers a reminder of the darker, Dionysian side of the novel, where music and silence conspire to reinforce an allegorical link between the voluntary submission to a wilfully destructive muse and the vicious cycle of domination and submission produced by the colonial bloodknot.

Yet although music has the power to disrupt or destroy, and silence the capacity to collude in that disruption/destruction, both retain the potential to transform and recreate. By transmuting his hidden language into the subliminal music of his 'hutches', spiral constructions of shells, driftwood and seaweed that channel the generative forces of wind and tide, Simon demonstrates his seemingly limitless capacity to reconstruct his own origins. And not just his own origins, for the elemental music that emanates from the hutches also reproduces the organic patterns of Maori creation myth. In the hutches, life and death are inextricably interwoven; the music that issues forth at the end of the novel from the round shell house that holds Simon, Kerewin and Joe in its 'spiralling embrace' (442) similarly includes within it both creative and destructive potential, the capacity both for 'noise and riot' and for 'peace and quiet' (442). This music contains, and is contained by, Simon's silence; but it cannot as yet bring him to speech. While Simon's silence is incorporated, like Baba's, into the mythical pattern that embraces the narrative, it is also disengaged from it. Room is thus left for the tracing of further possible connections and for the fabrication of alternative versions of a story that, however many times it is told, will always fall short of completion.

In *Clear Light of Day* and *the bone people*, silence and music play active roles in a transformation of the coercive forces of history into the revitalizing energies of myth. But in J. M. Coetzee's *Foe*, myth is demonstrated to be no less oppressive than history: the variations on the Crusoe myth provided by Coetzee's text seem only to prove that the myth itself is as enslaving as the exemplary tale of 'grateful servitude' it relates. In the context of this myth, Friday's very silences are spoken for, absorbed within a narrative that, in whatever version it is told, apparently perpetuates the very cycle of domination and subjection from which it seeks to liberate itself. As Susan Barton tells Foe, Friday's version of the story, like his mutilated tongue, is missing:

> The story of Friday's tongue is a story unable to be told or unable to be told by me. That is to say, many stories can be told of Friday's tongue, but the true story is buried within Friday, who is mute. The true story will not be heard till by art we have found a means of giving voice to Friday. (118)

The task Susan sets herself, however, is not that of bringing Friday to speech but that of speaking Friday's silences: the voice she wishes to give him is her own.

Yet if Susan 'speaks' Friday, so she too is spoken by him. For Friday's expressive range of music, gesture and silence not only constitutes an alternative language to Susan's, but also provides a set of counter-discursive strategies designed to undermine the authority of verbal language and to challenge the supremacy of those like Susan – and Foe – who have arrogated that authority to themselves.[5] Like Philomela, Friday is forced to find an indirect way of accusing his oppressors. Deprived of speech, he turns his attention to subverting the language that has been imposed upon him.[6] He mocks Susan's attempt to teach him to write, just as he mocks her attempt to accompany his music. The 'o's' and 'sh's' that Friday scrawls repeatedly on his slate, like the monotonous notes he plays over and over again on his flute, do not just indicate his disdain for, but his effective negation of, the signifying systems of Western chirographic culture (written script/musical notation). But Friday's role is not a purely destructive one; he is also creative in his own right. In the final, dreamlike scene of the novel, the narrator takes his turn to search for Friday's 'buried' story. In a submerged environment 'where bodies are their own signs' (157), the bloated corpses of Susan and the ship's captain seem only to signal their own obsolescence; but from Friday's mouth, the site of his previous violation, 'the sounds of [Crusoe's] island' issue forth in a constant stream (154). As in Desai's and Hulme's texts, silence is thus transmuted into a kind of 'elemental music' in a process which also re-enacts the rites of Indigenous creation myth. The myth links back in Coetzee's text to the sacred ceremony in which Friday scatters a series of white petals across the face of the waters in an attempt to invoke, or possibly appease, his Maker. The sacred act is also desacralizing: Friday symbolically fragments and disperses a page of the Good Book on which Crusoe, and Crusoe's colonialist myth, so heavily rely. And there is a further implied blasphemy; for the regenerative process set in motion by Friday's act stands in ironic counterpoint to the Christian paradigms of genesis and resurrection. The 'natural' music issuing forth from Friday's mouth thus subverts the imperatives of a culture based on the teachings of, and dependent upon the stable origins of, the Word; at the same time, it celebrates the capacity of the oppressed to make themselves heard in spite of being denied the right, or being dispossessed of the means, to speak.[7]

I have suggested in this chapter that the transformative strategies implemented in Desai's, Hulme's and Coetzee's novels mark them out as postcolonial texts whose re-inscription of the history of their own formerly colonized countries, or whose re-exploration of the conceptual framework of colonial relations, involves a reaction against the self-privileging practices of European colonialism. These practices include the 'muting' of the colonial subject[8] and the production and perpetuation of a system of mutual dependence in which individual creativity is surrendered to the control of the presiding 'colonial muse'. Much of my argument has been based on an assumption that what constitutes the particularity of Desai's, Hulme's and Coetzee's postcolonial texts is their adaptation of the legend of Philomela to a context in which the disempowered colonial subject must find an indirect medium through which to relate his/her past experience. Two questions arise here that might threaten the validity of such an assumption: first, the applicability of a paradigm of patriarchal enslavement to a series of texts that feature not female, but male victims (Baba, Simon, Friday); and second, the desirability of using a European myth as a 'master code' through which to read postcolonial texts whose sentiment, if not anti-European, is certainly anti-Eurocentric, and whose cultural specificity is apparently ill-served by a catch-all critical vocabulary that ironically re-imposes the very totalizing structures those texts seek to challenge and dismantle.

The first of these objections seems all the more legitimate in that a large number of postcolonial texts posit a correlation between the subordinating practices of colonialism and those of patriarchy. That the three Philomela-figures in the novels I have been discussing are all male does not necessarily invalidate this correlation; indeed, I would argue that it is paradoxically upheld, not so much through the text's presentation of a battle between the sexes in which female desire pits itself against institutionalized male authority, as through an implied resistance in the text to the binary construction of gender. It is significant in this regard that Baba, Simon and Friday are all perceived as sexually ambiguous. The unresolved sexual orientation of Baba, Simon and Friday raises further questions that go beyond the boundaries of this essay: the problematic issue of homophobia in Hulme's novel, for instance, or the persistent (if reversible) typecasting of 'dominant male' and 'subservient female' roles in Coetzee's.[9] Suffice to say here that Desai, Hulme and Coetzee are each concerned in their respective novels to break down the hierarchical structures of power by which dominant groups promulgate and perpetuate their authority. In this context, the victimization of a male Philomela whose ambiguous sexuality contributes towards his ostracism from 'normal' society, or whose disempowerment is partly dependent on the removal of his manhood – (the case of the 'doubly mutilated' Friday) – can be seen in terms of a rigidly conformist patriarchal system that seeks to impose its own male authority on its subjects. That authority is called into question, however, by the discovery in the text of an alternative discursive site from which to challenge the 'natural' privileges granted by the male (vocal/ sexual) organs, a site in which the silence of disenfranchisement doubles as a silence of dissent.

The second possible objection to the use of the Philomela legend as a conceptual framework for the exploration of colonial relations in Desai's, Hulme's and Coetzee's texts, that it represents a further imposition of European models on literatures/cultures striving to break away from European hegemony, strikes at the very heart of contemporary postcolonial criticism. Attacks on Fredric Jameson for his totalizing theories about the Third World, or on Helen Tiffin for the persistently Eurocentric bias of her work on postcolonial literary revisionism, indicate the perils involved in attempting to formulate a cross-cultural framework within which to view literatures/cultures whose diversity and complexity make a mockery of such dubiously unifying causes as 'the common reaction against colonialism'. Postcolonial critics, it could further be argued, run the risk not of interrogating European assumptions of cultural leadership but of reinforcing them: the comparative approach to postcolonial literatures is vitiated by a tendency towards reductionist generalizations about, say, the function of allegory or the operations of canonical counter-discourse that depend on the pre-existence of European norms. The Empire may write back to 'the centre', but Europe remains the 'centre': postcolonial critics are thus found guilty, at best, of an attitude of condescension towards literatures/cultures that continue to be perceived as marginal and, at worst, of an act of imperialism in which a vast body of heterogeneous literatures is incorporated within the grand design of postcolonial theory, ironically 'silenced' by the very critics who believe they speak on its behalf.[10] The argument is a forceful one, but the postulation of comparative postcolonial criticism as a falsely homogenizing practice overlooks the dialectical nature of the work done by many of its most prominent practitioners. Moreover, the tendency of some of the more extreme nationalist critics to wish away the existence of a European cultural heritage, however distorting and/or debilitating that heritage may have been, seems not only to divest postcolonial writing of much of its oppositional power in exposing and critiquing the material conditions that govern its cultural production, but also to risk coralling nation- or race-based literatures into separate, jealously protected territories that resist intrusion to the extent that they become accessible only to those 'exclusive insiders'[11] possessed by virtue of birthright or immediacy of experience of an intimate knowledge of their own 'field'. Wilson Harris has perhaps done more than any other critic to promote a cross-cultural approach to postcolonial literatures that does not deny their cultural specificity, but that reaches beyond polarized structures and unified models to promulgate a 'ceaseless dialogue [...] between hardened conventions and eclipsed or half-eclipsed otherness' (Harris xviii). It is within the context of that cross-cultural enterprise that I believe Philomela's legend can retain its legitimacy, not as a 'universal' story that can be applied to any given period or socio-cultural context, but as a 'retold' story that is taken from one context and adapted to another. The legend is oblique in Desai's, Hulme's and Coetzee's novels; it is also necessarily incomplete. If we are not given full access to the different postcolonial versions of the legend that tell of Baba's rejection, Simon's violation, and Friday's enslavement, that is also because the non-verbal languages of silence and music employed to tell them are themselves subject to a verbal narrative that testifies to the continuing dominance of the word and of the societies or social groups that control it. Silence and music remain subject to the word, then, but if they cannot escape its controlling agency, they can at least suggest an alternative framework within which a history not just of verbal but of physical and mental subjection can be expressed and imaginatively transformed.

Works Cited

Ahmad, Aijaz. *Social Text* 17 (1987): 8–18.

Ashcroft, Bill, Gareth Griffiths and Helen Tiffin. *The Empire Writes Back: Theory and Practice in Postcolonial Literatures*. 2nd edn. London: Routledge, 2001.

Brink, André. *Mapmakers: Writing in a State of Siege*. London: Faber & Faber, 1983.

Coetzee, J. M. *Foe*. Harmondsworth: Penguin, 1987.

Dale, Judith. 'The bone people: (Not) Having it Both Ways'. *Landfall* 39.4 (1985): 413–28.

Desai, Anita. *Clear Light of Day*. Harmondsworth: Penguin, 1980.

Dodd, Josephine. 'Naming and Framing: Naturalization and Colonization in J.M. Coetzee's *In the Heart of the Country*'. *World Literature Written in English* 27.2 (1987): 153–61.

Huggan, Graham. 'Opting Out of the (Critical) Common Market: Creolization and the Post-Colonial Text'. *Kunapipi* 11.1 (1989): 27–40.

Harris, Wilson. *The Womb of Space: The Cross-Cultural Imagination*. Westport, CT: Greenwood Press, 1983.

Hulme, Keri. *the bone people*. London: Pan, 1986.

Jameson, Fredric. 'Third-World Literature in the Era of Multinational Capitalism'. *Social Text* 15 (1986): 65–88.

Larousse Encyclopedia of Mythology. London: Batchworth, 1959.

Lee, Dennis. 'Cadence, Country, Silence'. *Boundary* 2.3.1 (1974): 151–68.

Macherey, Pierre. *A Theory of Literary Production*. London: RKP, 1978.

Tiffin, Helen. 'Post-Colonial Literatures and Counter-Discourse'. *Kunapipi* 9.3 (1987): 17–38.

Said, Edward. 'Orientalism Reconsidered'. In *Postcolonial Criticism*. Ed. B. Moore-Gilbert, G. Stanton and W. Maley. London: Longman, 1997. 131–42.

Spivak, Gayatri Chakravorty. *In Other Worlds: Essays in Cultural Politics*. London: Methuen, 1987.

Notes

1   See Lee, who gives a specific cultural context to Pierre Macherey's general remark that 'the [literary] work cannot speak of the more or less complex opposition which structures it; though it is its expression and embodiment. In its every particle, the work manifests, uncovers what it cannot say. This silence gives it life' (Macherey 84).

2   The narratives of *The Tempest, Robinson Crusoe* and *Heart of Darkness* come immediately to mind. See Ashcroft, Griffiths and Tiffin's brief discussion of the influence of these (de)formative texts on postcolonial writers, and their argument that postcolonial writing is situated in the context of an ongoing 'struggle for the control of the word' (87).

3   Although postcolonial literatures are grounded in colonial history insofar as they are subject to the socio-economic conditions governing cultural production under the colonial system (and although they can be said in this sense to participate in the wider struggle for cultural decolonization), they are by no means bound to thematize that history. The sheer diversity of postcolonial writing – its vast range of different cultural contexts – necessarily outmanoeuvres ill-advised critical attempts to reduce it to a 'literature of resistance'; it goes without saying that a great deal of postcolonial writing ostensibly has little or nothing to do with colonialism. The issue of the critical straitjacketing of postcolonial literatures and of the uncertainty, or even the undesirability, of the term itself, will be discussed at a later stage of this essay.

4   Apollonian/Dionysian tensions clearly underscore *Clear Light of Day* and *the bone people*; both writers appear to subscribe to the Nietzschean view of music as creative principle/destructive force.

5   For a more detailed study of counter-discursive strategies in Coetzee's text, see Tiffin.

6   The parallel with Caliban is obvious here; indeed, *Foe* can be considered as much a postcolonial reworking of *The Tempest* as it is one of *Robinson Crusoe*. Note in particular the affiliation between (enforced) silence and (imposed) music as strategies of disempowerment in Shakespeare's play; and the way in which these strategies are eventually turned against Prospero, reminding him of the limits of his own – predominantly verbal – authority. Prospero claims that he intends to 'drown' his book (Act V, Scene i); but as Coetzee and other postcolonial writers have shown, the story it tells, and those alternative stories that are themselves 'submerged' beneath the surface of the master narrative, will come back (like the lurking sea monster of *Foe*) to haunt him. A further comparison might be made here between *Tempest* motifs in *Foe* and those in *the bone people*: (see, for example, my own discussion of the connections between Hulme's novel and Shakespeare's play in Huggan, 'Opting').

7   I have chosen here not to dwell on the analogy between mutism in Coetzee's text and censorship in contemporary South Africa, or on the particular dilemma faced by white liberal writers who wish to pledge their support for the cause of black liberation without presuming to act as the blacks' mouthpiece. The connection between Friday's mutilated tongue and the disenfranchisement of the black majority in South Africa is, of course, an obvious one. More interestingly, perhaps, Coetzee suggests that the white liberal in South Africa is faced with a double bind: he wishes to side with Friday, but cannot speak for him; he wishes to dissociate himself from *Foe*, but cannot help but speak for him. Another white liberal writer in South Africa, André Brink, has spoken thus of his own commitment in the face of government oppression: 'When the conspiracy of lies surrounding me demands of me to silence the one word of truth given to me, that word becomes the one word I wish to utter above all others' (165). But what is that 'word of truth'? And who decides when, or if, it should be spoken?

8   I am indebted here as elsewhere to the work of Gayatri Spivak (e.g. *In Other Worlds*) on strategies of (dis)empowerment in colonial discourse; and to Ashcroft, Griffiths and Tiffin's adoption/adaptation of Spivak in *The Empire Writes Back*, where the

writers make the (somewhat exaggerated?) claim that silence is 'the active characteristic linking all postcolonial texts' (187).

9   Essays which investigate these issues in more depth include those by Dale and
Dodd.

10 See the critique of Jameson by Aijaz Ahmad, and of Tiffin by Arun Mukherjee (in an
unpublished seminar paper on postcolonial theory given at the Canadian Learneds
Conference, Victoria, BC, 1990). See also the original essays by Jameson and Tiffin.

11 The phrase is Edward Said's: see the final section of 'Orientalism Reconsidered'.

CHAPTER 10

Ghost Stories, Bone Flutes, Cannibal Counter-memory

The Ghost is the fiction of our relationship to death.

(Cixous 542)

Face to face with the white man, the Negro has a past to legitimate, a vengeance to exact; face to face with the Negro, the contemporary white man feels the need to recall the times of cannibalism.

(Fanon 225)

Moving between literature and history, this chapter has three objectives. First, it seeks to forge an unholy alliance between the cannibal and the ghost, and to explore their interworkings in the context of revisionist Caribbean history. Second, it examines the cannibal and the ghost as textual mediators, as means by which Caribbean writers re-imagine their European literary ancestry. And third, it charts the attempt through the shape-shifting cannibal/ghost alliance to transform the orthodox, largely negative perception of Caribbean history, and to set up a counter-memory to the hegemonic European record. The primary texts are the creolized ghost stories of two modern Guyanese writers: Edgar Mittelholzer's *My Bones and My Flute* (1955) and Wilson Harris's *Palace of the Peacock* (1960). In both of these stories the ghost – the 'uncanny cannibal' – has a dual function, reasserting the presence of a past (or pasts) that had previously been repressed while estranging that past and converting it into forms that sublimate material exploitation.

Uncanny Cannibals

It is little wonder that Derek Walcott, the Caribbean's best-known poet, begins an essay on the region's past by citing Joyce's familiar epigraph, 'History is the nightmare from which I am trying to awake'. For the Caribbean region is haunted by ghostly presences, reminders of a history seen as loss, distress, defeat. Walcott takes as his artistic task the deliverance from this collective trauma:

> The New World originated in hypocrisy and genocide, so it is not a question for us of returning to an Eden or of creating Utopia; out of the sordid and degraded beginning of the West Indies, we could only go further in indecency and regret. Poets and satirists are afflicted with the superior stupidity which believes that societies can be renewed, and one of the most nourishing sites for such a renewal, however visionary it may seem, is the American archipelago. (Walcott 13)

Walcott drives out the ghosts that crowd in upon ancestral memory, clearing the space for history to direct its gaze towards the future. Other writers, however, from the Caribbean region – a region defined as much by discursive ties as by history or climate – have found themselves repeatedly, even obsessively, drawn back to the past. Kamau Brathwaite, Édouard Glissant, Alejo Carpentier, Wilson Harris: all of these writers have explored the hidden recesses of Caribbean history, rejecting the Eurocentric claim that the region has no past to speak of, and uncovering instead the 'traces of historical experience [that have been] erased from the collective memory of an oppressed and exploited people' (Webb 7).

Caribbean literature, in this context, enacts a struggle over origins. Where does the past begin? What might be seen as the region's heritage? And can this heritage – acknowledged as multiple, fluid and syncretistic – be re-invented to suit the purposes of emancipation and renewal? (Caribbean cultural origins clearly predate the European record, stretching back beyond 'discovery' and the history of slavery to engage with folk mythologies that have survived in adapted forms despite the decimation of both the islands' and the mainland's indigenous peoples.) Modern Caribbean writing participates in a process of perceptual transformation: it submits itself to its own haunting but with a view to overcoming it, and with an aim of converting a spectral past into a speculative future.

It seems appropriate, then, that among the region's most prolific forms is the ghost story, or a hybrid variant of it, at least, derived both from African/Amerindian oral sources and from the repository of Western (Euro-American) literary fantasy. This chapter deals with two novel-length ghost stories set in 'ancestral' Guyana: an area of the Caribbean whose complex racial intermixture owes both to 'mestizo' (Euro/Amerindian) and 'mulatto' (Euro/African) forms of cultural creolization.[1] Before turning to the works themselves, however, a few prefatory remarks seem necessary, both on the properties of the genre and its ambivalent stance to history.

Ghost stories, according to Gillian Beer, 'elide the distance between the actual and the imagined': they speak, literally and figuratively, of an intrusion into the everyday world. In ghost stories, says Beer, 'the fictional takes place in the everyday: it takes space, and it is this usurpation of space by the immaterial which is one of the deepest terrors released by the ghost story. [...] [G]host stories are to do with the insurrection, not the resurrection of the dead' (260).

The return of the undead may act as a trigger for personal memories; for the ghost, as Helene Cixous reminds us, is 'the direct figure of the uncanny' (542). Ghosts are uncanny in the Freudian sense that they register the familiar: they belong, as Freud puts it in his 1919 essay 'The Uncanny', to 'that class of the terrifying which leads us back to something long known to us' (369–70). Yet the ghost, and its ambiguous return, also have far-reaching social consequences. History is reintroduced into the arena of the present, but in such a way that it threatens the fixity of existing social structures.[2] Ghosts bring with them a knowledge other than that ratified by social charter: they make a mockery of the institutional respects we pay to satisfy the dead. And to keep ourselves separate from them – for ghosts have contempt for boundaries, for all our cherished social distinctions. They walk through historical walls, co-existing with the present, and literalizing the memories we consecrate in metaphor in order to contain them. (Ghosts, after all, are indiscreet: they scorn the blandishments of the tombstone, or the solemn rites that attend the passing of the funeral hearse.) Ghosts bring the past into our midst that we might recognize it. But they also estrange the past: their relationship to the history that they reinstate is inherently uncertain. What renders the ghost intolerable, according to Cixous, is not so much that it is an announcement of death nor even the proof that death exists, since it 'announces and proves nothing more than [its] return. What is intolerable is that the [g]host erases the limit which exists between the two states, neither alive nor dead; passing through, the dead man returns in the manner of the Repressed. It is his coming back which makes the ghost what he is, just as it is the return of the Repressed that inscribes the repression' (543).

Ghosts are the unwelcome carriers of an occluded history; they show us how we screen, and thus protect ourselves from, the past. They function, to be sure, as agents for the reconstruction of historical memory. But they are double agents: they are working for the 'other' side. They make us recognize another past to the one we might have chosen: they transform, not the past itself but our 'normal', socialized perception of it. This set of preliminary observations on the disruptive properties of ghosts suggests that ghost stories might be effective as vehicles of historical revisionism, or as means by which repressed histories can be brought back to the surface. It also suggests that ghost stories might help construct a kind of counter-memory, in Foucault's sense of the transformation of (linear) history into a different form of time.[3] In the Caribbean context, this need to transform the past becomes an urgent imperative. Denis Williams states the dilemma well:

> We are all shaped by our past; the imperatives of a contemporary culture are predominantly those of a relationship to this past. Yet in the Caribbean and in Guyana we think and behave as though we have no past, no history, no culture. And where we do come to take notice of our history it is often in the light of biases adopted from one [racially] thoroughbred culture or another,

of the Old World. We permit ourselves the luxury [...] of racial dialectics in our interpretation of Caribbean and Guyanese history and culture. In the light of what we are this is a destructive thing to do, since at best it perpetuates what we might call a filialistic dependence on the cultures of our several racial origins, while simultaneously inhibiting us from facing up to the facts of what we uniquely are. (qtd. in Harris, 'History' 13)

Ghost stories in the Caribbean thus often have a dual purpose: they revive in order to dispel the ghosts of a past conceived by Europe, a history couched in the paralysing terms of dispossession and defeat (Huggan, 'Tale'). At the same time, they reclaim a past anterior to European conquest, a history whose outlines blend with those of originary myth, and whose ghosts are not horrifying apparitions from another, unwanted era but welcome catalysts for the recovery of a buried ancestral consciousness. Ghost stories, like ghosts themselves, shift the shape of the past(s) that they engage with; they are co-opted, in the Caribbean, into a discourse of conversion, whereby a history of exploitation is estranged even as it is confronted, and a pattern is established for the transformation of individual trauma into the inspiring recollective force that bonds a whole community.

This discourse of conversion goes by many names. It might refer, for instance, to Kamau Brathwaite's project of cultural creolization, whereby the appeal to ancestors other than the European (such as the African and Amerindian) involves the writer in a 'journey into the past and hinterland which is at the same time a movement of possession into present and future' (*History* 42). Or then again it might take in Denis Williams's model of catalysis, whereby an interaction between the region's racial groups qualifies each other's self-image, and a history of race-based conflict is turned into a valuable source of artistic creativity. For Wilson Harris, too, adversarial contexts can be productive. Harris's experimental fictions are exercises in what he calls a 'dialectic of alteration': historical antagonisms are converted into a volatile symbiosis (Huggan, 'Tale'), with the Old World and the New nurturing each other's creativity; meanwhile, history itself is turned into a set of 'architectural complexes', spatial frameworks offering alternatives to a linear vision of time and to a 'block' perspective on the past that blindly serves self-interest – the obsessive pursuit of material goals that only strengthen social divisions, the obstinate refusal to acknowledge 'visionary' schemes other than one's own (Harris, 'History' 32). There is an ethical dimension, then, to all of these projects of conversion, which present a challenge to the teleology of imperial conquest, asserting in its place a dialectical or processual view of (cross-)cultural interchange. In proposing what Harris calls 'a treaty of sensibility between alien cultures' (19), each writer recognizes the need for continuing self-critique. Caribbean counter-discourses (in Helen Tiffin's useful gloss on Harris) 'evolve textual strategies which continually "consume their own biases" [Harris's term] at the same time as they expose and erode those of the dominant discourse' (Tiffin 18).

Harris's arresting metaphor of 'consuming one's own biases' is linked throughout his work to the symbolic practice of cannibalism. Cannibals, according to Harris, do not merely feed on the dead; they absorb the dead into themselves, drawing on their enemies' strength but suggesting, at the same time, that the declaration of material hostilities might eventually give way to an uneasy metaphysical truce. Harris explains this process further in his preface to *The Guyana Quartet*. Here he refers the reader to the Carib/cannibal bone flute, an instrument traditionally made from the hollowed-out bones of the Caribs' war-victims and whose music, in releasing the ghosts of victories past, works to sublimate them. The relevant passage is as follows:

> The Carib bone flute was hollowed out from the bone of an enemy in time of war. Flesh was plucked and consumed and in the process secrets were digested. Spectres arose from, or reposed in, the flute. [The anthropologist Michael] Swan identifies this flute of soul with 'transubstantiation in reverse.' In parallel with an obvious violation ran therefore, it seems to me, another subtle force resembling yet differing from terror in that the flute became the home or curiously mutual fortress of spirit between enemy and other, an organ of self-knowledge suffused with enemy bias so close to native greed for victory. (Harris, *Guyana* 9–10)

Harris's language is characteristically metaphor-laden and oracular. Peggy Sanday's anthropological analysis helps put it in perspective: 'When projected onto enemies, cannibalism [...] becomes the means by which powerful threats to social life are dissipated. By consuming enemy flesh one assimilates the animus of another group's hostile power into one's own' (Sanday 6). Harris's description of the bone flute also reflects on Dean MacCannell's more speculative distinction (derived from Montaigne) between economic and symbolic cannibalism: the former motivated by the selfish desire for material gain; the latter, paradoxically, by the mutual need for human kinship.[4]

The flute, which Harris seems to see as an organizing metaphor for his work, integrates the cannibal and the ghost – the phobic creatures of a paralysed unconscious – into an alchemical process where they act in tandem as catalysts of transformation. The flute works to sublimate the physical violence it embodies; its spectral music provides both for the rehearsal of cannibal urges and for their translation into an ephemeral form that dematerializes the act of conquest. The flute functions as a mnemonic device whose range is atavistic: to play it is to summon the ghosts of an ancestral past into the present, submitting oneself to one's primal fears and fantasies of the 'other'. It embodies the cannibal act but then converts it into ghostly music; in the process the threat of cannibal destruction is not diminished, but is dispersed in the re-enactments of former cannibal confrontations, dismemberments now remembered in a disembodied form. The flute transforms the cannibal, the West's irreducible 'other', into a free-floating manifestation of the Freudian uncanny. This cannibal ghost is a blueprint for fantastic liminality: neither alive nor dead, both physical and spiritual; it absorbs the 'other' only to reassert it as a powerful 'absent presence'.[5] By trading on the interplay between containment and dispersal – between the incorporated body and the unassimilable ghost – the bone flute records and regulates the violence of the past while acknowledging that this violence can never be fully controlled.

Letting in the Demons

In Mittelholzer's *My Bones and My Flute* (1955), the eponymous flute and its ghostly music are associated with the Dutch planter Jan Peter Voorman, victim of a slave revolt in mid-eighteenth-century (British) Guyana. Voorman's ghost still roams abroad, it seems, hounded by demonic spirits – spirits whose presence his magic flute had originally summoned, but who now leave him, and all those who associate with him, no rest. A parchment he leaves for posterity draws its readers into a pact: either they must find his bones and flute and give them a Christian burial or they, too, will be lured by the flute's nefarious music to their death. Enter the novel's protagonists, the aristocratic mill-owner and part-time antiquarian Ralph Nevinson, and the narrator Milton Woodsley, an aspiring writer and painter and, like the Nevinsons, from old Coloured – and thus respectable – Guyanese stock. Billed both as a 'good thrilling sort of old-fashioned ghost story, with the mystery solved at the end' and as a 'true record, including nothing that might be attributed to [its narrator's] imagination' (5–6), *My Bones and My Flute* tells the story of Woodsley's and the Nevinsons' quest to lay Voorman to rest. At the same time, the novel reads as an allegory of Guyana's mixed racial ancestry and as an attempt to come to terms with the country's violent colonial past.

From the outset, Mittelholzer's ghost story acquires racial dimensions. 'I curse these black wretches', Voorman says of the slaves who work for him, 'even as I curse the Blacker Ones', the demons his flute has summoned (29). These demons turn out to be a cross between neanderthals and extraterrestrials; they shift in shape and form, now ghosts, now beasts, now cannibal vampires. They are, in short, a composite of the white man's racial phobias, phobias linked in Voorman's case to the justified fear of insubordination, and in Woodsley's to the guilt instilled by a puritanical religious education. (The Day of Judgement, says Woodsley's grandmother, might come at any moment, with 'the Righteous lifted as they sleep and transported up to Heaven while the Unrighteous are cast into Eternal Flames with Satan and his *Black Angels*' [57–58, my emphasis].)

The Blacker Ones also have another, literary, ancestry. In recalling the ghostly predators of Poe's and M. R. James's fictions, they remind us of the paranoid racial myths endemic in Western fantasy.[6] James's *Ghost-Stories of an Antiquary* is cited as an intertext, as is, almost inevitably, Poe's *Tales of Mystery and Imagination*. And another text of Poe's appears to lie beneath the surface: *The Narrative of Arthur Gordon Pym*, with its spectral visions of Blackness and its projections of the writer's pathological fears of Southern slave rebellion.[7] *My Bones and My Flute* locates itself squarely within this dubious tradition, not to reinforce the white man's racial fantasies, but rather to reassess their function within a specific historical context. And the context here is that of British Guyana's colonial history – a record of the drudgery, cruelty and violence of the planta-tions, but also of the hybrid cultural forms thrown up by that encounter.

Kamau Brathwaite distinguishes usefully here between two forms of New World creolization: 'A mestizo-creolization, the interculturation of Amerindian and European (mostly Iberian) and located primarily in Central and South America; and a mulatto-creolization, the interculturation of Negro-African and European (mainly Western European) and located primarily in the West Indies and the slave areas of the North American continent' (*Development* 30). Guyana's history intersects these two different forms of cultural creolization. In *My Bones and My Flute*, Woodsley and the Nevinsons are the 'olive-coloured' products of racial intermixture: their ancestors, Woodsley tells us, go back to the late eighteenth century, after which time they acquired the 'strain of Negro slave blood that runs in them today' (8). It is significant, though, that each of them downplays this aspect of their cultural ancestry, choosing instead to emulate their (white) European forebears and accepting their 'superior' status within a (post)colonial pigmentocracy.

It is tempting, in this context, to read the novel as an allegory of acculturation and of the 'lactification complex' that afflicts Caribbean societies (Fanon).[8] Such a reading might account for the Nevinsons' condescension towards their black and/or Indian workers; it might also help explain Mr Nevinson's and Woodsley's taste for European art. Most importantly, it might rationalize their joint decision to save the planter from perdition, for Voorman's blood is in their veins: theirs is a common history. Woodsley and the Nevinsons stake their claim on a European ancestry; yet as they stave off Voorman's demons, other ghosts come into their midst. These are their 'other' ancestors, the enslaved blacks on the plantations, and their 'absent presence' within the text signals a return of the repressed. By the end of the novel, Woodsley and the Nevinsons are confronted with a subal-tern history; they are made to recognize the past they had disclaimed as being their own. Voorman ends his diary, which also ends the novel, with a premoni-tion of slave rebellion. Still haunted by demons – the Blacker Ones – Voorman becomes increasingly desperate:

> Last night I heard them speaking in varied languages – languages I know not and yet which I myself spoke. I heard French and German and English and Italian and other tongues I could not identify [...]. They babbled about me in a clamour too deafening to describe. They fumed and wreathed [*sic*] and turned in spirals [...] and the air thundered about me. [...] A catastrophe threatens. I sense it in the air. I am a thwarted, craven soul, a human tottering on the edge of ultimate darkness. To whom, to what, must I turn for salvation? (174)

Voorman's demons speak in European tongues: they ape the colonizer's language. Yet they also foreshadow an imminent end to white planter autoc-racy: they usher in, like Poe's Madeline, the downfall of an era, as the white man's fears of violent black revenge are reconfirmed. For Voorman's necro-mancy converges with the Berbice Slave Rebellion, an uprising that results in his own death and the slaughter of other white families. The white man's spell is broken; the otherworldly Blacker Ones – the emanations of a troubled unconscious – bring with them the ghostly tidings of a decisive break in history. (The date listed for the rebellion – 1763 – is all the more ironic in that it coincides with the year of the post-Seven Years War Caribbean Peace Treaty.[9] Thus, at the very apex of British mercantile achievement comes a revolt that prefigures the fall of their, among other white, fortunes in Guyana.)

Mittelholzer's ghost story, then, seems to clear the space for an emancipatory history. It drives out one kind of demon in order to let in another; but these latter 'demons' are not just the incubi of white colonial history, they are the catalytic agents of revolutionary change.[10] In laying Voorman's bones to rest and relieving themselves of the White Planter's Burden, Woodsley and the Nevinsons are forced to recognize a history they had previously suppressed. Mittelholzer, similarly, delivers himself from his white literary ancestors, acknowledging the influence of Poe and James but taking possession of them, either to turn their ghosts against themselves and render them insubstantial or to redeploy their racial fears as a means of reclaiming black agency.

My Bones and My Flute turns the tables on its literary predecessors. Rather than submitting to a Western (Euro-American) 'anxiety of influence' (Bloom), Caribbean texts such as Mittelholzer's use the conventions of the ghost story to expose the West to the anxieties of its own imposed authority.[11] The flute – a Prosperan wand – is a generator of illusion; but it is equally deceptive for the person who controls it. Its primary function in the novel seems to be as a conductor for Voorman's evil thoughts and intentions; turning against him, it eventually becomes the instrument of his perdition. The flute also provides the means, however, for Voorman's own salvation and for the reconciliation of his followers to an 'inconceivable' past. Its function is therefore similar to that of the Carib/cannibal bone flute, even though Voorman's flute is made of metal and has no obvious 'tribal' affiliation. (Its closest symbolic connection, perhaps, is to the slave-owner's branding-iron – on more than one occasion, the invisible flute sears its victim's flesh.) The bone flute remains peripheral to Mittelholzer's text: it is a spectral presence hovering around the novel's title credits. Nonetheless, the flute (like Mozart's, to which it more obviously alludes) works a generalized kind of intertextual/cultural alchemy.[12] It releases the collective ghosts of Guyana's ancestral past; not all of these ghosts are a figment of the white imagination. *My Bones and My Flute* is, after all, a creolized form of the Western ghost story: it owes as much to Amerindian as to European sources (see 41–42, 61–62). It is precisely in the syncretism of its forms that Mittelholzer's novel works its magic: in the weaving together of disparate, nominally hostile creative traditions, and in the production of a counter-memory to Caribbean material history – one which willingly rehearses the traumas of a brutal past, but then transmutes them into a vision of change that moves beyond catastrophe (174).

Transubstantiating Hostility

In *My Bones and My Flute*, Woodsley's and the Nevinsons' quest is eventually cathartic: it allows them to confront and accept a hidden aspect of their past by staging the in/resurrection of their ghostly slave ancestors. In Harris's *Palace of the Peacock*, ancestral memory stretches back further, taking in the European myth of the New World El Dorado and uncovering behind it a rich array of different 'sources'. Ostensibly, Harris's novel recounts the quest for El Dorado within the context of a latter-day journey to (and beyond) an Amerindian mission. The plot, however, like the journey, is impossibly convoluted, not least because Harris's novel oscillates between past and present. The journey takes place in a dreamtime where story merges with myth and legend, and where the fated expeditions of de Berrio, de Vera and Raleigh are interlaced with creation myths from both Amerindian and Judaeo-Christian traditions. El Dorado is the meeting-place, the Source of all these sources. But the City of Gold remains, as of course it must, just out of reach; and each successive quest to find it is condemned to re-enact defeat. V. S. Naipaul has captured well the compulsiveness of the delusion, as the 'original' story passed from mouth to mouth, leaving more deaths in its wake:

> There had been a golden man, el dorado, the gilded one, in what is now Colombia: a chief who once a year rolled in turpentine, was covered in gold dust and then dived into a lake. But the tribe of the golden man had been conquered a generation before Columbus came to the New World. It was an Indian memory that the Spaniards pursued; and the memory was confused with the legend, among jungle Indians, of the Peru the Spaniards had already conquered. (Naipaul 18)

For Naipaul, El Dorado presents a cautionary tale of repeated New World failure. The story outruns, outlasts, and eventually engulfs its actors, revealing the spiritual vacuum behind their dreams of material wealth. Harris's view of El Dorado is, however, somewhat different. He sees an 'instinctive idealism' associated with the adventure, even though he recognizes that these ideals usually give way to greed and cruelty.[13] El Dorado represents a chain of contradictory correspondences; in uncovering these correspondences in *Palace of the Peacock*, Harris gestures towards the reversal 'of the "given" conditions of the past, freeing oneself from catastrophic idolatry and blindness to one's own historical and philosophical conceptions and misconceptions which may bind one within a statuesque present or a false future' (Harris, *Tradition* 36).

The ghost is a primary instrument of this historical reversal; for the mixed-race crew that sets off up-river in search of the Mariella Mission are ghosts returned from the dead to confront, once more, their own mortality. Mariella, the expedition leader Donne's former Amerindian mistress, now pursued by him to the secluded jungle mission that bears her name, is herself described as a phantom, a ghostly object of desire. Mariella, at once executioner and victim, pursuer and pursued, becomes a symbol in the novel for the circularity of desire. Her presence, restored in the figure of the ancient Arawak woman, is a reminder to the crew not of what they might gain but of what they have already lost. For as they move beyond the mission into increasingly dangerous territory, they condemn themselves to a 'second death', as inevitable as the first:

> It was all well and good they reasoned, as inspired madmen would to strain themselves to gain that elastic frontier where a spirit might rise from the dead and rule the material past world. All well and good was the resurgence and reconnoitre they reasoned. But it was doomed again from the start to meet endless catastrophe: even the ghost one dreams of and restores must be embalmed and featured in the old lineaments of empty and meaningless desire. (Harris, *Guyana* 80)

The ghost is the lack inscribed in their material ambitions; and it is the talisman that presages their own repeated destruction. It reminds them, too, that the past returns to batten on the present; that there is no escape from the phantoms (re)produced by a guilty conscience. (Each of the crew-members is in some way attempting to escape his responsibilities, fleeing a personal history that, just as irresistibly, binds them all together.)

The ghost – that which returns – reinscribes a legacy of shame and fear (69): a legacy associated elsewhere with the involuntary memory of cannibalism. The cannibal act is linked most closely to the expedition leader Donne, whose relentless greed and cruelty amount in the novel to 'an incalculable devouring principle' (79). Yet Donne draws others, too, into a blasphemous communion: the fish the narrator eats becomes 'a morsel of recollection', a 'memory spring[ing] from nowhere into [his] belly and experience' (48); while Donne, the spectre released from a history of cannibal savagery, becomes 'an apparition stoop[ing] before him and cloth[ing] him with the rightful nature of the jungle', striking him dumb with the knowledge that he has swallowed 'a morsel of terror' (52). Donne, here, is the uncanny cannibal, forcing the past into the present, bringing with him unwanted memories and previously ingested secrets. The terror he induces owes to the yoking of two forces: the all-devouring incorporative principle of the ferocious cannibal and the uncontainable mnemonic power of the surreptitious ghost. Violent assimilation, inexorable repetition: these are the forces that propel the crew towards renewed destruction. And they are also the forces that lock them in an incestuous alliance. For the crew are all related: they are, quite literally, 'one spiritual family' (39) – and cannibalism, as resurrected through the figure of the predatory ghost, is, as Lévi-Strauss reminds us, 'the alimentary form of incest' (141). Cannibalism, like incest, is a rudimentary form of violation: it transgresses the social boundaries that separate us from kith and kin.[14] And yet, as Harris suggests, it is also born of the need for kinship: cannibalism, again like incest, is a disallowed form of symbiosis. It is this conjunctive aspect to the cannibal infraction that Harris draws upon and absorbs, in turn, into his own 'cannibalistic' text. Thus, whereas in *My Bones and My Flute* the 'cannibal ghost' is a primarily phobic entity, a manifestation of the white man's racial fears and paranoid fantasies, in *Palace of the Peacock* it provides the reminder of a productive violation, displaying the incestuous ties that bond together a Creole (Caribbean) people.[15]

Over and against the Donnean principle of cannibal devoration, Harris asserts a counter-principle of alchemical transformation. The cannibal/ghost alliance – a Donnean conceit if there ever was one – forms the bonding agent that produces an unlikely metamorphosis. This metamorphosis, as Michael Gilkes, among other critics, has suggested, is best seen in alchemical terms as a process of psychic reintegration. Here it is Jung, rather than Freud or Lévi-Strauss, who captures best the nature of Harris's project. Historically, says Jung,

> [Alchemy] was a work of reconciliation between two apparently incompatible opposites which, characteristically, were understood not merely as the natural hostility of the physical elements but at the same time as a moral conflict. Since the object of the endeavour was seen outside as well as inside, as both physical and psychic, the work extended as it were through the whole of nature, and its goal consisted in a symbol which had an empirical and at the same time a transcendental aspect. (Jung 554)

The relevance of Jung's quotation to Harris's novel need hardly be stressed; it might serve, indeed, as an epitaph to the novel's final, epiphanic sequence, where the crew-members, meeting their second deaths, consumed by their own will-to-consumption, realize that 'the wall that had divided [them] from their true otherness' is nothing other than 'a web of dreams' (114). The recognition of 'otherness', and of the 'otherness' in themselves, allows them to cancel the 'forgotten fear of strangeness and catastrophe in a destitute world' (116), and to free themselves from their obsessive desire for material possession. Reborn to themselves, they are reawakened to the world which they see now in its unity; their need for each other fades into the vision of 'one muse and one undying soul' (117). This vision seems to hold as well for the novel's intertextual project: its integration of Western writers working within the Symbolic tradition (the Metaphysicals; Hopkins; Eliot, Yeats and Conrad) into a unifying pattern of regenerative myth.[16] What is interesting in Harris's case, however, is the attention he pays to context: the violent New World encounters that act as a backdrop to Donne's devotionals; the savagery that Conrad locates at the heart of modern European civilization. Like Mittelholzer, then, Harris plays on the fears of his European ancestors: inhabiting their texts, preying upon them like a ghost, but also transforming them into actors in a New World spiritual drama, a kind of passion-play that moves beyond the Manichaean categories of Good and Evil. So whereas Mittelholzer releases the racialized spectres that lurk behind the Western ghost story, giving them material form as agents of revolutionary vengeance, Harris invites the cannibal and the ghost to link their otherworldly fingers and to perform together the alchemical work of transubstantiation.

In *Palace of the Peacock*, the cannibal ghost is an inspiring, muse-like figure; it is transformed from a source of terror into a vehicle of reconciliation. This transformation both resubstantiates the immateriality of memory and dematerializes the act of conquest by giving it a spectral form. The cannibal and the ghost are, in this sense, collaborators in paradox: the one breaks down divisions between the eater and the eaten, 'creat[ing] a total identity between [them] while insisting on the unreciprocal and yet ultimately total control – the literal consumption – of the latter by the former' (Kilgour 7); the other bridges the gap between the actual and the imaginary, producing a hybrid entity that straddles ontological realms. The cannibal ghost, along with the instrument that brings it into being, the Carib bone flute, produces an uneasy harmony from apparently incompatible elements. At the same time, it is a symbol of radical discontinuity (the internalization of the fragmented body; the defiance of solid form). In this second sense, it features as an agent of counter-memory, disrupting a view of history that insists on continuous progress. Counter-memory, in Michel Foucault's formulation, consists of three components: 'The first of these is parodic, directed against reality, and opposes the theme of history as reminiscence or recognition; the second is dissociative, directed against identity, and opposes history given as continuity or representative of a tradition; the third is sacrificial, directed against truth, and opposes history as knowledge' (Foucault 93).

The cannibal ghost inhabits the interstices of the recognizable past; its discontinuous form eludes attempts at historical identification. The countermemory it instantiates functions on a principle of uncontrollable heterogeneity; the history it perceives 'will not discover a forgotten identity [...] but [rather] a complex system of [...] multiple elements, unable to be mastered by the powers of synthesis' (Foucault 94). For Harris, cannibal counter-memory opposes European history: it fragments the vision of time that underpins an ideology of conquest. The cannibal ghost, however, re-institutes a form of collective remembrance; it absorbs and synthesizes, if in a new substantive, form. Here, then, are the two conflicting aspects of Harris's 'dialectic of alteration': on the one hand, a counter-memory that challenges reminiscence, and that delivers itself from the 'origins' that Europe has imposed upon it; on the other, an equal and opposite move towards mythic transcendence, restoring collective memory but elevating it to a higher form. This dialectic remains unresolved. The cannibal absorbs the 'other'; the 'other' returns – as a ghost. Yet this cycle of repetition, this pattern of what Harris calls 'infinite rehearsal', need not be seen in terms of alienation or imprisonment; instead, it asserts the principle of creole transmutation, as Caribbean writers, inspired by the bone flute, reinvent their region – and themselves.

I began this chapter by invoking the powerful ghost of Frantz Fanon; it seems appropriate, then, to end it by bringing Fanon back out of the shadows. For Fanon, the cannibal – the alibi for a history of race oppression – must be confronted, then surmounted, before being banished into the past. For blacks, meanwhile, the past, restored, ignites the fires of vengeance. But the smoke then clears to yield a glimpse of Fanon's great utopian vision: 'self' and 'other' converge, until there is no 'self', no 'other'; 'white' and 'black' worlds coalesce, until there are no 'whites', no 'blacks' – only people, disabused of the history that once defined them, working together for the creation of a liberated future:

I am not a prisoner of history I should not seek there for the meaning of my destiny. [...] I should constantly remind myself that the real leap consists in introducing invention into existence. [...] In the world through which I travel, I am endlessly creating myself. [...] I, the man of color, want only this: That the tool never possess the man. That the enslavement of man by man cease forever. That is, of one by another [...] Why not the quite simple attempt to touch the other, to feel the other, to explain the other to myself? (Fanon 229–31)

Works Cited

Abraham, Nicolas. 'Notes on the Phantom: A Complement to Freud's Meta-psychology'. *Critical Inquiry* 13 (Winter 1987): 287–92.

Beer, Gillian. 'Ghosts'. *Essays in Criticism* 28.3 (1978): 259–64.

Bloom, Harold. *The Anxiety of Influence: A Theory of Poetry*. New York: Oxford University Press, 1973.

Brathwaite, Kamau. *The Development of Creole Society in Jamaica 1770–1820*. Oxford: Clarendon Press, 1974.

——. *History of the Voice*. London: New Beacon,1984.

Cixous, Helene. 'Fiction and its Phantoms: A Reading of Freud's "Das Unheimliche"'. *New Literary History* 7.3 (1976): 525–47.

Drake, Sandra. *Wilson Harris and the Modern Tradition: A New Architecture of the World*. New York: Greenwood Press, 1986.

Fanon, Frantz. *Black Skin, White Masks*. Trans. Charles Markmann. New York: Grove Weidenfeld, 1967.

Foucault, Michel. 'Nietzsche, Genealogy, History'. In *The Foucault Reader*. Ed. Paul Rabinow. New York: Pantheon, 1984. 76–100.

Freud, Sigmund. 'The "Uncanny"'. In *Collected Papers*. Ed. Ernest Jones. New York: Basic Books, 1959. 368–407.

——. *Totem and Taboo*. London: Ark Paperbacks, 1983.

Gilkes, Michael. *Wilson Harris and the Caribbean Novel*. London: Longman, 1975.

Girard, René. *Violence and the Sacred*. Trans. Patrick Gregory. Baltimore: Johns Hopkins University Press, 1977.

Glissant, Edouard. *Caribbean Discourse: Selected Essays*. Ed. Michael Dash. Charlottesville, VA: University Press of Virginia, 1989.

Harris, Wilson. *Tradition, the Writer, and Society*. London: New Beacon, 1967.

——. 'History, Fable and Myth in the Caribbean and Guianas'. *Caribbean Quarterly* 16 (1970): 1–32.

——. *The Womb of Space: The Cross-Cultural Imagination*. Westport, CT: Greenwood Press, 1983.

——. *The Guyana Quartet*. London: Faber & Faber, 1985.

Howard, W.J. 'Wilson Harris's "Guiana Quartet": From Personal Myth to National Identity'. *Ariel* 1.1 (1970): 46–60.

Huggan, Graham. 'A Tale of Two Parrots: Walcott, Rhys, and the Uses of Colonial Mimicry'. *Contemporary Literature* 35.4 (1994): 643–60.

——. 'Cannibal Rights: Intertextuality and Postcolonial Discourse in the Caribbean Region'. In *Eating Dis-orders: Cannibalism in Contemporary Latin American Culture*. Ed. A.L. Andrade and G. Huggan. (forthcoming).

Jackson, Rosemary. *Fantasy: The Literature of Subversion*. London: Methuen, 1981.

James, C. L. R. *The Black Jacobins: Toussaint L'Ouverture and the San Domingo Revolution*. New York: Vintage, 1963.

James, M. R. *Ghost-Stories of an Antiquary*. London: Edward Arnold, 1915.

Kilgour, Maggie. *From Communion to Cannibalism: An Anatomy of Metaphors of Incorporation*. Princeton, NJ: Princeton University Press, 1990.

Lévi-Strauss, Claude. *The Naked Man*. Trans. J. and D. Weightman. London: Harper and Row, 1981.

MacCannell, Dean. *Empty Meeting Grounds: The Tourist Papers*. London: Routledge, 1992.

McWatt, Mark. 'The Two Faces of Eldorado: Contrasting Attitudes Toward History and Identity in West Indian Literature'. In *West Indian Literature in its Social Context*. Ed. M. McWatt. Barbados: UWI, 1985. 33–47.

Mittelholzer, Edgar. *My Bones and My Flute*. London: Longman, 1955.

Naipaul, V. S. *The Loss of El Dorado* [1969]. New York: Vintage, 1984.

Rowe, John Carlos. 'Poe, Antebellum Slavery, and Modem Criticism'. In *Poe's Pym: Critical Explorations*. Ed. R. Kopley. Durham, NC: Duke University Press, 1992. 117–40.

Sanday, Peggy Reeves. *Divine Hunger: Cannibalism as a Cultural System*. Cambridge: Cambridge University Press, 1986.

Tiffin, Helen. 'Post-Colonial Literatures and Counter-Discourse'. *Kunapipi* 9.3 (1987): 17–34.

Todorov, Tzvetan. *The Fantastic: A Structural Approach to a Literary Genre*. Trans. Richard Howard. Ithaca, NY: Cornell University Press, 1975.

Walcott, Derek. 'The Caribbean: Culture or Mimicry?'. *Journal of Interamerican Studies* 16 (1974): 3–13.

Wasserman, Renata. 'Reinventing the New World: Cooper and Alencar'. *Comparative Literature* 36 (1984): 130–45.

Webb, Barbara. *Myth and History in Caribbean Fiction*. Amherst, MA: University of Massachusetts Press, 1992.

Williams, Eric. *From Columbus to Castro: The History of the Caribbean* [1970]. New York: Vintage, 1984.

Notes

1   On creolization in the Caribbean context, see Brathwaite, *Development*; also Glissant, especially Book Three. In a specifically Guyanese context, see Harris's essay 'History, Fable and Myth'.

2   See Jackson's discussion of the social implications of the fantastic in the opening chapters of her study *Fantasy: The Literature of Subversion* (1981).

3   Counter-memory, says Foucault, loosely following Nietzsche's *Untimely Meditations*, presents an alternative to the 'traditional' historical view of a continuous past. Counter-memory opposes the holistic pursuit of historical retrieval; instead, it traces a genealogy of breaks, fissures, disruptions. The purpose of counter-memory – a genealogically guided history – is not to recover the origins of personal/cultural identity; it is to chart the faultlines that cross-hatch the remembered past, and to register the discontinuities that traverse the (social) body. Counter-memory is disruptive, but it has creative uses – as in the Caribbean, where the compulsion to rehearse a history of deprivation is a spell that must be broken, revealing in the break a different future.

4   See the introduction to Sanday's *Divine Hunger* (1986); also the first essay in MacCannell's *Empty Meeting Grounds* (17–73).

5   On the ghost as a liminal figure and a looming 'absent presence', see Freud's essay 'The "Uncanny"'; also the discussions of Freud in Todorov and Jackson, and the psychoanalytical debates surrounding the figure of the (Freudian) phantom in Abraham and Cixous. Phantoms, says Abraham (following Freud), are not representations of the dead but collective metaphors for the 'gaps left within us by the secrets of others' (287).

6   Surprisingly, neither Todorov nor Jackson, in the standard introductions to fantasy, has very much to say on the subject of race. Fantasy, as a privileged site for race-based traumas and delusions, would clearly benefit from a more sustained (Fanonian?) cultural analysis.

7   On racial paranoia in Poe, see Rowe.

8   In *Black Skin, White Masks*, Fanon's classic study of interracial neurosis based on his research in the Caribbean, he speaks of the 'lactification' or 'whitification' complex as being among the foremost of an 'arsenal of complexes that has been developed by the colonial environment' (30). For Fanon, the lactification complex – the desire of blacks to wear white masks – is emphatically *not* the projection of a collective psyche predisposed towards dependency; instead, it is the product of colonial brainwashing: of a systematic attempt to lower blacks' self-expectations, and to force them to see themselves in the distorting mirror of the white (wo)man's world (34).

9   See Williams' account of eighteenth-century Caribbean history (chapters 10–14). Here, Williams outlines both the conflicts of the European imperial powers over Caribbean trade and the growing resistance of Caribbean plantation workers to their European 'masters'. This culminated in the mid-eighteenth century in a sequence of slave revolts – including one in Surinam in 1763.

10 The slave revolts of the mid-eighteenth century arguably culminated in the revolution in San Domingo in 1791, which eventually led in 1804 to the establishment of the world's first black republic (see Williams: chapter 15; also C. L. R. James's magisterial study of the Haitian Revolution).

11 See Huggan, 'Tale'. Here I argue that one reason for the plethora of revisionist texts in the Caribbean is the writers' collective attempt to turn the tables on their European precursors: 'Far from submitting to a Bloomian anxiety of influence toward the Great Tradition of European literature, [these texts] subject that tradition to its own anxiety: first, by charting the contradictions and inconsistencies within a European colonialist discourse which has co-opted the "otherness" of "non-European" cultures in order to consolidate Europe's own sense of self; and second, by taking up that "otherness" and using it as "the sign of systematic opposition to the [European] metropoles and of affirmation of an independent identity"' (658). The embedded quotation comes from Wasserman (13).

12 For a reading of *The Magic Flute* informed, via Jung, by alchemical symbols, see Koenigsberger. Koenigsberger sees Mozart's opera as tracing 'the search for self-perfection': its main characters are alchemically fused in 'one being, one psyche, one soul' (231). *The Magic Flute*, of course, is known for attracting contradictory readings: the flute itself, like Voorman's (and, before it, the bone flute of the Caribs), can be seen both as a fatal lure and a medium of reconciliation.

13 For a comparison of Naipaul's and Harris's views on El Dorado, see the opening chapter of the former's *The Loss of El Dorado* (1984) and the latter's *Tradition, the Writer, and Society* (1967: especially 35–36). For a comparative critical treatment, see also McWatt.

14 See Freud, *Totem and Taboo* (1983), especially the final chapter; also Girard: 192–222, 274–80. Although the Oedipal dimensions of *Totem and Taboo*, as Girard points out,

are understated, Freud nonetheless links cannibalism to the patricide prohibition and to its incarnation in the surrogate sacrifice of the totem feast.

15 For a celebration of the Caribbean's mixed cultural heritage, see Harris, 'History'; also, in a broader context, the 'miscegenated' aesthetic theory of his *The Womb of Space* (1983).

16 See the early critical essay by Howard; also the later studies of Gilkes and, particularly, Drake.

CHAPTER 11

Cultural Memory in Postcolonial Fiction: The Uses and Abuses of Ned Kelly

Remembering Kelly

The story of the Irish Australian bushranger Ned Kelly has become paradigmatic for the selective retelling of history as folk legend, and for the ideological processes by which social memory may be reworked into the fabric of a nation's founding cultural myths. As John Ryan among others has pointed out, the 1880s, a period of radical nationalism in Australia, allowed Ned Kelly to be brought into conjunction with a number of more or less compatible legends (101). Among these were the twin legends of the 'noble bushranger' and the 'noble convict': victims both of a palpably unjust penal code, these figures could be grafted – with the help of a little historical sleight of hand – onto a long line of morally ambivalent 'good badmen' whose romanticized outlawry embodied libertarian ideals within an oppressive colonial system (102–03).[1] To these might be added a number of legends surrounding Irish nationalist insurgency,[2] not forgetting the now-stereotypical 'bush legend' itself with its virtues of endurance and self-reliance, and its celebration of mateship as a marker of loyal adherence to the bushman's code (106). These legends, needless to say, have been endlessly re-interpreted and challenged, with revisionist accounts variously puncturing the Kelly myth by stressing the vicious criminality of the gang, stripping them of their (self-)glorified guise as frontier-society 'Robin Hoodlums' (Greenway); by using the camp theatrics of some gang members to upset the standard narrative of rugged male adventure-heroism; and by emphasizing the racism underlying Kelly's mythicized status as a 'moral European' (Rose), a racism now generally acknowledged as being built into the structure of the so-called 'Australian legend' itself.

As with other mythic narratives surrounding oppositional figures such as the outlaw, the Kelly legend continues to depend on a manipulation of collective memory more notable for its strategic omissions than for its 'keeping alive

[of] pasts that story [has] obliterated' (Hamilton 14), and for its highly selective reading of a number of often far from reliable historical sources. At the same time, the sheer quantity of Kelly material currently available on the market testifies not just to the durability of the legend, but also to its continuing profitability as a commodity circulating within an increasingly globalized memory industry. These products indicate the powerful role played by popular culture and its representations in shaping social memory (Hamilton 25). Among them we might include several Kelly films and television programmes, ranging in quality from the abysmal *Ned Kelly* (starring Mick Jagger as Ned), to the widely acclaimed 1980 TV mini-series *The Last Outlaw*; a wide array of popular songs, from contemporary ballads such as Midnight Oil's 'If Ned Kelly Were King' and Redgum's 'Poor Ned', to the revived *Ned Kelly, the Musical*; and an even larger number of books and other printed works, many of them designed for mass-market distribution, including Thomas Keneally's children's tale *Ned Kelly and the City of Bees* (1995), and Monty Wedd's hugely successful comic strip *Ned Kelly*, which ran uninterrupted for over two years in the mid-1970s. Meanwhile, as one might expect, the Internet has become a fertile source for Kelly memorabilia, spawning a variety of electronically connected Kelly fan clubs and helping to produce that latter-day variant on the figure of the Victorian collectomane, the starstruck nerd.[3]

A feature of the Kelly industry has been its ability to mobilize popular sentiment for ostensibly high-brow representations, such as – probably most notably – Sidney Nolan's vivid paintings or, more recently, the New York-based novelist Peter Carey's fictionalized *True History of the Kelly Gang* (2000), winner of many literary awards, among them the 2000 Commonwealth Writers Prize and the 2001 Booker Prize, and his most commercially successful work to date. These items, and many others like them, suggest that it matters less how faithfully Kelly and his legend have been remembered than how effectively they have been remodelled to meet a variety of changing ideological interests and consumer needs. In what follows, I want to focus on two recent *literary* representations: Carey's *True History of the Kelly Gang* and Robert Drewe's less well-known but equally intriguing fictive exploration of the Kelly legend, *Our Sunshine* (1991). These novels, I will argue, illustrate the importance of the literary text in structuring the individual/collective memory process, while also drawing attention to the ways in which memory is dependent on metaphor – more specifically, metaphors of the body – to actualize remembered experience.[4] Both works, I will also suggest, are postcolonial renderings, not just of one of Australia's most powerful national narratives, but also one of its most enduring and yet paradoxically amnesiac cultural myths. In remembering Ned Kelly, both writers draw attention to alternative histories, inscribed upon the wild colonial body, through which the nation's chequered past can be creatively transformed and its present critically reassessed. The conclusion of the chapter goes on to offer reflections on the malleability (and current fashionability) of the legend of Ned Kelly, assessing its implications for a Western ex-settler society whose own thriving memory industry bears so many of the contradictory signs of the nation's colonial past.

Claiming Kelly

Robert Drewe's novel *Our Sunshine* ranks as one of the most inventive literary attempts to date to grapple with the Kelly legend. Drewe's 'chronicle of the imagination' (183) rejects the standard teleological account of Ned Kelly as doomed folk-hero; instead, it employs a pared-down style to assemble a collage of impressionistic fragments in which the Kelly legend, in keeping with the visceral language used to relate it, is not just effectively dismantled but violently torn apart. More specifically, the text stages a struggle over the uses and abuses of Kelly's memory, a struggle in which the fictionalized figure of Kelly himself claims the right to remember people and events that others have appropriated in his name (5). It soon becomes clear, however, that Kelly's memories are themselves impossibly belated. Even the most private of reminiscences has been re-assigned in advance as public property, as in the ironically patriotic claim – our sunshine – implicit in the novel's title.[5] The legend has outstripped the life, dictating the pattern in which it is remembered (183); the life, in a sense, is already relived, the story since retold.

This 'belatedness' of memory accounts for the second-hand quality of a text that playfully rehearses the clichéd scenarios of colonial melodrama as black farce and journalistic self-parody. Consider, for example, Kelly's mocking incantation of the litany of atavistic names given to him by the press, a list he succeeds in turning into an ironic fanfare for his own 'monstrous' achievements:

> Devil incarnate of the Antipodes, Satan's right hand, our Mephisto, the Vulture of the Wombat ranges, beast of prey, outback monster, rural sadist, flash young ghoul, savage yokel, bog-Irish fiend, homicidal maniac, corpse robber, cheap assassin, man of blood, bog butcher, jumped-up bush butcher, brute creation, crawling beast, jungle gorilla, creeping thing, reptile, viper in society's bosom, sewer scum, vermin, bog worm, peat maggot [...] pack wolf, shark, spineless jellyfish, strutting rooster, scrub bull [...] cut-rate highwayman, champion of the [...] street-corner loungers, evil marauder, predator, common thief, desperado, thug [...]. Things he'd been called by the gentlemen of the press, *ta rah!* [...] A corner of the faintest memory flickered. Hadn't Dad called him Sunshine? (5–6)

Here, as elsewhere in the text, Drewe summons up a repertoire of demonized animal imagery to stress not so much the brutality of the Kelly gang, nor the fine line that divides them from their equally vicious captors, but rather the predatory aspect that links the legend itself to those who continue to use it to compete for scraps of Kelly's legacy in the name of 'science', the 'national interest' or the 'public good' (49).

The apparent interchangeability of human and animal worlds also gives the novel a surreal twist, as the theatricality already present in the legend tips over into performances of circus-act grotesquery and vaudeville show (4). This carnivalistic spirit is embodied in a form of what we might call, after the American anthropologist Michael Taussig, *colonial wildness*. Wildness, for Taussig, is a figure that, deployed in a wide variety of colonial contexts, has the potential to combine 'the anarchy of death with carnival, in a process that entertains yet resists the seductive appeal of self-pity and redemption through suffering' (467), Certainly, Drewe's novel endorses Taussig's view that the performativity of colonial wildness allows 'the space of death [to] incorporate the laughter of carnival as oppositional practice' (466). Yet the novel, as if in defiance of its title, also amply demonstrates the 'dialectics of terror' (466) on which performances of colonial wildness, however liberating these might appear, so obviously depend.

This terror is represented in the text in graphic images of bodily penetration and mutilation that dispel the myth of remembrance as redemption, uncovering memory instead as a violent, sexually encoded mechanism of powerful repression and explosive release. For beneath the bright surface of Kelly's memory games is a deep structure of displaced colonial trauma, captured in surrealistic visions of the hell of transportation: 'a greasy winter shore bisected by a loamy rivermouth, a city's slimy bay, froth-stained with tar and sawdust, phlegmy flotsam, puffy things with pecked-out eyes. And on the high-tide line, strings of smelly sea-grapes pretending to be rosaries' (58). This trauma is also visible in the destructive convergence of memory and history represented in one of the novel's closing scenes, in which Kelly, tragicomic armour pierced, envisions his own transformation from self-glorifying wild colonial boy into abject colonial mimic man (Naipaul), the shift from first- to third-person narration also suggesting that he is no longer subject of his twice-told tale, but rather second-hand object of derisive contempt:

> Why are parrots pecking his shins? Lorikeets scaling his legs, parakeets dancing up his calves, hanging from his kneecaps. Feathery body heat rustling in his pants, legs worse than mice. Hot beaks nibbling at his veins, claws gripping. Any deeper and they'll be pecking his bone marrow. Creeping up and ripping his foreskin off, Holy Mother! In the rising light, he gets to his feet, whacks and whacks his shins with his rifle butt to smash the little pecking parrots. (172)

The symbolism of castration, as in the death of Joe Byrne (168), that accompanies scenes such as this one further critiques the Kelly legend, puncturing a surface of male bravado to reveal deep-seated anxieties within. This 'un-manning' of the legend reminds us that memory is frequently connected in the text with Freudian metaphors of dismemberment and severance. Probably the most gruesome of these is the severed head of the notorious bushranger Dan Morgan, paraded through the streets of Melbourne in a scene remembered from Kelly's childhood (49). A not dissimilar scene takes place after the final showdown at Glenrowan, when an angry crowd attempts to wrest the charred remains of two former Kelly gang members, like Morgan's head scarcely recognizable as human, from the police who had previously killed them, while in a parallel incident another police officer, responsible for guarding the barely conscious Kelly, claims the prisoner's bullet-riddled body for his own (176–77).

The scene reminds us of the commodified discourse of claim and counterclaim – of custodial rights – surrounding conflicting versions of the Kelly legend, an appropriative discourse on which Drewe's novel skilfully plays and into which we, too, as readers of his text are drawn. The novel emerges in this context as a ferocious, if also fiercely comic, anti-requiem which, in refusing to mourn the death of Kelly, points rather to the ways in which his memory has been co-opted for individual and collective (national) ends. At the same time, Drewe himself self-ironically replicates these predatory tactics: *Our Sunshine* performs less a recuperative version of Kelly's life told by Kelly himself than a further staged invasion of his body. By metaphorically penetrating the body of Kelly – by aggressively inserting itself into the corpus of Kelly folklore – Drewe's novel fulfils the contradictory tasks of re-animating a worn-out legend, thereby ensuring its transmission to the 'grandchildren of the next century' (2), while wrenching it free from the collective memory on which it feeds – and tearing it apart.

Speaking Kelly

Like *Our Sunshine*, Peter Carey's *True History of the Kelly Gang* offers a self-reflexive account of the Kelly legend that, playing fast and loose with historical sources, emphasizes the ambivalent and, above all, commodified status of Kelly as national icon and anti-imperial resource. From the outset, the novel cheerfully acknowledges its debts by making a connection between the archival source on which it draws, a fictive version of the incomplete manuscript handed over by Kelly to the schoolmaster, Tom Curnow, who betrayed him, and the 'wholesale souveniring of [Kelly gang] armour and guns and hair and cartridges that occurred at Glenrowan on June 28th 1880' (Carey 4). However, the written manuscript upon which the novel claims to draw can hardly be considered a reliable documentary item; rather, it acts as the trigger for a sequence of highly entertaining picaresque adventures in which the inscribed narrator, Kelly, doubles as comic 'remembrancer' (Burke 10) and tragic protagonist of his (mock-)heroic quest.[6] Not for the first time in his work, then, Carey deliberately dissolves the boundary between oral and written, fictional and non-fictional sources, thereby maintaining a dynamic balance between competing versions of the historical past.

Throughout Carey's novel, history slides imperceptibly into the more distant recesses of folk memory, while the documented discoveries of archival research converge with the fabrications of the adventure tale. This structural ambivalence is reinforced by the remarkable act of sustained ventriloquism by which Carey is able to give voice to Kelly's memories of his ancestral Irish, as well as his more immediate Australian, past. The narrative is consistently *doubled*, as the subjective recounting of Australian colonial history encounters half-buried memories of an Irish ancestry – an ancestry that clearly causes Kelly as much pain as pride, and through which the repetitive patterns of a larger 'historic memory of UNFAIRNESS' (299, Carey's capitals) can be seen inexorably to emerge. In addition, Kelly's perception of ancestral memory itself is presented as being deeply riven. On the one hand, he scorns the attitude of those (such as his fellow gang member Steve Hart) who nourish themselves on the stories of the rebel Irish martyrs, describing Hart witheringly at one point as 'like a girl living in Romances and Histories always thinking of a braver better time' (196). On the other, he is by no means immune himself from such forms of anti-colonial revenge nostalgia, as when he likens the gang to legendary Irish warriors such as the all-conquering Cuchulainn in his apocalyptic war chariot (326), or when he romantically enlists his latest recruits to a hallowed tradition of victims of British imperialism:

> men who had been denied their leases for no other crime than being our friends men forced to plant wheat then ruined by the rust men mangled upon the triangle of Van Diemen's Land men with sons in gaol men who witnessed their hard won land taken up by squatters men perjured against and falsely gaoled men weary of constant impounding on & on each day without relent. (328)

For Kelly, the superimposition of Irish folk memory onto recent Australian colonial history produces a double effect in which the fear of renewed betrayal lurks beneath the sanctioned pride of violent dissent. The contradictory desires to revisit and to purge the past are reflected in the text in a dialectical interplay between metaphors of burial/unearthing (49, 327, 352) and containment/expulsion (309). Through this interplay, a series of secret histories are temporarily brought to light, only to be further suppressed. A paradigmatic example here is the buried trunk containing a dress worn by Kelly's father, which turns out to be a sign not of his 'effeminacy' but, on the contrary, of his membership of a secret society of Irish rebels feared for their excessive use of force (17).[7] These metaphors are reinforced by the idea of memory itself as a kind of malignant parasite, insinuating itself into the bloodstream and building its destructive strength from within (12), and by the similarly embodied notion of memory as a bruise that slowly forms upon the body, providing evidence of recent affliction but also suggesting a much longer history of incubated anger now recorded on the surface of the skin (98).[8] These alternative metaphors – memory rising within the body, memory inscribed upon the body – mirror Carey's attempt to create an inner biography that, as it were, gradually takes over Kelly's body, getting inside the historical character in an effort to articulate its pain, to make it speak.

What is at stake here, as in Drewe's novel, is not just a recovery of memory mapped onto the wild colonial body, but an *implantation* of memories designed to bring a collective history of destruction to the fore. Thus, while Kelly prefers to envision himself as an actor in a violent history of his own making (245), he also seems predestined to become the pathological host for malevolent ancestral forces that, nourishing themselves on his body, slowly destroy it from within. These forces are conjured up in the text in a number of grisly stories, such as those associated with the ominous Banshee (86–87), or the tale served up to the twelve-year-old Kelly by the policeman O'Neil about the atrocious consequences of a Certain Man's (Kelly's father's) perfidious acts in Ireland, which plants the seed in his young mind of a recurring history of treachery and self-defeat (11–12).[9] Memory, whether unconsciously absorbed or deliberately implanted, is thus potentially lethal – literally so when the *Monitor*, the fondly remembered battleship that provides the inspiration for the Kelly gang's ludicrous armour, eventually becomes the symbol of invincibility that kills (327, 349). Quotational memory (Plett),[10] Carey implies, is scarcely less dangerous to Kelly, whose rebel fantasies are nurtured by his reading of Shakespeare – whom he comically fails to see at one point as being quoted in support of the very imperial Englishness against which he believes himself to be fighting (340) – and the similarly ambiguous West Country historical romance, *Lorna Doone*.

It is highly ironic, of course, that Kelly entrusts his memoirs to the man who turns out to betray him, more ironic still that this same man painstakingly attends to the manuscript, his own personal 'keepsake of the Kelly Outrage' (4), only after its author's death. And most ironic of all is that Carey, who, like Drewe, certainly cannot be accused of not being aware of capitalizing on Kelly's legacy, seems himself to have taken on the role of a latter-day Curnow. The manuscript emerges in this context as another souvenir – perhaps the most valuable souvenir of all – from the siege at Glenrowan (350), lovingly restored by an owner who now brings back to life the very subject he himself had helped to kill. This dialectic is maintained through the device of a fictional memoir that inhabits its chosen subject. Is ventriloquism to be seen here as a related form of parasitism? Is 'speaking Kelly' to be understood as a sympathetic gesture of remembrance, or should it rather be seen as a surreptitious act of treachery and destruction? These are open questions; more certain is that Kelly's narrative, while idiosyncratic enough, is always inflected by other half-remembered narratives: the voice through which it claims to speak is never Kelly's own. Drewe's novel reinforces this obvious point by presenting a burlesque of multiply mediated Kellys; Carey's strategy is rather to offer a complex network of competing ventriloquisms in which the fiction of 'Kelly's voice' is projected onto other, equally fictional narrative voices, and in which the simulated memoir – the 'true history' with 'no single lie' (7) that Kelly has written for his daughter – ultimately pays tribute to neither history nor truth, but the generative mendacity of tall tales (Huggan 87).

Why Bother with Ned? Soundings from the Memory Industry

'Why bother with Ned', fumes Dennis Loraine in a characteristically vituperative letter reacting to government prevarication over the purchase of the last piece of Kelly armour in private hands.[11] The letter, one of a number of similar responses published in the *Herald Sun* (23 May 2001), reads as follows:

What kind of Australian government would legislate to ensure a piece of scrap iron from Ned Kelly's armour remains in this country?

Especially when governments have privatised, or sold, power companies, telecommunications companies, hospitals, railways, train routes, major roads, manufacturing and service icons, airlines and shipping companies.

The privatisation and selling off of Australia has placed this and future generations in jeopardy and at the mercy and greed of overseas owners.

Thus it is that Kelly, pitched into his starring role as protective symbol of an endangered Australian cultural heritage, is once again summoned up from the mists of history at the moment he might seem likely to disappear. And thus it is that Kelly's left shoulder plate, the improbable missing link in a renewed struggle over the privatization of cultural memory, must join other 'souvenirs from Glenrowan' in being restored to its rightful place as an indispensable national resource.

This latest attempt to remember Kelly raises the usual questions, though, as to what continues to be forgotten. It seems fair to assume that for a growing number of Australians, the national narrative embodied in Kelly – and, through Kelly, enshrined in the Australian legend – is embarrassingly exclusive, and that the history of Aboriginal genocide and dispossession, increasingly institutional-ized in a number of official events, museum exhibits and state memorials, now constitutes the most significant form of memory work being undertaken in postcolonial Australia today. All the same, there are numerous signs that the folk memory associated with the Kelly gang has made a recent comeback. Why? One reason may lie in the current appeal of a variety of nation-based outlaw mythologies to a transnational memory industry – an industry in which nostal-gically rebellious figures such as Robin Hood, Jesse James and Kelly himself circulate as iconic representations of an oppositional history that disguises other, probably more significant, oppositional histories, ensuring that these latter remain ignored or inadequately understood.

It is in this context that the American historian Kerwin Lee Klein declares, at the beginning of a recent essay: 'Welcome to the memory industry', for who can now dispute that 'memory has become the leading term in our new cultural history?' (128). Why the memory boom? And why the ambivalent response to it? Several factors may be cited here:[12] the recent revitalization of attempts – many of them within the framework of the Holocaust – to come to terms with personal and collective trauma, releasing deep-seated anxieties not just over the past, but over the specific forms in which it should be recalled; the further anxiety that with the much-vaunted 'acceleration of history' (Nora) in contemporary postmodern culture, the art of remembrance might itself run the risk of being lost;[13] the centrality of memory to contemporary discourses of personal and cultural identity, and the linkage of these discourses to emancipa-tory social movements, victimized individuals and embattled ethnic groups; the quasi-religious belief in the power of collective memory to act as an antidote to the worst excesses of history, and to counteract baleful 'postmodern reckonings of history as the marching black boot and of historical consciousness as an oppressive fiction' (Klein 145); and, not least, the increasing commodification of memory as the function of a consumer-driven late-capitalist society in which historical consciousness has been eroded by nostalgia – a society of the souvenir as much as the spectacle, in which an ever-growing number of commercially viable memorabilia and pseudo-historical reconstructions has granted the illusion of access to, while effectively substituting for, the lived experiences of the past.

Klein's concerns, however exaggerated, about the negative implications of the current memory industry should certainly not be underestimated. Such implications might include, for instance, the paradoxical reification of bourgeois subjectivity in the name of postmodernist relativism (24);[14] the romanticization, even sanctification, of atrocity victims and 'people without history' (Wolf) as global standard-bearers for the oppressed; and the manipulation of memory for authoritarian purposes, as in falsely inclusive national projects of commemoration that primarily serve the powerful in society, consolidating the agenda of the state – as appears to be the case with the Kelly legend – or protecting the interests of a nation's ruling elite. Collective myths like Kelly's are, after all, among the most significant of those raw materials through which any national(ist) struggle over the uses of cultural memory may be expressed. For as Kate Darian-Smith and Paula Hamilton argue in their introduction to a collection of essays on memory and history in twentieth-century Australia,

> It is through the simplified and selective narratives of collective myths that historical events are rendered emotionally comprehensible and memorable. Mythic narratives are thus the wellspring of nationalism and they are constantly mobilised to serve differing ideological and political interests. (2)

Memory, on the other hand, is always likely to supersede state-sanctioned attempts to regulate it. As Andreas Huyssen suggests, it is in the 'tenuous fissure between past and present' that memory is constituted, and this tension makes it 'powerfully alive and distinct from the archive or any other mere system of storage and retrieval' (3). Memory continually re-invents itself in a multiplicity of different representations, and these representations are at once a powerful creative force for the transformation of the past in the present, and a reminder of the large number of different positions we may inhabit in relation to our own, as well other people's, histories. This more positive view is shared by those who work towards an enabling definition of *cultural memory* as a collective 'activity occurring in the present in which the past is continuously modified and re-described even as it continues to shape the future' (Bal *et al.* vii).

This notion of 'cultural memory' has been at the forefront of a great deal of recent interdisciplinary research, taking in the work of (oral) historians, sociologists, anthropologists, cognitive psychologists, literary/cultural critics, and many more. Much of this research, drawing on the pioneering work of the French sociologist Maurice Halbwachs, has operated on the premise that memory is a social/collective, rather than a personal/individual, phenomenon. Cultural memory needs to be distinguished, though, from Halbwachs' 'collec-

Here, as so often in his work, Said lets his impatience get the better of him, launching into an all-out attack on the 'programmatic ignorance' of readers, like Daniel Pipes, who are mere lackeys of US neo-imperialism or, like Bernard Lewis, who are tacit apologists for Zionism, despite their hypocritical insistence that their studies of the Orient, Arabs and Islam are not 'political' at all (133–35). Better not to read at all, Said implies, than to read in this reprehensibly expedient fashion, exhibiting in the process a 'sheer heedless anti-intellectualism unrestrained or unencumbered by the slightest trace of critical self-consciousness' (133). It is worth noting here that Said tends not to attribute 'critical self-consciousness' to those who happen to disagree with him – to those who have 'read' him but not read him, as it were, or to those who have read him but either had the temerity to rebuff him or to filter his work in such a way as only to see what they have expressly wanted to see. Said's own reading of his work oscillates, similarly, between the very form of political partisanship he is so quick to deride in others and his cultivation of a 'decentred' critical consciousness based, unlike Orientalism, on 'investigative, open models of analysis', and committed to 'the dismantling of systems of domination', like Orientalism, that are 'collectively maintained' (141–43). The type of reading Said favours, though does not necessarily practise himself, thus gestures not only towards the possibility of new beginnings, but towards 'nothing less than the creation of new objects for a new kind of knowledge' (129).

Two further attempts on Said's part to begin *Orientalism* again – to take a 'dominating system of knowledge' and prise it apart to create the conditions for a 'new kind of knowledge' – should be mentioned here. These are the afterword to the 1995 edition of *Orientalism* and the preface to the 2003 edition, one of the last pieces of writing Said completed before he died. In the 1995 afterword, Said carries on where he left off in '*Orientalism* Reconsidered'. Recognizing that *Orientalism*, 'in almost a Borgesian way, has become several different books', Said sets out to account for nearly a decade of reception, 'reading back into the book' what his many appreciators and detractors have said (*Orientalism* 330). As in '*Orientalism* Reconsidered', Said gives short shrift to those who have seen the book as resolutely 'anti-Western' or as an unadulterated celebration of the collective Arab cause. 'One scarcely knows what to make', Said complains, 'of [such] caricatural permutations of a book that to its author and in its arguments is explicitly anti-essentialist, radically sceptical about all categorical designations such as Orient and Occident, and painstakingly careful about not "defending" or even discussing the Orient and Islam' (331; emphasis in original). Much of the argument of '*Orientalism* Reconsidered' (and, indeed, *Orientalism* itself) is repeated: the 'Orient' and the 'Occident' are a 'combination of the empirical and the imaginative', and should in no way be understood as corresponding to a stable ontological realm (331); Orientalism is not 'just the antiquarian study of oriental languages, societies, and peoples', but is an evolved 'system of thought [that] approaches a heterogeneous, dynamic, and complex human reality from an uncritically essentialist standpoint' (333); Orientalism presupposes a non-Oriental reader insofar as '[t]he discourse of

Orientalism, its internal consistency [*sic*] and rigorous procedures, were all designed for readers and consumers in the metropolitan West' (336). This familiar roll-call is then followed by an equally familiar demolition of Bernard Lewis, Said's intellectual nemesis, whose 'verbosity scarcely conceals both the ideological underpinnings of his position and his extraordinary capacity for getting nearly everything wrong' (343). Lewis and his followers, fumes Said, specialize in the 'elaborate confection of ideological half-truths [intended] to mislead non-specialist readers' (346), thereby reconfirming the very prejudices his own book had been explicitly designed to contest. These are the arguments one finds, again and again, in *Orientalism*: that routine misreadings and misinterpretations can have devastating consequences for those routinely misread and misinterpreted; that erudition in the service of ignorance is another form of ignorance; that reading itself may produce knowledge – as in knowledge of the Orient – that confirms the authority of the knower without creating new possibilities for understanding or extending the boundaries of the known.

As in 'Orientalism Reconsidered', Said concedes a few points, namely the 'scholarly and humanistic achievements' (*Orientalism* 342) of at least some Orientalist practitioners, or the tendency of Orientalism to confess its own attraction to the works of writers, scholars and administrators who clearly 'condescended to or [actively] disliked the Orientals they either [studied] or [ruled]' (336). In general, though, the 1995 afterword has a confirmatory ring to it. This is corroborated by Said's view that some of his later work – *Culture and Imperialism*, for instance – was primarily an amplification of, rather than a departure from, *Orientalism*'s governing 'cultural' theses: on the symbiotic link between culture and empire; on the constitutive hybridity of cultures; and on the continuing existence of Orientalism as a willed form of human activity – as cultural work (349). But if Said himself was always more likely to revisit than to revise *Orientalism*, he was also appreciative of others' efforts to push their readings of the text into libertarian initiatives of their own. As Said says proudly in the afterword:

> I intended my book as part of a pre-existing current of thought whose purpose was to liberate intellectuals from the shackles of systems like Orientalism: I wanted readers to make use of my work so that they might then produce new studies of their own that would illuminate the historical experience of Arabs and others in a generous, enabling mode. That certainly happened in Europe, the United States, Australia, the Indian subcontinent, the Caribbean, Ireland, Latin America, and parts of Africa. The invigorated study of Africanist and Indological discourses, the analyses of subaltern history, the reconfiguration of postcolonial anthropology, political science, art history, literary criticism, musicology, in addition to the vast new developments in feminist and minority discourses – to all these, I am pleased and flattered that *Orientalism* made a difference. (340)

The updated 2003 preface re-issues the compliment, with an important clarification. The clarification consists of an impassioned defence of humanism

Benterrak, Krim 135, 136
Bhabha, Homi 3, 22, 37, 133
bioethical abuses 71
'biosphere', *see* 'ecosphere'
'biotic communities' 66
black liberation, South Africa 164 nn6, 7
Boehmer, Elleke 37
bolekaja criticism, Nigeria 109
bone flutes, Caribs 170–1, 173
book industry, Africa 118
Botswana, *see* Head, Bessie
Brathwaite, Kamau 167, 169, 172
Brink, André 164 n7
Britain, and empire 8, 206–7
British Guyana
   and history 168–9, 172–3
   literature 166, 171–3
Brody, Hugh, *Maps and Dreams* 142, 147,
   148, 149
Brossard, Nicole 28
Buell, Lawrence 89 n37

Cambridge Survey of World Migration 36, 43
Campbell, Marion 28
Canada
   literature 27–30
   Native Indian culture 48 n15, 143–5
Cannadine, David, *Ornamentalism* 206–8
cannibalism, in Harris's *The Guyana Quartet*
   170–1, 175–7
Carey, Peter, *True History of the Kelly Gang*
   183, 186–8, 192–3
Caribbean literature, ghost stories 166–7
Caribs 170
Carpentier, Alejo 101, 167
   Los pasos perdidos 97–9
Carter, Paul 34, 40–3, 136
cartography, feminist 28–9
   see also maps
Castles, Stephen and Miller, Mark J. 36, 43
censorship
   African writers and 126 n1
   South Africa 156
Chambers, Iain 34, 35, 38–40
Chatterjee, Partha 68
Chatwin, Bruce 58
   The Songlines 142, 145–9
cities, and migrants 39–40
Cixous, Helen 168
Clifford, James 36–7, 96, 101, 110, 114,
   143, 147, 198
Coetzee, J.M.
   Disgrace 89 n30
   Foe 156, 160, 161, 163

The Lives of Animals 71–4
Cohen, Robin 36, 43
'colonial' fiction 28
colonial miscegenation 133
colonialism 6, 17
'colonialist criticism', African literature 121
commemoration ceremonies, and elites
   192
commodity fetishism 131
comparatism, and postcolonialism 1–2
Conrad, Joseph 176
conservation, Africa 52
   Kenya 54, 55, 56, 59, 60
'contradictory coherence' 24
counter-memory 177
creative revisionism 29
creolization, Guyana 172
criticism 64–5
   African literature 109–10, 121
   ecocriticism 64, 65, 66, 84 n1
   postcolonial 10, 64, 66, 162, 191
   Said's *Orientalism* 196–7, 198, 201,
     203–6
cultural consumerism 40
cultural creolization 169
cultural decolonization 27
cultural heritage, African, satires on 94–6
cultural identity, Canadian and Australian
   literature 28
cultural memory 189, 190–3
cultural studies 130, 138
culturalism, and postcolonialism 1–2
culture
   Africa 109
   'non-Western' 112
   Samoa 100–1
Cuna Indians 132–4
Currey, James 120
Curtin, Deane 65, 84 n1

Darian-Smith, Kate and Hamilton, Paula 190
'Dark Continent' imagery 119, 127 n8
deep ecology 84 n1, 85 n8
Deleuze, Gilles and Guattari, Félix 28, 29,
   151 n12
Derrida, Jacques 24, 25, 29
Desai, Anita, *Clear Light of Day* 156–8, 160,
   161, 163
Devall, Bill and Sessions, George 89 n38
development
   Third World 65
   India 69
di Leonardo, Micaela 9–10, 126 n4
'dialectic of alteration' 169, 177

Dobson, Andrew 84 n1
Dreamtime
   Australian Aborigines 145, 146
   in Harris's *Palace of the Peacock* 174
Drewe, Robert, *Our Sunshine* 183–6, 192–3

Eagleton, Terry 11–12
eco-travel writing 51
ecocriticism 64, 66, 79–80
ecofeminism 78–9
'ecological refugees', India 86 n19
ecology 64, 79–80
'ecosphere' ('biosphere') 84 n7
ecotourism, Africa 57, 59
ecotopia 89 n38
Egbuna, Obi 107
egocentrism 51
El Dorado 174
English language and African literature
   106–7
   Heinemann African Writers Series
      (AWS) 117–22
environmental criticism 65
'environmental imagination' 89 n37
environmentalists 84 n1
'ethnic' writers 47 n13
ethno-criticism, African literature 109
ethnographic discourse 142, 147–8
ethnographic realism 113
ethnographies
   as allegories 147
   as fiction 148
   'salvage' 96, 138
Europe, and African literature 122
   see also Westerners

fables 71, 72, 74, 75, 77, 89 n37
Fanon, Frantz, *Black Skin, White Masks*
   177–8, 180 n8
feminist cartography 28–9
feminist critiques, Orientalism, *see*
   Yeğenoğlu, Meyda
fetish-objects, *see* mud sculptures
figurines and mimicry 132–4, *see also* mud
   sculptures
'first-wave' postcolonialism 10
folktales, Africa, *see* Head, Bessie
Foucault, Michel 150 n1, 177
Freud, Sigmund 168
Frobenius, Leo 94

Gallmann, Kuki, *I Dreamed of Africa* 51,
   52–6, 59, 60
Gavron, Jeremy 76

Geertz, Clifford 100, 110, 142, 151 n13
geographers, need for 61
geography, postcolonial 15, 49–51, 61
ghost stories, Caribbean 166–78
   Harris, Wilson 169–71
   Mittelholzer, Edgar 171–3
Gikandi, Simon 110, 113
Glissant, Édouard 167
Glotfeldy, Cheryll 84 n1
González Echeverría, Robert, on
   Carpentier's *Los pasos perdidos* 98
Gowdy, Barbara, *The White Bone* 74–9
Graebner, Fritz 95–6
Grass, Günter 38
Green movements and play 86 n20
Grossberg, Lawrence 4
Guattari, Félix, *see* Deleuze, Gilles and
   Guattari, Félix
Guha, Ramachandra 66, 67, 85 n12
   and Martinez-Alier, Juan 90 n39
Gunew, Sneja 43, 44
Guyana, *see* British Guyana

Halbwachs, Maurice 190–1
Hamilton, Paula, *see* Darian-Smith, Kate
   and Hamilton, Paula
Hardin, Garrett 84 n2
Harris, Wilson 27, 98, 162, 167
   Guyana Quartet 170–1, 175
   Palace of the Peacock 166, 174–7
Hart, Kevin 25
Hasluck, Nicholas 29
Hauka ceremonies, Niger delta 134–5
Head, Bessie, *The Collector of Treasures*
   111–12, 114, 115–17
Heinemann African Writers Series (AWS)
   117–21
Hill, Alan, and Heinemann African Writers
   Series 118–19, 121
historians and interdisciplinarity 7–8
historicism, European 16
history
   British Guyana 172–3
   in Carpentier's *Los pasos perdidos* 98
   and ghosts 168, 169
   postcolonial 15, 16
Hodge, Bob 43–4
Hodgkins, Jack 27
Hoffmann-Nowotny, Hans-Joachim 35
Houbein, Lolo 47 n13
Hulme, Keri, *the bone people* 156, 158–9,
   160, 161, 163
hunters
   Africa 51, 56

British Columbia 144–5, 147
Hutcheon, Linda 48 n15

identity, *see* 'other'
Igbo culture, Nigeria 112, 113, 114, 134
imagination
   and animals 75
   and everyday life 12–13
immigration policies, Australia 43
imperial history and colonial theory 8
imperialism
   and language 37
   as metaphor 6
'imperialist nostalgia' 66
India
   and cartography 23
   'ecological refugees' in 86 n19
   'ecosystem people' in 86 n19
   Narmada Valley Development Project
      68–71
   and neocolonialism 67
   Partition, *see* Desai, Anita, *Clear Light of Day*
indigenous peoples 65
   see also Aborigines, native peoples
interdisciplinarity
   definition 5
   and postcolonialism 4–10, 14
Interventions (journal) 3
Irish nationalism 182
irony
   in Achebe's *Things Fall Apart* 114
   in Chatwin's *The Songlines* 145
   in Desai's *Clear Light of Day* 157
   in Head's *The Collector of Treasures* 116
ivory trade, Africa 89 n33

James, M.R., *Ghost Stories of an Antiquary*
   171
James, Wendy 131
Jameson, Frederic 162
Jeyifo, Biodun 109
Jung, Carl Gustav 176

Kafka, Franz 71
Kaplan, Caren 37, 47 n8
Kelly, Ned 182–9, 192–3
Kennedy, Dane 7–8
Kenya
   conservation 54, 55, 56, 59, 60
   native peoples 53, 55, 60
   travel writing 51–60
Kingston, Maxine Hong 38
Kipling, Rudyard 75

Klein, Julie Thompson 5
Klein, Kerwin Lee 189
Kotei, S.I.A. 108
Krishnaswamy, Revathi 47 n8
Kroetsch, Robert 27, 28, 29
Kundera, Milan 38

'lactification', Caribbean 172
language 141 n12
   African literature 106
   and colonization 172
   dominated and dominant societies 105
      n14
   in Harris's *Guyana Quartet* 170
   and human/animal rights 72–3
   and imperialism 37
   and migrants 37, 39, 40–1
   and mimetic behaviour 141 n12
   music and silence as 160, 163
   written and spoken word 143
Lawson, Alan 44
Lefevere, Andre 107
legends
   Kelly, Ned 182–9, 192–3
   Philomela 155, 161
   see also myths
Les maîtres fous (film) 135
Lévi-Strauss, Claude 97–9
   Tristes Tropiques 96–7
Lindfors, Bernth 120
literacy, transnational, *see* transnational
   literacy
literary criticism
   African literature 109–10, 121
   postcolonial 10, 64, 66, 162, 191
   Said's *Orientalism* 196–7, 198, 201,
      203–6
literary critics and postcolonial criticism
   10
literary studies and postcolonialism 12–17
Lizarríbar, Camille 118, 119
Loomba, Ania 66
Lucas, Robert E.B. 35

MacCannell, Dean 170
McClintock, Anne 50
McCully, Patrick 69
Macherey, Pierre 163 n1
McLeod, John 2–4
magic 131
Malawi 126 n1
Malouf, David 27
Maori culture, *see* Hulme, Keri, *the bone people*

maps
    Australian Aborigines and 146, 148
    decolonization of 21–30
    as metaphors 26, 27
    and mimesis 21–2, 23
    Native Indian 144–5, 147
    Western 143, 144, 145, 146–7
Martinez-Alier, Juan, *see* Guha,
        Ramachandra and Martinez-Alier,
        Juan
Marxist critiques, ecology 84 n1
materialist analysis, postcolonial studies
        61
Maugham, W. Somerset 99
mbari houses, Owerri Igbo 134
Mead, Margaret, *Coming of Age in Samoa*
        99–101
media and anthropology 9
memory 185
    in Carpentier's *Los pasos perdidos* 98
    in Desai's *Clear Light of Day* 156, 158
    and El Dorado 174
    and ghosts 167
    and metaphor 168, 183
    and Ned Kelly legend 182–3, 185, 186,
        187–9
    see also counter-memory
memory industry 189–90
Mercator, Gerardus 23, 24–5
metaphors 108
    anthropological 109
    colonialism as 6
    maps as 26, 27
    and memories 168, 187
    and nomadic instincts 143
    participant-observation as 122
    and time and space 143
Michener, James 99
migrant aesthetics 34–45
    Australia 40–5, 43
    cities 39–40
    language 37, 39, 41
    writing 37–8, 43
migrant writing 37–8, 43
migrants
    'Anglo-Celtic', Australia 43
    and 'first-wave' postcolonialism 10
    and poetics of movement 42
migration, metaphor of 36–7
Miller, Christopher L. 109–10
Miller, Mark J., *see* Castles, Stephen and
        Miller, Mark J.
mimesis
    cartography 21–2, 23

    in Chatwin's *The Songlines* 148
    and mimicry 130–8
mimetic excess 57, 87 n22
mimicry
    and colonial discourse 22
    and mimesis 130–8
Minh-ha, Trinh T. 9, 130
miscegenation, *see* colonial miscegenation
Mishra, Vijay 43–4
missionaries, publishers as 119
Mittelholzer, Edgar, *My Bones and My Flute*
        166, 171–3
movement, poetics of 42
mud sculptures, Owerri Igbo 134
Muecke, Stephen 135, 136
Muehrcke, Philip 143
Mukherjee, Pablo 10–11
'multicultural' writers, *see* 'ethnic' writers
Murnane, Gerald 29
music
    and silence in Coetzee's *Foe* 160–1
    see also songs and maps, Australian
        Aborigines
musical motifs, in Carpentier's *Los pasos
        perdidos* 98
mythologies, Western and Oceanic 100
myths
    Africa 95–6
    Australia 190
    Canada 151 n10
    creation 160
    El Dorado 174
    see also legends

Naess, Arne 84 n7
Nagel, Thomas 74
Naipaul, V.S. 174
Narmada Bachao Andolan (NBA) 85 n12,
        86 n13
Narmada Valley Development Project
        (India) 68–71
narrators
    in Coetzee's *Foe* 160
    in Head's *The Collector of Treasures* 116
    in Nyoongah 's *Master of the Ghost
        Dancing* 137
'national progress', India 68
Native Indians, Canada 48 n15, 143–5
Native peoples
    India 68
    Kenya 53, 55, 60
    see also Aborigines, Australia
Nelson, Cary 4
New Zealand literature, *see* Hulme, Keri

Roth, H.L., *The Aborigines of Tasmania* 141
   n10
Rowell, Andrew 69, 85 n12
Roy, Arundhati, 'The Greater Common
   Good' 67–71
Rushdie, Salman 38, 86 n15

Said, Edward 6, 9, 10, 22, 93, 101
   Beginnings 199–200
   Orientalism 196–206, 208
   'Orientalism Reconsidered' 200, 201
   'salvage ethnography' 96, 138
   Samoa 99–101
Sanday, Peggy 170
satire, ethnographic 102
   in Nyoongah 's *Master of the Ghost*
    Dancing 136–7
Schmidt, Nancy 112
Schmidt, Father Wilhelm 95–6
'second-wave' postcolonialism 10–12
Senghor, Léopold 94
Sessions, George, *see* Devall, Bill and
   Sessions, George
'settler cultures' 44, 66
   and maps, British Columbia 145
sexism and Orientalism 206–7
sexuality in postcolonial novels 161–2
Shakespeare, William, *The Tempest* 163 n1,
   164 n6
Shiva, Vandana 66, 67, 86 n14
silence and music, postcolonial texts
   155–63
   Desai's *Clear Light of Day* 157–8, 160
   Hulme's *the bone people* 158–9, 160
Singer, Peter 88 n28
slave revolts 180 nn9, 10
Songhay workers, Niger delta 134–5
songs and maps, Australian Aborigines
   145–6
South Africa
   black liberation 164 nn6, 7
South Asian studies 66
Soyinka, Wole 109, 126 n1
space and maps, Native Indians 144
Spivak, Gayatri 10, 23, 66
Steedly, Mary 131
stereotyping
   African literature 108, 120, 121
   Samoan culture 99–101
Stoller, Paul 134
'Subaltern Studies Project' 85 n10
Swift, Jonathan 24
Symbolic tradition 176
synoptic interdisciplinarity 5–6

Taussig, Michael 71–2, 131–3, 135, 184–5
Third World and First World 38–9, 65,
   66–7, 70–1, 84 n2
Thomas, Nicholas 131
Tiffin, Helen 104 n13, 162, 169
Torgovnick, Marianna 9
tourism, *see* ecotourism
transnational literacy 14
travel writing 50–60
   Africa 51–60
   Australia 58, 142, 145–9
'travelling theory' 36, 42, 44
Treichler, Paula 4
Tswana society, Botswana 115
Tylor, Edward, preface to Roth's *The*
   Aborigines of Tasmania 141 n10

universities and 'anxiety of interdisciplinarity' 6–7
utopianism 13

Van Herk, Aritha 27
Vance, Linda 78
Villemaire, Yolande 29
vivisection 88 n28

Walcott, Derek 166–7
Webster, Steven 100
Wendt, Albert 99, 100–1
Werbner, Richard 191–2
Westerners and African literature 110
   see also Europe
whiteness and power 134
wilderness narratives 51
wildness 59, 184–5
Williams, Denis 168–9
witchcraft, Botswana 115–16
Wolff, Janet 5
women and Orientalism, *see* sexism and
   Orientalism
World Bank
   and dam building 86 n14
   and publishing industry 126 n3
writers
   African 107, 120, *see also* Achebe,
    Chinua; Head, Bessie; Soyinka, Wole
   Caribbean 166–78
   postcolonial 155–61
   travel 50–60, *see also* Chatwin, Bruce .

Yeğenoğlu, Meyda, *Colonial Fantasies* 205–6
Young, Robert 3, 4, 11, 133

Zolberg, Aristide R. 34

Nǧuǧi wa Thiong'o 13
Niger delta, *Hauka* ceremonies 134–5
Nigeria
  Igbo culture 113, 114
  publishing industry 126 nn2, 3
  state repression 126 n1
nomads 136, 151 n12
'non-Western' cultures 112
nostalgia 66, 97, 190, 207–8
Nyoongah, Mudrooroo, *Master of the Ghost Dancing* 136–8

Okai, Atukwei 107–8
Old and New Worlds, in Carpentier's *Los pasos perdidos* 97–9
omnivores and environment 86 n19
Omotoso, Kole 108, 121
'oral' cultures 147, 148
Orientalism 196–208
  Cannadine, David, *Ornamentalism* 206–8
  defined 201–2
  feminist critiques, *see* Yeğenoğlu, Meyda
  Said, Edward, *Orientalism* 196–206, 208
'others' 80, 177–8
  Africa 53, 122
  ancestors 172
  animals 57–8, 79
  anthropology 9
  British Empire 207
  Caribs 170
  cultures 96, 102, 104 n3, 135
  in Harris's *Palace of the Peacock* 176
  humans 87 n21
  Native cultures 148–9, 180 n11
  see also 'non-Western' cultures
Ouologuem, Yambo 101
  Le Devoir de violence 94–6
overpopulation 84 n2
Owerri Igbo, Nigeria 134

parody
  in African literature 113
  in Chatwin's *The Songlines* 149
  in Drewe's *Our Sunshine* 184
  ethnographic 102, 103 n3
  and mimesis 133
Parry, Benita 16
Partition, India, *see* Desai, Anita, *Clear Light of Day*
Pepper, David 84 n1
play, radical strategy 86 n20
Plett, Heinrich E. 194 n10
poaching, Africa 89 n33

Poe, Edgar Allan, *Tales of Mystery and Imagination* 171
political intervention, African literature 111
Porritt, Jonathon 84 n1
postcolonial criticism 10, 64, 66, 162, 191
postcolonial fiction 28, 101–2
postcolonial literature/culture 43–4, 162–3
postcolonial writers 155–61
postcolonialism 8–10
  as comparatism 1–2
  as culturalism 2–4
  'first-wave' 10
  and generalization 3
  and interdisciplinarity 4–10
  anthropology 8–10
  and literary studies 12–17
  'second-wave' 10–12
  transnational models of 3
power
  and cultural studies 138
  and whiteness 134
power groups, and maps 24, 25–6
power relations, and anthropology 114, 115, 116
publishing industry
  Africa 117–21
  and African literature 107, 108, 112, 117–22
  Nigeria 126 n3

Quayson, Ato 5–6, 12, 13

Rabasa, José 23, 24
race, Africa 94–5
racial superiority, white 206–7
  Kenya 53, 54
readers
  and African literature 112, 113, 114, 115, 118, 120, 121
  and maps 143
  and Said's *Orientalism* 201
Reading the Country, Australian landscape 135–6
reason, and mistreatment of animals 72
religion
  Botswana 115–16
  late-capitalist Western culture 131
resistance, *see* 'Subaltern Studies Project'
Ridgeway, Rick, *The Shadow of Kilimanjaro* 51–2, 56–60
Rilke, Rainer Maria, *Duino Elegies* 77–8
Roe, Paddy 135
Rosaldo, Renato 85 n9
Rose, Gillian 49